PUERTO RICO

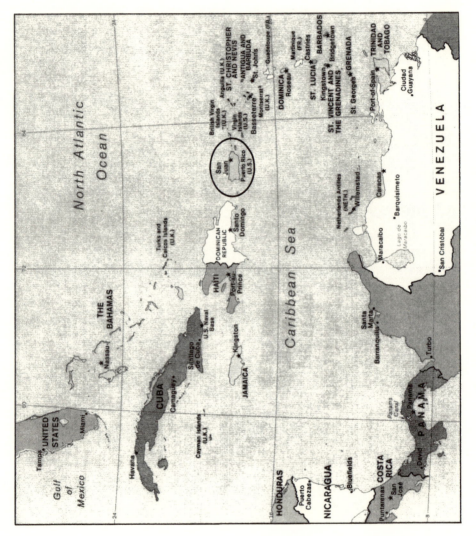

Map 1. Location of Puerto Rico in the Caribbean

PUERTO RICO

Culture, Politics, and Identity

Nancy Morris

Westport, Connecticut
London

Library of Congress Cataloging-in-Publication Data

Morris, Nancy.
    Puerto Rico : culture, politics, and identity / Nancy Morris.
        p.   cm.
    Includes bibliographical references (p.   ) and index.
    ISBN 0–275–95228–2 (alk. paper).—ISBN 0–275–95452–8 (pbk.)
    1. Puerto Rico—Politics and government—1898–1952.   2. Puerto
Rico—Politics and government—1952-   3. Identity (Psychology)—
Puerto Rico.   4. Nationalism—Puerto Rico.   5. Ethnicity—Puerto
Rico.   6. Political culture—Puerto Rico.   7. Puerto Rico—
Relations—United States.   8. United States—Relations—Puerto
Rico.   I. Title.
F1975.M67   1995
972.9505′2—dc20   95–14416

British Library Cataloguing in Publication Data is available.

Library of Congress Catalog Card Number: 95–14416
ISBN: 0–275–95228–2
        0–275–95452–8 (pbk.)

First published in 1995

Praeger Publishers, 88 Post Road West, Westport, CT 06881
An imprint of Greenwood Publishing Group, Inc.

Printed in the United States of America

∞™

The paper used in this book complies with the
Permanent Paper Standard issued by the National
Information Standards Organization (Z39.48–1984).

10 9 8 7 6 5 4 3 2 1

To the memory of my uncle

Jim Davidson

Contents

PART II: IDENTITY IN CONTEMPORARY PUERTO RICO

PART III: IDENTITY UNDER CHALLENGE

List of Maps, Tables, and Figures

MAPS

TABLES

FIGURES

Acknowledgements

This book owes its existence and its shape to many people. It is a pleasure to acknowledge them.

I am enormously grateful to the interviewees and focus group participants who contributed the substance of this study; their willingness to participate and the thoughtfulness of their responses far exceeded my hopes. Without their generosity with their time and ideas this book would not exist.

Everywhere in Puerto Rico I was met with the hospitality that is so often mentioned as characteristic of Puerto Ricans. Luis R. Dávila Colón, Jorge Duany, Víctor García San Inocencio, and Manuel Rodríguez Orellana provided insightful observations, valuable feedback, and moral support, as well as friendship. I would also like to express my appreciation to Casandra Badillo Figueroa, Ricardo Barahona, Evelyn Cedeño Piñero and her sister Ruth, Rosa Corrada, Irmarilis González, Carlos Gorrín, Kenneth McClintock, George McDougall, Jaime Platón, Yolanda Platón, Marco Rigau, Pedro Rosado, Hilda del Toro, Linda Schaffer and family, Luis Vega, and to the Pabón family for a wonderful Puerto Rican Thanksgiving and much more.

A number of friends have helped in the complicated task of completing a book about Puerto Rico while based in Scotland. I greatly appreciate the readiness to comb various libraries and the tireless good humor of Robin Andersen, Nell Booth, Joe Davidson, Vince Ercolano, Eliut D. Flores Caraballo, Víctor García San Inocencio, Marilee Schmit Nason, María Pabón, Irma Rodríguez Morales, Deborah G. Stinnett, Jaime E. Toro Monserrate, Charley Vick, and Kristen Whitney.

For invaluable comments on portions of the manuscript, I am indebted to Jorge Duany, Vince Ercolano, Jamie Hall, Sandy Kyrish, Doug Vick, Henry Wells, and my University of Stirling colleagues Philip Schlesinger, Raymond Boyle, and Peter Meech. I am grateful to everyone in Stirling's Film and Media Studies department for creating a supportive and enjoyable working environment.

This book was enriched by the resources of the Hunter College Centro de Estudios Puertorriqueños library. The training to undertake the study and funding for the field research came from the Annenberg School for Communication. I would especially like to thank three University of Pennsylvania professors whose teaching and friendship have been and continue to be immensely important to me: Larry Gross, Robert Hornik, and Henry Wells.

Finally, infinite thanks to Doug. Meeting him was the most significant outcome of this project.

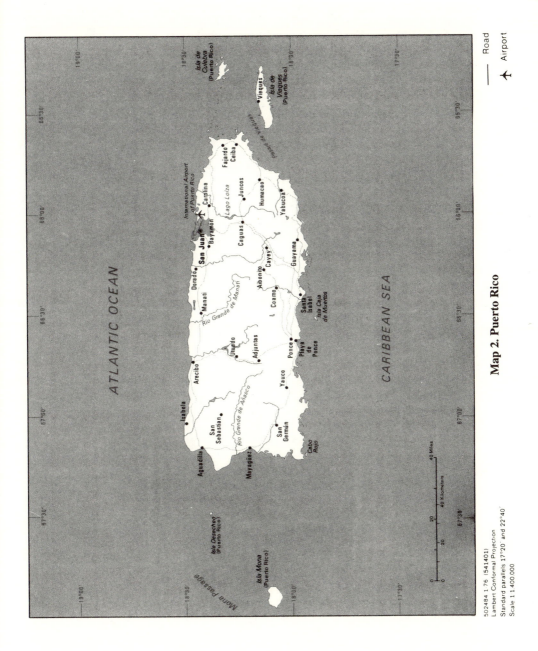

Map 2. Puerto Rico

502484 1 76 (541401)
Lambert Conformal Projection
Standard parallels 17°20' and 22°40'
Scale 1:1,400,000

——— Road

✈ Airport

Introduction

The concept of national identity is as elusive as it is pervasive. Although it constitutes a basic axis of global political organization, it has defied systematic analysis. Scholars, philosophers, and politicians have been unable to agree on what national identity is, much less explain its persistence as a central reference for individuals and groups. This book examines national identity through the lens of Puerto Rico and through the voices of Puerto Ricans. It asks how members of an influential group in Puerto Rican society—political elites—have perceived and expressed their own identity in the century of U.S. sovereignty over Puerto Rico. This focus on the experience of national identity provides a way to examine aspects of identity that have been largely overlooked in theoretical considerations of the topic.

Puerto Rico lends itself to a study of collective identity because of the prominence of identity issues in its recent history. The smallest and easternmost of the Greater Antilles island chain that forms the northern boundary of the Caribbean Sea, Puerto Rico was a Spanish colony for 400 years. The island passed to U.S. control in 1898. For almost a century, Puerto Ricans have been directly exposed to the political, social, and economic influence of the United States. Puerto Ricans hold U.S. citizenship and travel between the island and the U.S. mainland with no restrictions. The island population is 3.5 million; another 2.5 million Puerto Ricans reside in the continental United States temporarily or permanently, many of them making frequent visits to the island in a continual cross-migration. The extent and nature of U.S. influence on islanders' identity—through political sovereignty, institutional links, commercial culture, and mass media—are topics of constant debate.

This study explores national identity through archival and field research. It first uses primary and secondary historical sources to describe the political interaction between Puerto Rico and the United States since the turn of the century. It then presents interviews with present-day Puerto Rican political leaders to examine the components of contemporary Puerto Rican identity.

Many observers have noted the importance of elites in the invention and shaping of national identity (Hobsbawm 1990: 10; Hroch 1985: 181; Smith 1991: 93–98; 1983: 83; Boerner 1986: 14). The role played by political elites in this regard is particularly prominent in Puerto Rico. Puerto Rican society is strikingly politicized, with the citizenry attentive to, and involved in, formal electoral processes. More than 90 percent of eligible citizens are registered to vote (Luciano 1993b) and voter turnout is consistently high—between 73 and 88 percent in every gubernatorial election since 1948 (R. Anderson 1988: 5). Political leaders do not simply inject their messages into the populace, but, in this robust democratic system, they both influence and articulate notions of what it means to be Puerto Rican. As policymakers they have access to channels for shaping identity, and as vote seekers they must be sensitive to their constituents' attitudes toward identity. The feedback process between political leaders and the public can blur the origination point of trends and messages, insofar as they can be said to have an origination point. But in a system like Puerto Rico's, politicians focus societal feelings as a magnifying glass focuses sunlight.

Any discussion of Puerto Rican politics quickly bumps up against Puerto Rico's political parties. Each of the island's three principal parties—the Popular Democratic Party, the New Progressive Party, and the Puerto Rican Independence Party—uses ideas of national identity in its electioneering. Each party reflects a different concept of national identity, as each advocates a different political future for the island—commonwealth status, statehood, or independence. With the exception of the Puerto Rican Independence Party, however, the parties' names do not indicate the political status they advocate. For clarity when discussing current Puerto Rican politics, I refer to each party not by name but rather by the political status position it promotes. Although it has been argued that status is not the defining issue in Puerto Rican politics and does not determine voting behavior (R. Anderson 1988: 25–26), the three parties are so closely identified with their respective status positions that I believe it is legitimate to designate the parties in these terms, particularly in a discussion centered on political status preferences. Using status preferences to designate the parties avoids the befuddlement that can result from the similarity of party initials and makes it easier to follow the story. The designations I use for the political parties, and their official names, are:

commonwealth party:
Partido Popular Democrático–PPD
(Popular Democratic Party)

statehood party:
Partido Nuevo Progresista–PNP
(New Progressive Party)

independence party:
Partido Independentista Puertorriqueño–PIP
(Puerto Rican Independence Party)

For the contemporary component of this study, I interviewed nineteen politicians and conducted group interviews ("focus groups") with eleven groups of young political activists. Interviewees and focus group members represented each of the three principal political parties and several other political organizations. When I began the interviewing process in 1990, I did not have a predetermined entry point. As I approached people in Puerto Rico and discussed my interests, I was repeatedly referred to high-level officials, many of whom agreed to be interviewed. Several party leaders suggested other possible interviewees and made the necessary introductions. This seemed to stem from a genuine interest in the project and was by no means partisan; politicians often referred me to members of parties other than their own. This snowball sampling led to officials in higher positions than I had anticipated being able to reach.

In these interviews, political leaders wore two hats: at one level they responded as professional politicians for whom identity issues are part of the daily agenda, and at another level they responded as individuals living in a society that has had a complex and often conflictive relationship with the United States. During the discussions of these topics, interviewees and focus group participants appeared to be engaged in the conversation, and none exhibited any impatience or evident desire to be elsewhere. In most cases they seemed to enjoy the chance to explain their views as well as to explore aspects of their self-identification as Puerto Ricans that may not have been daily conversational fare.

Because the language of Puerto Rico is Spanish, all of the focus groups and all but two of the interviews were conducted in Spanish. Interviews were then transcribed and translated into English, but certain crucial terms commonly used in the island are not readily rendered into English-language equivalents. A key term in this book is *puertorriqueñidad*, a common Spanish noun that means "Puerto Ricanness," or, as defined in *Vocabulario Puertorriqueño*, a dictionary of Puerto Rican usage, the "totality of the sentiments and traits characteristic of the Puerto Rican people" (Rosario 1980: 58). "Puerto Ricanness" is perhaps an awkward term in English, but it conveys the essence of the word, which is central in Puerto Rican thinking. I have translated *puertorriqueñidad* as "Puerto Ricanness" throughout.

Puerto Ricans often use the word *país* to refer to the island. *País* translates as "country" in English, and that is what Puerto Ricans mean when they use the term. This, of course, is tricky, as Puerto Rico is not an independent political entity. I have nonetheless translated *país* as "country," which most faithfully captures the sense of the word as it is used in Puerto Rico.

The final problematic translation issue involves the Spanish word *estadounidense*, which means a person from the United States. This term has no neat translation into English. Rather, the terms "America" and "American" are commonly used throughout the world to refer to the United States and its people. Some Latin Americans and Canadians have felt themselves excluded from a term that technically applies to all of North, Central, and South America but has been appropriated by the United States alone. This was noted by Puerto Rican focus group participants in this study.

> *Commonwealth party focus group:*
> I was talking the other day to some guys from Costa Rica, Honduras,
> Nicaragua, and I think one from Paraguay. They were asking
> themselves "why do the Americans call themselves Americans?
> Why don't they use another name; we are the Americans. They
> should call themselves something else; we're the Americans."

> *Commonwealth party focus group:*
> American. That's different from North American. I see America as a
> single continent. I don't see it as divided into North, Central,
> South. We're America from, I suppose, Canada, Alaska, to
> Patagonia, Tierra del Fuego, down there.

> *Independence party focus group:*
> I try to call Americans *estadounidenses*. Unfortunately in English
> there is no such word.

In translating Puerto Ricans' comments, I have followed their usage. When a respondent used the term *americano*, I have translated it as "American"; *norteamericano,* I translate as "North American." When respondents used the word *estadounidense*, I have left it in italicized Spanish.

One additional language note concerns the Spanish-language system of surnames, which differs from the English-language norm. In Spanish-speaking countries, a child takes both the mother's last name and the father's last name. The "first last name" is the father's and is the name used in alphabetizing and for short references. The "second last name" is the mother's and may be used in conjunction with the first last name, abbreviated by an initial, or dropped. Luis Muñoz Marín, for example, may be referred to as Muñoz Marín or simply as Muñoz.

I write as an outsider. I am not Puerto Rican, and I do not have a personal stake in the Puerto Rican political process. This has its advantages and disadvantages; the disadvantage of lacking intimate, lifelong familiarity with the issues and personalities of Puerto Rican politics may be offset by the corresponding advantage of approaching the subject from outside the partisan vortex. In describing Puerto Rican politics, I have done my best to represent the political positions of parties and of the people I interviewed fairly and accurately. Respondents' comments, which are presented anonymously, must be taken as a snapshot of their views in late 1990 and early 1991. The Puerto Rican political situation is volatile, and subsequent events and realignments may have led to shifts in individual or party positions since the time of the interviews. There will doubtless be disagreements with my interpretations of Puerto Rico, past and present. If objections come from different corners of the political ring, I will take this as an indication that I have presented an overview of the Puerto Rican political labyrinth that gives evenhanded consideration to the views of Puerto Ricans across the political spectrum.

1

National Identity and Puerto Rico

Puerto Rico was a Spanish colony from 1493 to 1898. The United States gained sovereignty over the island in 1898 and undertook a sustained "Americanization" campaign designed to make Puerto Rico "in its sympathies, views, and attitude toward life and toward government essentially American" (Davis 1899: 656). This campaign was waged actively for fifty years before Puerto Ricans were granted a measure of self-rule. Since then, the island has remained integrated into the legal and economic systems of the United States, which retains sovereignty over Puerto Rico. Despite the direct and indirect pressures to "Americanize" felt throughout the twentieth century, Puerto Ricans do not, on the whole, regard themselves as "essentially American." The collective identity of Puerto Ricans has been influenced by the island's relationship with the United States, but Puerto Ricans have retained an identity that is distinct and separate from their sovereign power.

This book examines the complexities of Puerto Rican collective identity, with particular attention to how islanders define themselves in relation to the United States. Through a century of substantive and symbolic conflicts over such issues as language, education, and political structure, Puerto Rican identity has remained distinct, while adapting to the pressures placed upon it. Such resilience demonstrates that identity, while malleable, is also durable. Moreover, it suggests that contrary to commonly held assumptions, external pressure on collective identity may strengthen that identity rather than diminish it.

Throughout the twentieth century, Puerto Ricans have debated what their relationship with the United States should be. The island's political system is arranged around this issue, with each of the three major political parties advocating a different political arrangement for Puerto Rico: full integration into the United States as a state, a continuation of the present, partially autonomous "commonwealth" relationship, or complete political independence. The fate of Puerto Rican identity—"Puerto Ricanness"—under each political status option is part of the debate. The central role of identity concerns in the island's complex political situation and the deliberateness of the U.S. attempt to influence Puerto Rican attitudes offer unique opportunities for a study of collective identity under challenge.

COLLECTIVE IDENTITY IN THE MODERN WORLD

The term "identity" as a feature of individual psychology was brought to prominence by child psychologist Erik Erikson in the 1950s. Selecting this word to describe "much of what has been called the self" by Freud and others (1959: 147), Erikson conceived of identity as a multifaceted aspect of personality. As Erikson's psychological model became known, it was adapted and referred to by sociologists in analyses of the individual's relationship to social groups. Political scientists then contributed to the "spill-over by analogy of 'personal identity' into 'collective identity' " (Mackenzie 1978: 166), employing the notion of "identity" in the investigation of the establishment of new states in the wake of European decolonization in the 1960s. As leaders of the new states set about modernization, the prevailing view was that "nation building" would require not only institutional change but also changes in individual attitudes. Political scientist Lucian Pye drew on Erikson's psychological insights throughout his large body of work on modernization. Pye postulated that a society's successful transition from traditional to modern required that the populace have a "clear sense of identity" and allegiance with the new government (1962: 52–53).

The conflation of the identity of the state and of the individual citizens in it was emblematic of the widespread use of the word "identity" that led a historian to conclude that "by the late 1960s the terminological situation had gotten completely out of hand" (Gleason 1983: 915). This situation was further complicated by the coining of such terms as cultural identity, political identity, ethnic identity, and national identity. These overlapping terms refer to some of the many forms of collective identity, ways that individuals may define themselves as members of groups.

A key part of defining collective identity involves establishing the distinction between group members and outsiders, "us" and "them." Collective identity in general and national identity specifically are becoming signally visible in the contemporary world as "us and them" judgments proliferate. At the same time that the growth of mass communications and global interdependence in the late twentieth century have brought knowledge of other communities to almost every doorstep, local allegiances have gained prominence; the assertion of collective will by national, religious, and ethnic groups in various combinations is increasing. Few areas in the world today are exempt from confrontations with groups making secessionist, autonomist, or territorial claims related to some form of collective identity. In Eastern Europe and the former Soviet Union, the ongoing turmoil centers on historic nationalities that were not eradicated by decades of centralized communist rule. China faces independence demands from Tibet, and, in Inner

Mongolia, a clandestine movement to reassert a separate cultural heritage (Kristof 1992). In the Middle East, the campaign of the Palestinian people for territory and autonomy has been founded on their self-identification as a nation. Kurdish leaders in Turkey are seeking formal recognition of a "Kurdish identity" as part of efforts to end their ten-year war of independence (*Guardian* 1994). In Western Europe, violent separatist groups have been active in the Basque region of Spain and until recently in Northern Ireland, and autonomist demands are heard in Catalonia and other Spanish regions, in Belgium, in Scotland, and in Corsica. In Africa, Eritrea fought to secede from Ethiopia on grounds that Eritreans are a distinct people (Perlez 1991) and declared independence in 1993. India, Sri Lanka, and Burma are among the Asian states confronting separatist claims based on national, linguistic, and religious groupings. Throughout South and Central America, indigenous peoples are calling for recognition and autonomy (Zamosc 1994: 38–39). In North America, Quebec's demand to be recognized as a "distinct society" from Anglo-Canada is characteristic of national identity struggles.

These conflicts involve groups of people whose desire for formal differentiation from existing states is based on the belief that realization of their ethnic, linguistic, or religious identities requires separate territory or self-government. Such movements for political independence often activate forces of political and military coercion, as a means either to further or to suppress them. A prominent recent example is the bloody conflict between the Russian military and Chechen separatists.

Conversely, the voluntary affiliation of groups of countries seeking increased political and economic strength places quite distinct pressures or perceived pressures on identities. Agreements between countries to exchange some degree of autonomy for the benefits drawn from multinational organization can generate fear that existing, realized identities will be eroded by the resultant partial integration. The most prominent contemporary example of this trend is Western Europe, where the objective of maintaining national identities while fostering regional cooperation has been an issue in negotiations over ongoing economic and political consolidation within the European Union. The Foreword to a European Commission policy discussion paper squarely posed this concern: "How can European cultures be promoted without causing any individual country to lose its identity?" (European Commission 1994).

The issue of national identity has also arisen in a context unrelated to geographical relationships: international controversies over the flow of information and mass media products. Claims that imported mass media products damage identity in receiving countries have been made by politicians, diplomats, and scholars (Camargo and Noya Pinto 1975; International Commission for the Study of Communication Problems 1980; McPhail 1987; Schiller 1976). The debate over the susceptibility of national identity to external influence was taken up in 1977 by the UNESCO-sponsored International Commission for the Study of Communication Problems (1980: 31), which concluded that "imported models reflecting alien life-styles and values" posed a danger to national and cultural identities.

The perceived threat to identity occasioned by imported mass media products, especially those from the United States, is not attributable to overt coercion or negotiated arrangements. Rather, imported mass media programming and other cultural products are claimed to deliberately or incidentally undermine the cultures of receiving countries by bringing ideas and products that erode authentic and traditional lifestyles, values, and identities. This notion—variously termed cultural imperialism, media imperialism, cultural domination, cultural homogenization, globalization, or, at times, Americanization, in reference to the principal source of the imported media[1]—has been much discussed, if little researched.[2] Such concerns were implicit in Dorfman and Mattelart's (1972: 155–56) critique of the impact of Disney comics in Latin America: "Why is Disney a threat? . . . [B]ecause this product of Disneyland . . . is imported, along with so many other consumer objects, to the dependent country. . . . [B]y importing a product . . . we are also importing the cultural forms of that society." Brazil's communications minister perceived a like problem with television: "Instead of acting as a factor of creation and diffusion of Brazilian culture, TV is playing the role of a privileged medium of cultural import, and is denaturing Brazilian creativity" (quoted in Camargo and Noya Pinto 1975: 31).

Concerns about the effects of imported media products on national identity have not been limited to developing countries. Canada's proximity to broadcast signals from the United States has long been a source of unease. As early as 1957 a governmental study of broadcasting stated

> [A]s a nation, we cannot accept, in these powerful and persuasive media, the natural and complete flow of another nation's culture without danger to our national identity. Can we resist the tidal wave of American cultural activity? Can we retain a Canadian identity, art and culture—a Canadian nationhood? . . . [W]e could have cheaper radio and television service if Canadian stations became outlets of American networks. However, if the less costly method is always chosen, is it possible to have a Canadian nation at all? (Bird 1988: 252–53).

This unease has not abated in the ensuing decades; one analyst recently termed the continued dominance of U.S. television programming in Canada a "crisis in national culture" (Starowicz 1993: 85).

Controversy over imported media nearly derailed the 1993 General Agreement on Tariffs and Trade (GATT) treaty reducing barriers to international trade. Economics may have been at the forefront of European broadcasting and film industries' wish to exclude audiovisual services from trade liberalization, but cultural concerns appeared as well. A French film director explained, "[c]inema is . . . a vehicle for a way of life, a language, customs, and questions. . . . To the French, film is an expression of an individual's origins and the creation of a country's imagination. . . . A country . . . can't entrust the imagination of its entire population to a foreign culture. . . . [W]e have to protect our own identity" (Z. Hall 1993). In a similar vein, the European Broadcasting Union, a voluntary association of public service broadcasters, asserted in 1993 that too much imported television would threaten Europe's cultural identity and would injure the new Central and Eastern European democracies, "for which broadcasting plays a decisive role in the affirmation of their new identity" (Luce 1993).[3]

Puerto Rico has experienced all of the forms of pressure on identity and culture discussed here. It was subjected to political coercion by the United States in the early twentieth century. As part of the "Americanization" campaign, U.S. institutional models were substituted for the existing Spanish ones. Theodore Roosevelt Jr., who was Puerto Rico's appointed governor from 1929 to 1932, described this process: "[O]ur currency replaced that of Spain, our stamps the Spanish stamps, etc. We took at once certain actions that are very characteristic of our people. We established a Board of Health and a Department of Education, we did away with such punishments as chains, stocks, etc., and we organized an insular police force; then, as a tribute to our underlying Puritanism, we abolished the government lottery and outlawed cockfighting" (Roosevelt Jr. 1937: 93). In the second half of the twentieth century, overtly coercive efforts to "Americanize" Puerto Ricans were abandoned. Since the institution of the commonwealth arrangement in 1952, Puerto Rico has been exposed to a different type of potential pressure on identity through its partial integration with the United States. In addition, Puerto Rico has imported the cultural products that are held to weaken national identity, receiving large quantities of films, television programs, and recorded music from the United States virtually since the invention of those technologies.

As a ward of the United States for nearly a century, Puerto Rico is a rich setting to study the perceived effects of various pressures on identity. As much as any society, Puerto Rico has been exposed to forces of globalization, through deliberate coercion, through integration into U.S. market culture, and through continuous exposure to imported media products.

THE DEFINITIONAL MAZE

A stumbling block in discussions of national identity is the difficulty of defining such key terms as nation and identity. These everyday words may at first seem transparent, but there is no consensus on the meanings of what one prominent writer on the topic calls the "complex and ramified . . . set of phenomena [that] we subsume under the elusive concepts of ethnicity, nation, and nationalism" (Smith 1983: xxiii). Because the human emotions and social arrangements described by such terms shade into one another, and because they involve subjective judgments, it has proven impossible to establish an airtight, mutually exclusive set of definitions. Nonetheless, it is possible and necessary to place definitional cornerstones.

Nation and State

The terms "nation" and "state" are sometimes used synonymously, but there are important conceptual distinctions to be made between them. The fundamental distinction is between nation as people and state as government.

Nation. The term "nation" does not enjoy clarity of definition,[4] yet it is the foundation for the ideas and terms under discussion here. Eric Hobsbawm points out that "no satisfactory criterion can be discovered for deciding which of the many human collectivities should be labelled in this way" and that whatever the specified criteria may be, there will always be cases that do not fit (1990: 5–8). In the face of this difficulty, many analysts have highlighted the centrality of group allegiance to the concept.[5] This book starts from that point and, following leading writers in the field, regards a "nation" as *a self-defined community of people who share a sense of solidarity based on a belief in a common heritage and who claim political rights that may include self-determination.* Certain aspects of this definition require elaboration. First, it centers on a subjective, internal self-definition by members of the nation. Second, a group's self-recognition as a nation is usually based on some combination of objective characteristics of history, language, culture, and territory. Third, the claim to political self-determination is not necessarily tantamount to a desire for political independence.

The importance of a perceived common descent to the self-definition of some groups as nations requires a differentiation between nation and ethnic group. Nations are often held to be the descendants of ethnic groups (Smith 1988: 8), and the two terms are typically defined with respect to one another.[6] A common distinction made between the two is that the term "nation" carries the connotation of a separate political identity and desire for self-determination, whereas "ethnic group" refers to a group that sees itself as culturally distinct without demanding self-determination. Jason W. Clay's definition makes this clear: "Ethnic groups . . . retain their cultural identity while accepting and operating within the political, institutional framework of the state" (Clay 1989: 224). Such a definition describes, for example, Mexican Americans in the United States or the Douala, Bulu, and others in Cameroon (Bjornson 1986: 134).[7]

By these definitions, Puerto Ricans in Puerto Rico are a nation; Puerto Ricans in New York may still be part of the Puerto Rican nation, depending on who is doing the defining, but in the U.S. mainland they constitute an ethnic group.

State. "State" is the least contested of the terms under consideration here. In Hugh Seton-Watson's neat definition, a state is "a legal and political organization, with the power to require obedience and loyalty from its citizens" (1977: 1). A state and its territory make up what is ordinarily called simply a country. Countries are commonly understood to be the big, differently colored areas on world maps: the landmasses, governments, and people or peoples of a certain geographical area, recognized as such by residents, international organizations, and therefore mapmakers. Although border disputes between states and challenges to legitimacy within states may exist, these are based on recognized borders and political bodies.

The term "nation-state" might appear to be useful at this point. On the surface, this designation seems precise but, in fact, it muddies the definitional waters with its implication of congruence of nation and state. As few states are ethnically homogeneous or consist of one self-defined group,[8] "nation-state" is seldom an accurate description. Further confounding this issue is the fact that the term "nation-state" is used at times as a synonym for "country."

"Nation" and "state," as defined here, may overlap partially or completely. Within or across states may reside various ethnic or other groups, some or all of which may consider themselves to be nations. States that comprise several nations include the former Czechoslovakia, now divided into the Czech Republic and Slovakia; the former Yugoslavia; Canada; and the United States, within whose borders live the entire populations of several Native American nations. Nations divided across states include the Basques in France and Spain and the Kurds in Iraq, Turkey, Iran, and Syria. The breakup of multinational states, notable of late in Eastern Europe and the former Soviet Union, is an effort on the part of collectivities that consider themselves to be nations, as defined here, to become nation-states. However, these collectivities are seldom the sole occupants of a geographic area, complicating the process, as in the former Yugoslavia, and calling into question the possibility of creating a state that is also a nation.

Nationalism and National Identity

The concepts of nationalism and national identity concern human emotions and perceptions. The terms are often used interchangeably, but, like nation and state, they are more useful when they are conceptually separated.

Nationalism. As with the other concepts under consideration, the definition of nationalism is confused, and the word has been applied to several linked phenomena. In everyday parlance, the word "nationalism" describes an emotional attachment to one's country.[9] But the term "nationalism" also has a specialized meaning: it is a doctrine that holds that the political organization of the world should be based on nations, and it describes any political movement whose aim is national independence (Kedourie 1960: 9, 115).

Nationalism of both types—emotional attachment and organized movement—is found in nations as well as in states, and, indeed, tension between nation and state may be manifested as one or another sort of nationalism on the part of either or both. The state may invoke nationalist arguments in the attempt to quell internal disputes caused by subgroup militant nationalism within its borders.

National Identity. The term "nationalism" is not only burdened with two distinct meanings but is also often pressed into service in yet another way, as a descriptor of peoples' sense of affiliation with their nation or state. Critics have noted that many authors do not distinguish nationalism from "national sentiment," "national feeling," or national identity (Smith 1983: 174; Schlesinger 1991: 168; Rossbach 1986: 187). Philip Schlesinger, a careful analyst of existing material on nation and identity, argues that "the sole category of 'nationalism' is too large a receptacle to do justice to the range of variation of collective sentiments" found in nations and that "national identity" is a useful term for describing the way a nation can serve as a referent for individual or group self-definition. This frees the term "nationalism" to indicate some extent of community mobilization and establishes a basic condition for national identity: related to the idea that a nation entails a sense of community, national identity designates an individual's sense of membership in the nation, the use of the nation as a cognitive "point of reference" (Schlesinger 1991: 168).

The flurry of attention to national identity in recent years has prompted various approaches to defining it. In the book *National Identity*, Anthony D. Smith (1991: 9, 14) devised a complex, multipart definition. In contrast, at a conference on national identity, participants, "in recognition of the futility of such an undertaking," chose not to attempt "to establish a definition of the term 'national identity' that would satisfy all demands placed on it" (Boerner 1986: 14). The term "national identity," like the others considered here, has many shades of meaning in the many contexts in which it appears. Nonetheless, a simple working definition of national identity can be *an individual's sense of belonging to a collectivity that calls itself a nation.* Like the term "nation" itself, national identity is defined from within, based on the beliefs of the members of the purported nation. The subjective feeling of national identity is generally (although not entirely) expressed in a way that can be perceived by those both inside and outside the nation through what Schlesinger calls the "mythico-cultural apparatus": symbols such as language, flags, and anthems (1991: 168). This apparatus is often constructed partly from what Eric Hobsbawm has termed "invented traditions"—ritual socializing practices with implicit historical roots that are created to establish, symbolize, and legitimate group membership or certain behaviors (Hobsbawm and Ranger 1983: 1, 9).

National identity may refer to a sense of belonging to a nation that does or does not have its own territory, that does or does not have political autonomy. The condition of the nation—stateless, territorial, dominant, dominated, colonized, and so on—is one factor in the way national identity is experienced and manifested.

PUERTO RICO

Under the definitions set forth here, Puerto Rico is a nation—a self-defined community of people who share a sense of solidarity based on a belief in a common heritage, and who claim the right to political self-determination. Eight of the fourteen Puerto Rican politicians interviewed in depth for this book used the words "nation" or "nationality" in describing Puerto Rico (see Figure 1, page 71). Puerto Rico has a clearly defined territory and half a millennium of shared history and language. Its residents share an identity as Puerto Ricans—a sense of the island and its culture as a fundamental "point of reference." As one Puerto Rican political leader explained, "We have a common territory, a common past, a history, a language, and an identity as members of a nation, the Puerto Rican nation."

Puerto Rico's contemporary political situation is different from that of many self-defined nations: while peoples throughout the world are seeking independence, most Puerto Ricans are not. No candidate from the political party that advocates independence has garnered more than 12.5 percent of the vote in the last thirty years, and in a 1994 ballot on the island's future, the independence option received just 4.4 percent of the votes. Yet, the low level of electoral support for independence does not carry with it a correspondingly low level of awareness of, or interest in, a distinct Puerto Rican identity. To the contrary, the importance of retaining Puerto Rican culture and identity is stressed by adherents of all political positions. Three principal factions are arrayed around the issue of Puerto Rico's political status, each with its own status preference, political party, and view of Puerto Rican identity. The political struggle over status provides an opportunity to examine differing viewpoints on identity from the perspectives of the actors in the debate. Comparing these views, as they developed historically and as they are expressed today, provides a foundation for considering issues of national identity.

As a site of contested identity, Puerto Rico is unusual in several ways: it is a small island with no border conflicts; its indigenous population was completely wiped out during the Spanish conquest, leaving no native groups to demand recognition; and its unambiguously Spanish colonial heritage left it with little suppressed ethnic, linguistic, or religious competition. Under Spanish rule, the slave and free black population was comparatively small and was never isolated, leaving Puerto Rico today with perceptible African cultural elements, but little in the way of a separate black culture (Wells 1969: 269–70). The relative homogeneity of the Puerto Rican population is unusual in the modern world.

This book examines the interplay of island political processes with aspects of Puerto Rican identity. It is divided into three parts. The first part describes nearly a century of Puerto Rican history, emphasizing Puerto Rican identity within the framework of Puerto Rico–United States interaction. It begins with early U.S. attempts to "Americanize" the Puerto Rican people and continues through recent decades in which the central issue in the island has been how to define Puerto Rico's relationship with the United States. This historical section is based principally on official documents and contemporary newspaper accounts, as well as secondary sources. The emphasis is on bilateral relations between Puerto Rico and the United States as expressed through formal political processes, with Puerto Rican internal politics as a secondary consideration.

The second part of the study presents a cross-sectional view of the ways in which current Puerto Rican identity is expressed across different political groups. The examination of contemporary Puerto Rico is based on interviews with Puerto Rican political leaders and focus groups with members of political party youth organizations. It provides a close-up view of island politics and is centered on the debate over Puerto Rico's relationship with the United States. This section emphasizes the struggles between competing groups within the Puerto Rican political system; United States–Puerto Rico relations are secondary.

This dual focus on changes over time and concurrent variation within a society seeks to expand understanding of the process of defining and perpetuating a collective sense of national identity. Both historical and contemporary parts of this case study are important to such an understanding, and each provides context for the other. The historical overview establishes the background to the current situation, which, in turn, reveals the modern outcomes of historical processes.

The final section of the book examines the Puerto Rican case for insights into collective identity formation that may have resonance beyond Puerto Rico. It highlights long-recognized concepts that merit greater attention, such as the centrality of perceived uniqueness to group identity and the dynamic nature of identity. It also develops ideas that emerge directly from this study of Puerto Rico—particularly the notions that reaction to a given element of imported culture may vary in relation to how much the import is perceived to be displacing its local equivalent and that pressure on identity can strengthen that identity.

National identity is not inborn and it does not fall from the sky. Like any form of collective identity, it is a product of socialization and communication processes. This study examines the operation of those processes in Puerto Rico, focusing on the perceptions of Puerto Ricans.

NOTES

1. Some careful analysts have specified differences in meanings of the different terms. John Tomlinson, for example, states that

> [g]lobalisation may be distinguished from imperialism in that it is a far less coherent or culturally directed process. . . . [T]he idea of imperialism contains, at least, the notion of a purposeful project: the *intended* spread of a social system from one centre of power across the globe. The idea of "globalisation" suggests interconnection and interdependency of all global areas which happens in a far less purposeful way. It happens as the result of economic and cultural practices which do not, of themselves, aim at global integration, but which nonetheless produce it. (Tomlinson

1991: 175)

2. The paucity of research may stem from the rootedness of assumptions about the damage wrought by imported cultural products, as well as from the difficulty of isolating the effects of mass media. Some studies have begun to appear, focusing on developed countries whose media are swamped by larger dominant neighbors or by exports from the United States (Lealand 1988; Garde, Gilsdorf, and Wechselmann 1993).

3. The concern that imported media will interfere with nascent national identities is the other side of the optimistic view expressed in 1950s and 1960s literature on political modernization that mass media and the modernization process would change peoples' allegiances from the village to the state level, pushing along the conversion of traditional societies into modern ones (Pye 1962; Lerner 1958; Lerner and Schramm 1967; Deutsch 1966).

4. As one author has noted, "the 'nation'—so formidably real in the real world of everyone's everyday existence—has eluded all efforts of scholars to agree on precisely what it is" (Isaacs 1975: 174). More than twenty years ago, Walker Connor expressed great frustration with the "careless use" of the terms "nation," "state," and "nationalism," and outlined detailed distinctions between them (1972: 332–36). The looseness of terminology that he decried continues to the present.

5. The oft-cited Ernest Renan, a nineteenth-century French academic, was among the earliest scholars to attempt to define the nation. In his 1882 essay "What Is a Nation?" Renan dismissed race, language, religion, geography, and community of interest as defining factors of a nation. Instead, he concluded, a nation is determined by a shared past and the "agreement and clearly expressed desire to continue a life in common" (203). Renan's assertion of the subjective character of nationality provided a basic foundation shared by many subsequent considerations of the nature of nationhood. Dankwart Rustow, in *A World of Nations* (1967: 22–23), noted the "dubious distinction" that some have made "between so-called 'objective characteristics' of nationhood—such as geography, political history, and economic structure—and so-called 'subjective characteristics'—such as consensus, loyalty, or will." Dubious distinction or not, Rustow clearly favored the "subjective" characteristics. "The relevant question," he asserted (28), "is whether there was any single group on which overriding loyalties in fact were focused, and whether every individual was conceived as having a direct relationship to that group." Ernest Gellner's definition also featured a concern for group membership: "Two men are of the same nation if and only if they *recognize* each other as belonging to the same nation" (1983: 7). For Hugh Seton-Watson, a nation is "a community of people, whose members are bound together by a sense of solidarity, a common culture, and a national consensus" (1977: 1). Benedict Anderson described a nation as an "imagined political community" whose members will never all meet one another but which is "always conceived as a deep, horizontal comradeship" (1983: 15–16). Key in all these definitions of nation is the notion of group identity: Renan's "life in common," Rustow's "overriding loyalties," Gellner's mutual recognition, Seton-Watson's "sense of solidarity," Anderson's "deep comradeship." Hobsbawm himself takes this path: "As an initial working assumption any sufficiently large body of people whose members regard themselves as members of a 'nation,' will be regarded as such" (1990: 8).

6. This relationship has been much battered by the definitional maelstrom. Anthony D. Smith (1981: 85) maintains that nations and ethnic communities are "closely related," Konstantin Symmons-Symonolewicz says that "ethnic consciousness cannot be compared to *national* consciousness" (1985: 220), and, at the far end of the spectrum, E. K. Francis asserts that "a nation is by no means based on shared ethnicity but on political relationships" (1976: 33). These definitional differences, of course, stem, in part, from the lack of an agreed-upon definition of nation. A typical sociological definition of ethnic group is a group of people who, because of "their shared cultural heritage, are regarded as socially distinct" (Robertson 1987: 286).

7. This definition would require stretching to include such groups as various hyphenated Americans whose ethnicity may be expressed at most by attendance at an annual parade. Konstantin Symmons-Symonolewicz (1985: 214) usefully uses the term "ethnic categories" to denote "all culturally distinct elements existing in modern society," that is, minorities and immigrant groups, however dispersed or assimilated they may be. This term could include, for example, Polish-Americans. The application of the term "ethnic group" to collectivities that are struggling for independence may stem from definitional disagreement or vagueness or from political differences. Kurds or Chechens may be referred to as ethnic groups, but their striving for political self-determination indicates that they do not accept and operate "within the political, institutional framework of the state" (Clay 1989: 224) and, indeed, are fighting to get outside it and establish their own states. They would define themselves as nations, not as ethnic groups, in this definitional scheme. In these cases, insiders and outsiders may, for political reasons, use different designations for the same group, with insiders defining themselves as a nation and opponents preferring to perceive an entity less threatening to the status quo—an ethnic group.

8. Complete correspondence between nation and state is rare in the modern world; among the few examples cited by Anthony D. Smith (1981: 9–10) are Iceland and Malta.

9. This understanding of nationalism is similar to, if not synonymous with, everyday conceptions of patriotism. Early nationalism scholar Carleton J. H. Hayes (1960: 2) defined nationalism as the "fusion of patriotism with a consciousness of nationality."

Part I

Identity in Puerto Rican History

2

The Americanization
Campaign, 1898–1948

PUERTO RICO AS A COLONY OF SPAIN

When Columbus claimed Puerto Rico for Spain in 1493, the island was inhabited
by Taíno and Carib Indians. The natives resisted attempts by the Spanish to
enslave them, but after an organized indigenous uprising of 1511 was put down,
according to Friar Iñigo Abbad, eighteenth-century chronicler of Puerto Rican
history, "the Indians were reduced to obedience and parceled out among the
conquerors, their muscles put to good use in the mines" (Abbad [1788] 1970: 57).
Brutal exploitation by the Spanish colonizers, along with epidemics and escape
through migration to other islands, quickly reduced the native population to
insignificant numbers.

From the sixteenth through the eighteenth centuries, Puerto Rico, lacking
riches or rumors of riches, became a military outpost for the Spanish empire at the
entrance to the Caribbean. The island developed a plantation economy based on
labor provided by the African slave trade. As was characteristic of Spanish
colonies, authority was centered in the governor-general, an appointee of the
Spanish crown. Puerto Rican essayist Antonio Pedreira, writing in the 1930s,
termed the first three centuries of Spanish rule a period of "faithful prolongation of
the Spanish culture" (Pedreira [1936] 1957: 15). During this period, according to
Abbad, the term "creole," typically used in Spanish colonies to denote children
born in the New World to Spanish parents, came to be used indiscriminately in
Puerto Rico to designate "every person born on the island, of any race or mixture.
The Europeans are called whites or, to use their own expression, *men from the
other side*" (Abbad [1788] 1970: 181).

In the nineteenth century, historians agree that a distinctly Puerto Rican culture
became increasingly perceptible (Maldonado-Denis 1972: 22–23; Morales Carrión
1983: 41). Pedreira termed the period from 1809 to the U.S. takeover in 1898 a
time of "awakening and beginning . . . during which Puerto Rico began to

discover an independent manner" within its Spanish culture. Without rejecting "his Puerto Rican Spanishness," the Puerto Rican "considered himself a Spaniard *from here* with ideas and reactions different from those *from there*" (Pedreira [1936] 1957: 15, 94). Members of the landowning and educated classes were the first to perceive that these different "ideas and reactions" also meant that their own interests differed from those of their Spanish rulers (Wells 1969: 52–56). Puerto Rican scholar José Luis González (1987: 77) describes the intellectuals of the time as making "a project" of the formation of a separate Puerto Rican identity.

The developing sense of difference between the native-born and the Spanish rulers was felt throughout Latin America and became a key factor in the independence struggles of the early nineteenth century. But while most of Latin America engaged in a war for independence from Spain, Puerto Rico remained outside the fray. Rather than take up arms against the Spanish, islanders who desired autonomy negotiated for political rights under the Spanish crown. Several explanations have been put forth for Puerto Rican leaders' tendency during this period to work for political reform rather than revolution. One factor was Puerto Rico's position as a military outpost and the resultant numbers of Spanish soldiers and police in the island, which rendered armed opposition infeasible (Morales Padrón 1962: 13; Wells 1969: 53). Further, as Spain lost control of its colonies, many Spanish partisans from South America took refuge in Puerto Rico. This influx of loyalist exiles made Puerto Rico less hospitable to revolutionary movements, and the weak economic position of Puerto Rican landholders inhibited them from promoting revolution (Morales Carrión 1983: 73).

The island's first pro-independence uprising, known as the *Grito de Lares*, took place in 1868, nearly half a century after most Latin American countries had won independence. Determined to hold on to what little was left of its empire, Spain promptly quashed that action and repressed subsequent Puerto Rican independence activities. A group of Puerto Ricans who favored independence congregated in New York, where in 1895 they formed a Puerto Rican section of the Cuban Revolutionary Party, which was promoting an armed insurrection for Cuba's independence from Spain. At the founding meeting, the fifty-nine members of the Puerto Rican group who were present agreed that Puerto Rico needed its own flag to replace the Spanish flag and to symbolize their aspirations. The flag they adopted was a visual echo of the flag used by the Cuban revolutionaries, identical in design but with the colors reversed. Both flags featured a single white, five-pointed star set in a triangle along the left side on a bed of five horizontal stripes. Cuba's triangle was red, Puerto Rico's blue; the stripes were white and blue for Cuba, white and red for Puerto Rico (*El Mundo* 1952d; Rosario Natal 1989: 44–45; Todd 1967: 16–18).

Within Puerto Rico, support for independence was minimal, but there was great dissatisfaction with islanders' lack of control over their own affairs. Proposals for a system to replace Spain's authoritarian rule were of two general types. One favored Puerto Rico's full political assimilation into Spain as a province, while the other advocated political and administrative autonomy with continued ties to the Spanish empire. In 1897, Spain granted the island the right to voting representation in the Spanish parliament and considerable self-government through a newly created Puerto Rican parliament.

On 25 July 1898, before this new political arrangement was fully implemented, U.S. troops fighting the Spanish-American War invaded Puerto Rico. The next morning, U.S. troops replaced the Spanish flag with the American flag in the harbor of Guánica (*New York Times* 1898). The war ended less than a month later; as part of the postwar settlement Spain relinquished sovereignty over Cuba and ceded Puerto Rico, Guam, and the Philippine Islands to the United States. The war had ostensibly been undertaken to liberate Cuba from Spanish rule. But, commented Theodore Roosevelt Jr., who was later appointed governor of Puerto Rico by President Hoover, "[b]esides Cuba, when the war was finished we had . . . Puerto Rico and the Philippine Islands. In neither case had we announced our intention of liberating them when we declared war. The problem, therefore, was just what status they should assume. We had no definite ideas, for when we declared war we had not thought of them" (Roosevelt Jr. 1937: 84).

With or without "definite ideas," the U.S. presence was welcomed by most Puerto Ricans. After centuries of neglect by the Spanish, the democratic ideology and material resources brought by the United States were favorably regarded. It was generally believed that Puerto Rico would be incorporated as a U.S. territory (Hunter 1966: 57), a prospect that seemed to promise statehood, as evidenced by examples in the North American mainland. Territorial status had preceded statehood for Florida and Louisiana, both of which were acquired by treaty as Puerto Rico had been, and was the status held at the end of the Spanish-American War by the future states of New Mexico, Arizona, and Oklahoma (Dávila Colón 1984: 147, 315, 671–722; Lewis 1963: 106).

Puerto Rico was the first Latin American property acquired by the United States since the 1823 Monroe Doctrine had proclaimed that the United States would not accept any European intervention in Latin America. The island represented not only a gain of territory for the United States but also a laboratory for ideas of proper civic arrangements. With respect to territorial expansion, L. S. Rowe, a political scientist who participated in the colonial administration in Puerto Rico, noted in 1904 (xi): "It is clear that the extension of our influence, both commercial and political, was inevitable; inevitable in the sense that the movement was inextricably bound up with our growth as a nation." In terms of spreading ideas, the U.S. major general who directed the invasion of the island had claimed: "This is not a war of devastation, but one to give to all within the control of its military and naval forces the advantages and blessings of enlightened civilization" (*Cong. Rec.* 1922c: 5914).

U. S. MILITARY OCCUPATION, OCTOBER 1898–MAY 1900

For the first eighteen months of U.S. sovereignty, Puerto Rico was occupied and ruled by the U.S. military. The internal autonomy that Puerto Rico had painstakingly negotiated from Spain soon ended. Major General Guy V. Henry was installed as governor, and U.S. military officers were put in place as mayors. The majority Liberal Party, which controlled the Puerto Rican cabinet that had been retained from the period of Spanish rule, tried to carry on, promoting the principle of "Puerto Rico for the Puerto Ricans." After several months in office, General Henry restructured the cabinet and placed it clearly under his authority (*New York Times* 1899a).

In 1899, a group of Puerto Ricans formed a new political organization, the Puerto Rican Republican Party, swearing loyalty to "our new nationality" and the American flag. The new party was ready to do whatever was necessary to achieve its primary objective of Puerto Rican statehood. Its founding manifesto argued that English, "which will soon be the official language," should be taught in schools in order to put Puerto Rico "in more favorable conditions soon to become a new state" of the union. But the party was not happy with U.S. military control, asserting that the Puerto Rican people were competent to govern themselves and that "we believe the time has come in the island for civil government" (Partido Republicano Puertorriqueño [1899] 1917: 4).

U.S. military authorities perceived not a competent electorate, but a poor agrarian society, with much illiteracy and little infrastructure. They set about bringing the island up to their standards, installing sanitation systems, building roads and railroads, and rearranging the legal system and other institutions (Rowe 1904: 122–26). "Like most countries," explained Theodore Roosevelt Jr. (1937: 85), "we were convinced that we had the best form of government ever devised in the world and that our customs and habits were also the most advisable." This unself-conscious belief in the superiority of everything from the United States drove the extensive reforms implemented by U.S. military administrators.

The remodeling of Puerto Rico was not simply a matter of providing material resources and technical expertise. U.S. leaders also sought to replace Spanish institutions. They had a clear agenda of "Americanization" of the island, a requisite, in their view, for the eventual self-rule and integration into the United States of a population that they perceived as politically immature and unequipped for self-government. The Americanization campaign in Puerto Rico had its antecedents in the "melting pot" ethos prevalent in the United States in the late nineteenth century. Among the U.S. policymakers publicly appraising techniques for assimilating the vast numbers of immigrants entering the country at that time (Talbot 1917; Harper 1980) was Theodore Roosevelt Sr., a vehement advocate of the melting pot model. The future president expressed in 1894 his belief in the necessity of full assimilation "of the newcomers to our shores. We must Americanize them in every way" (Roosevelt [1894] 1926: 20–21). This notion of Americanization was applied in Puerto Rico to a people who had not voluntarily entered the United States but rather had been annexed by force. Arturo Morales Carrión has described the process from the Puerto Rican point of view: "Americanization as a creed did not simply involve embracing the principles of American federalism or establishing the political institutions of a republican America, but of accepting with American tutelage the notion that one belonged to a decadent and inferior civilization, that the new tutors were the benevolent masters, that one had to undergo not simply a civic but a psychological transformation" (Morales Carrión 1990: 46).

In the spirit of the times, Americanization was undertaken, in Rowe's words (1904: 12), with "our unbounded faith in the benefits of American rule and the blessings of American institutions." Political institutions were early conduits for "Americanization" measures. When General Henry restructured the island cabinet in 1899, he unambiguously asserted that "heads of departments or others objecting to the introduction of American methods of business and progress or to the investigation of the affairs of the departments . . . will be relieved from office" (*New York Times* 1899a). U.S. administrators recognized, however, that they could not implant a new social and political system overnight. While some saw this as simply a logistical problem, Rowe, who participated in commissions charged with rewriting Puerto Rican legal codes, argued from a more relativistic position that the occupiers had a responsibility to consider the worth of established Puerto Rican institutions. But along with that, he expressed "a firm determination to bring the new peoples with whom we may be brought into close and intimate contact, by means of the slow process of education, to a free and willing acceptance of all that is best in our system of law and government" (Rowe 1904: 19).

The educational system was a primary target of the occupiers' efforts. Just 8 percent of the school-age population was enrolled in school (Osuna 1949: 341), many Spanish schoolteachers had returned to Spain (Negrón de Montilla 1990: 22), and the system was in disarray.[1] U.S. secretary of war Elihu Root (1899: 38) believed that education should be a priority of the occupation:

> A necessary element to the success of . . . any scheme of government in Puerto Rico is the complete establishment of a system of education which will afford the opportunity for every child of school age in the island to acquire elementary instruction. The cost of this should be defrayed from the insular treasury, if its revenues are sufficient, and if not it should be regarded as a duty of the highest obligation resting upon the United States and the expense should be borne by the United States.

In response to the evident need, Governor General Henry completely redesigned the educational system, stating among his objectives the hiring of competent English teachers for the children (Negrón de Montilla 1990: 26). By December 1899, each Puerto Rican municipality employed at least one teacher from the United States, and an English-language school had been established in San Juan

(*New York Times* 1899b). Victor S. Clark, appointed president of the newly established Puerto Rico Board of Education, made explicit the goals of the educational policy in an 1899 report to his superior: "If the schools are made American, and teachers and pupils are inspired with the American spirit, and people of both races can be made to cooperate harmoniously in building up the schools, the island will become in its sympathies, views, and attitude toward life and toward government essentially American. The great mass of Puerto Ricans are as yet passive and plastic. . . . Their ideals are in our hands to create and mold" (Davis 1899: 656). Within two years of the U.S. takeover, all Puerto Rican schools had reading material in English and Spanish, U.S. history books, and U.S. maps. Thanks to a donation by a Civil War veterans' organization, boasted the military governor, "nearly every school house in the island is provided with an American flag" (Davis 1899: 646).

CIVILIAN GOVERNMENT

After eighteen months of military occupation, the U.S. Congress enacted the Organic Act of 1900, instituting civil government in Puerto Rico. The Organic Act was known as the Foraker Act, after its sponsor, Senator Joseph B. Foraker. The civil government it mandated was seen as an improvement by Puerto Ricans who had been pressuring for an end to military occupation, but it was far from the self-rule they desired. The unwillingness of the United States to install a popularly elected government caused great disillusionment among Puerto Rican leaders and became a central factor in island politics (Lewis 1963: 106). The new administration was to be controlled by appointees from the U.S. mainland because, in the occupiers' view, as expressed by the island's military governor, "the social, industrial, moral, and intellectual condition of the people is such as to seem to me to demand, before local self-government can be granted, that they undergo a period of probation" (U.S. Senate 1900: 8) During this open-ended "probation period," Puerto Rico would be run by a governor and an eleven-member Executive Council, at least five of whose members were to be "native inhabitants of Porto Rico" (Foraker Act 1900, sec. 18). All of these officials would be appointed by the U.S. president. The Executive Council exercised both executive and legislative duties. It comprised the executive offices of secretary, attorney general, treasurer, auditor, commissioner of the interior, and commissioner of education, and also served as the upper house of the Legislative Assembly. The lower house, a thirty-five member House of Delegates, was to be elected by Puerto Rican voters. Legislative powers were constrained by the provision that "all laws enacted by the Legislative Assembly shall be reported to the Congress of the United States, which hereby reserves the power and authority, if deemed advisable, to annul the same" (Foraker Act 1900, sec. 31). Puerto Rican historian Arturo Morales Carrión (1983: 156) has described the government installed under the Foraker Act as "paternalistic . . . dominated by Washington, and run primarily by an American bureaucracy with a smattering of Puerto Rican participation."

A curious oversight in the drafting of the Foraker Act caused the name of the island to be officially misspelled. The law established a civil government for the island of "Porto Rico." In writing the bill, Congress followed the spelling in the English text of the Treaty of Paris, the document through which Spain had ceded the island to the United States. The U.S. Geographic Board changed the spelling of Puerto Rico "to conform to that found in the treaty of annexation," effectively causing the official designation of the island to be incorrect until 1930, when steps were taken to correct it (U.S. Geographic Board 1933: 622; U.S. War Department 1932: 14).

The Foraker Act included a provision for Puerto Ricans to elect a "resident commissioner" to represent island interests in the United States. In 1904, the post was upgraded; the resident commissioner would join representatives of Arizona, New Mexico, and other "incorporated territories" as a nonvoting delegate in the U.S. House of Representatives (Cabranes 1979: 43). A 1901 U.S. Supreme Court decision had designated Puerto Rico an "unincorporated territory," a new characterization that left the island's future undetermined (Morales Carrión 1983: 157; Hunter 1966: 65).

At the time of the Foraker Act, many island politicians favored the extension of U.S. citizenship to Puerto Ricans. This desire did not mean they were ready to discard their Puerto Ricanness. Political leader Luis Muñoz Rivera stated in 1900, "We continue in the fight for our rights, for a full American nationality and for a full Porto Rican personality" (in Negrón de Montilla 1975: 26). In the U.S. Congress, debate over the citizenship issue turned on several questions of the relationship between Puerto Rico and the United States, including whether granting citizenship would imply eventual statehood for the island. Rather than resolve the complex political and economic issues involved in granting islanders U.S. citizenship, the authors of the Foraker bill included a provision that made Puerto Ricans "citizens of Porto Rico, and as such entitled to the protection of the United States" (Foraker Act 1900, sec. 7).

The 1900 election of the House of Delegates was the first time since the Spanish-American War that Puerto Ricans had exercised a voice in choosing their leadership. When the first civilian governor of Puerto Rico, U.S. appointee Charles H. Allen, addressed the newly elected legislature, attendees entered the theater to the sounds of a U.S. military band playing "patriotic airs" (Allen 1900: 4). Governor Allen's comments to the legislators exemplified the paternalistic attitude of the United States. "Henceforth, you must move forward with the light of modern experience to guide your way. . . . You are today the masters of your own future," said Allen, as he made detailed suggestions for the organization of the municipal administration and judiciary and stressed the importance of education in creating "an enlightened citizenship" (5, 9–11, 17).

The fledgling civil government set out to follow Governor Allen's dictates. A contemporary observer noted that the United States-appointed commissioner of education faced "the task of greatest magnitude. . . . Not only had the department to be organized, but the system itself had to be created. Public education had been almost completely neglected by the Spanish Government" (Rowe 1904: 139). The education commissioner advocated establishing an educational system that would mirror the U.S. system, complete with English teachers brought in from the mainland (Negrón de Montilla 1990: 51).

The new education system needed buildings as well as teachers. In an early infrastructure project, eight schools were built around the island in 1901 and named after U.S. heroes such as George Washington and John Adams. The commissioner of education was greeted at official inauguration ceremonies by schoolchildren who sang "America" in English while the island's governor, an appointee from the mainland, raised the U.S. flag. U.S. holidays were pronounced official school holidays and were celebrated accordingly. The education commissioner claimed in 1901: "These exercises have done much to Americanize the island . . . it's one of the most gratifying results so far achieved in our work" (Negrón de Montilla 1990: 61; 1975: 45, 49).

While U.S. holidays were promoted, Puerto Rican holidays were downplayed. In 1903, on the occasion of the Puerto Rican holiday celebrating the 410th anniversary of Columbus's discovery of the island, the education commissioner grudgingly arranged a commemoration:

> Some recognition of this day should occur in public schools.
> I do not think advisable that we should have any elaborate exercises at that time and no special program will be issued by the Department.
> Exercises should be of a historical character making specially prominent the life and discoveries of Columbus. (Negrón de Montilla 1975: 87)

The issue of whether Three Kings Day should be a school holiday in the island arose periodically. In Puerto Rico, as in some other Latin countries, the Feast of the Epiphany, January 6, is an important part of Christmas celebrations. On January 6 children traditionally receive gifts, brought not by Santa Claus but by the Three Kings (the Magi). When the Puerto Rican school calendar was changed, Three Kings Day was removed from the list of holidays. Negrón de Montilla has documented notice of this action in 1907 and opposition to it in 1925 and 1928 (1990: 135, 237, 240); undoubtedly protest occurred on other occasions as well.

The school system was the key in the campaign for the universalization of the English language. Governor Hunt, who succeeded Governor Allen, reported in 1901 that teachers were "working assiduously to fulfill their duty" to learn English (Hunt 1902a: 43). At the same time, an article in a Puerto Rican teachers' magazine protested "the spirit of absorption and supremacy with which the English language is being imposed" (Negrón de Montilla 1975: 58).

Not only language was being imposed. In 1902, Governor Hunt told the Legislative Assembly: "The time seems ripe for the introduction of many changes in the present laws. The full benefits of American systems can only be realized through legislation sweeping away un-American principles and substituting American" (Hunt 1902b: 348). By mid-1902, the secretary of government reported the enactment of a "system of laws largely taken from the most modern and approved American statutes covering the same subjects" (Hunt 1902a: 83).

In the process of revamping Puerto Rico's political and legal system, the Executive Council passed the Official Languages Act, mandating that "the English language and the Spanish language shall be used indiscriminately" in all official and public activities, with translation provided as necessary (*Laws of Puerto Rico Annotated* 1982: 375). While this may have been part of the "Americanization" process, it has been interpreted by some Puerto Ricans as having been necessary for the functioning of the council, few or none of whose mainland appointees spoke Spanish (Cámara de Representantes 1991).

Governor Hunt resigned in 1903. In his farewell address he exhorted the Puerto Rican legislators to "let your conduct carry you toward ends which mean that you realize your share in the pride of the nation: that while properly cherishing in your hearts deep reverence for the honored traditions of your forefathers, yet in truth you are American in spirit, American in hope, American in sentiment" (Hunt 1903: 322).

The issue of Puerto Rico's relationship to the United States was crucial to Puerto Ricans at the beginning of the century. Political party leaders were not happy with their lack of political power and advocated self-government through statehood or territorial status (Hunter 1966: 65–66). The Unionist Party was founded in 1904 to advocate self-government (Morales Carrión 1983: 161). The party proposed three possible arrangements: "We find it feasible that the island of Puerto Rico be confederated with the United States of North America; that it be a State of the American Union, through which we will attain the self-government that we need and request; and we also declare that the Island of Puerto Rico may be declared an independent nation under the protection of the United States" (Pagán 1959, vol. 1: 107). This was the first time since the U.S. takeover that independence had been formally proposed as an option for the island, but independence was not the party's preference. While noting the possibility of independence, the Unionist Party, joined by the Republican Party, continued to favor statehood. These two parties accounted for the great majority of the Puerto Rican electorate (Lewis 1963: 115; Cabranes 1979: 59).

In 1911, Unionist Luis Muñoz Rivera, Puerto Rico's resident commissioner to the United States, reiterated the same three possibilities that had been put forward seven years earlier for resolving Puerto Rico's unsatisfactory political situation. Referring to Puerto Rico's status as a "problem," Muñoz Rivera made it clear that independence was listed only as a last resort and that statehood was preferred. "Our problem has three solutions: the proclamation of statehood . . . the concession of home rule . . . and the concession of independence. . . . Of these three solutions, we would prefer the first, we propose the second, and we reserve the third as the last refuge of our right and our honor" (Pagán 1959, vol. 1: 154).

During this period of political shifts, the teaching of English continued to be a priority for U.S. administrators. The language policy of commissioner of education Roland P. Falkner guided the school system from 1905 to 1916. Falkner's policy dictated the use of English as the language of instruction in all school classes, including nonlanguage subjects such as arithmetic and history, rather than simply teaching English as a class subject (Negrón de Montilla 1990: 111). Pedro A. Cebollero, who later became dean of the University of Puerto Rico College of Education, described the intensity of the project:

> During the years 1905–1913 all the resources of the Department of Education were mobilized to further the aims of the Falkner policy. Native teachers were feverishly trained in English under the threat of losing their certificates; an additional salary was paid to those teachers who qualified to teach English; pupils and teachers were required to answer in English examinations prepared by the Department of Education; and extraordinary emphasis was given in the annual reports of the commissioners of education to the progress made in adopting English as the medium of instruction. (Cebollero 1945: 11)

The "height of absurdity" of this policy, according to Cebollero, was reached in 1909, when first graders were taught to read in English but not in Spanish.

Despite the enormous problems of training teachers (Negrón de Montilla 1990: 112–16), Governor Beekman Winthrop claimed in his 1906 annual report that the "movement toward the use of English has always been of local origin. The Department of Education has had to restrain it, not to stimulate it. Wherever adopted it has given satisfaction, and no demands have arisen for a return to the old system" (U.S. Congress 1906: 34). This rosy view was contradicted by a local school superintendent: "The people did not sympathize completely with the plan and it has been difficult to assure the collaboration of competent American and Puerto Rico teachers" (Negrón de Montilla 1990: 118). Indeed, it seems clear that the policies were being carried out against the wishes of many Puerto Ricans who felt that the language policy was interfering with pupils' education (Cebollero 1945: 11). Nonetheless, by 1909 the school exit examination was administered in English, and in 1910 qualified teachers of English were awarded higher salaries (Negrón de Montilla 1990: 139). These moves were so unpopular among educators in the island that in 1913, at the request of the Puerto Rican Teachers' Association, the House of Delegates passed a law abolishing the requirement that teachers take an annual examination in English (Negrón de Montilla 1990: 147). The upper house of the Puerto Rican legislature, composed entirely of U.S. appointees, blocked this bill.

These events took place during a period of increasing frustration on the part of Puerto Ricans who had been petitioning continuously for statehood or some form of self-government. Disappointment in the United States' refusal to act on their petitions led the Unionist Party in 1913 to eliminate from its platform the demands for statehood and U.S. citizenship (Pagán 1959, vol. 1: 156). The extremism of the Falkner language policy was another factor in the rising separatist political sentiments. So connected were the issues that a person's position on school language was taken to represent his or her political orientation. Those who favored English as the language of instruction were called "assimilationists," with the implication that they desired that Puerto Rico become part of the United States, while those who advocated Spanish as the language of instruction were called "separatists" (Rodríguez Bou 1966: 161).

Bills providing U.S. citizenship to Puerto Ricans had failed to pass every Congress since 1900 (Cabranes 1979: 53–68). By the time the issue came up in 1914, separatist sentiments in Puerto Rico had ripened. The House of Delegates rejected U.S. citizenship in a statement addressed to the president and the Congress of the United States conveying "the sentiments and wishes of the vast majority of Porto Ricans":

> We firmly and loyally maintain our opposition to being declared, in defiance of our express wish or without our express consent, citizens of any country whatsoever other than our own beloved soil that God has given us as an inalienable gift and incoercible right. . . . [W]e have demonstrated that there is not the remotest necessity of declaring the people of Porto Rico citizens of the United States.

In a passage that may be interpreted either as revealing the self-image of at least some Puerto Ricans or as deliberately playing on U.S. prejudices, the statement continued:

> We, Porto Ricans, Spanish-Americans, of Latin soul, imaginative, high-strung, ardorous by reason of the sun of our climate and by the blood in our veins, separated from you by over four hundred years and by more than four hundred leagues, with a different historic process, diverse language, different customs . . . could we convert ourselves into American citizens, in that spiritual sense that the notion of citizenship requires, and feel, think, wish, and speak as you do, and have with you that solidary [sic] of life, of memory, of hope, of ideals. . . .
>
> [W]e are satisfied with our own well-beloved Porto Rican citizenship and proud to have been born and to be brethren in our mother island. (Cong. Rec. 1914: 6718–20)

Puerto Ricanness was asserted in another bill submitted to the House of Delegates in 1915, requiring the use of Spanish not only in schools but also in legal proceedings. A student caught collecting signatures on a petition supporting it was expelled from high school. This incident was followed by a student strike and the subsequent establishment of a Puerto Rican high school by disgruntled parents (Negrón de Montilla 1990: 154). Meanwhile, the executive council vetoed the Spanish language bill. Another symbol of Puerto Rico, the "single-star" flag that had been designed in 1895 by opponents of Spanish rule, was the object of unsuccessful petitions to the House of Delegates for official recognition in 1916 and again in 1921 (Rosario Natal 1989: 59).

Puerto Rican leaders were not concerned only with symbolic designations. In 1916 the U.S. Congress considered a proposal for increased self-government for the island. The proposal included U.S. citizenship for Puerto Ricans, a provision that was opposed by the majority Unionist Party and supported by the Republican and Socialist parties[2] (Pagán 1959, vol. 1: 175). Puerto Rico's resident commissioner, Luis Muñoz Rivera, a Unionist, had lobbied hard for the self-government bill but opposed the citizenship clause as possibly precluding future independence (Cabranes 1979: 74–75). During congressional debate on the issue, Muñoz Rivera proclaimed:

> [T]he people of Porto Rico have decided to continue to be Porto Ricans; to be so each day with increasing enthusiasm, to retain their own name, claiming for it the same consideration, the same respect, which they accord to the names of other countries, above all to the name of the United States. Give us statehood and your glorious citizenship will be welcome to us and to our children. If you deny us statehood, we decline your citizenship, frankly, proudly. (*Cong. Rec.* 1916: 7472)

Muñoz Rivera did not carry the forcefulness of this appeal into congressional committee, where, according to legal scholar José A. Cabranes (1979: 86), he offered only "halfhearted opposition" to the citizenship provision. In 1917 the Jones Act, granting increased self-government and U.S. citizenship to Puerto Ricans, was passed by the U.S. Congress.

U.S. CITIZENSHIP

Putting aside initial doubts, Muñoz Rivera's majority Unionist Party ultimately praised the Jones bill, "considering, first of all, that it gives us greater self-government." Unionists accepted U.S. citizenship "without reservation" because it came with the governmental reform that the party had sought for so long. An editorial in the party newspaper *La Democracia* (1917) consented to citizenship "because it defines today the political personality of this people before the world, because it redeems us from our inferiority as colonials, and because it places us in better conditions to continue working for full sovereignty." In contrast to the Unionists' polite tone, the response of the Republican Party of Puerto Rico to the Jones Act was wildly enthusiastic. When the bill passed, the Republicans devoted the entire front page of their newspaper, *El Tiempo*, to the story, illustrated with drawings of the American flag and an American eagle. "Today is a glorious day for Puerto Rico and especially for our party," rhapsodized *El Tiempo*. The passage of the bill "fills us now with joy and gratitude." The Republicans, believing that the Jones Act brought Puerto Rico a step closer to statehood, thanked the United States for "offering a new people, of a race and language different from their own, that which is most valuable and prominent in their national life, which is citizenship" (Partido Republicano Puertorriqueño 1917: 1–2).

Puerto Rican historian Arturo Morales Carrión and others have maintained that citizenship was a way to bring Puerto Rico, with its strategic Caribbean location and potential recruits for the armed forces, more tightly into the U.S. fold on the eve of World War I (Morales Carrión 1990: 53; Maldonado-Denis 1972: 108). Puerto Rican legal scholar Cabranes, however, points out that citizenship is not necessary for conscription of noncitizens under U.S. jurisdiction and states that he is "unaware of any evidence of a design by anyone in the American government during this period to . . . make Puerto Ricans citizens on the theory that they might be conscripted" (1979: 15–16). Whatever the motivation for the citizenship decision, as Morales Carrión (1990: 53–54) notes, it "did not equate citizenship with full political rights or the claim to self-determination." Under the Jones Act, the governor was still appointed by the president of the United States, with the advice and consent of the U.S. Senate, as were the attorney general, the commissioner of education, and the justices of the Puerto Rican Supreme Court. The governor was authorized to appoint the treasurer and the interior, agriculture and commerce, labor, and health commissioners, with the advice and consent of the Senate of Puerto Rico, which replaced the Executive Council as the upper legislative body. Both houses of the legislature were to be popularly elected by qualified voters, who at that time made up 30 percent of the population. The governor's veto of legislation could be overridden by a two-thirds vote of both houses, in which case the legislation would be automatically referred to the president of the United States, who would have absolute veto power (*Cong. Rec.* 1916: 7479).

U.S. citizenship was granted to all Puerto Ricans who desired it. Those who did not desire it could remain citizens of Puerto Rico by declaring under oath the "intention not to become a citizen of the United States" (García Martínez 1982: 159), thereby forfeiting the right to vote or hold office. Of a population of approximately 1.25 million, 288 Puerto Ricans declined U.S. citizenship (Cabranes 1979: 93, 97).

The Jones Act and U.S. citizenship did not resolve the question of Puerto Rico's status. While the English-language section of the Puerto Rican *Times* newspaper lauded the increased self-government and exulted that "the American citizen born in Massachusetts, New York, or Porto Rico are to-day, *in every respect,* equal before the law in this Territory," it recognized that some day, "[p]erhaps we shall all want independence, perhaps we shall all want Statehood; and perhaps we shall not want either one" (*Times* 1917: 7).

Citizenship brought with it continuing pressure to adopt U.S. ways and the English language, which, in turn, brought continued counterpressure to return to Spanish instruction in the schools. In 1919 the teachers' association passed another measure condemning the language policy and requesting that the Puerto

Rican legislature ask the U.S. Congress to permit the use of Spanish as the language of instruction in Puerto Rico's primary schools (Negrón de Montilla 1990: 174). The general structure of primary and secondary education, copied from the United States, was also under attack. Many educators opposed the arrangement of eight years of grade school followed by four years of high school, arguing that this model was inappropriate for Puerto Rico, where most children attended school for no more than four years. According to one authority on Puerto Rican education, despite the debate that "raged around the question of the reorganization of the schools," the Department of Education was not persuaded to alter its traditional scheme (Osuna 1949: 280).

The commissioner of education saw the U.S. entry into World War I as an opportunity to teach such subjects as geography and history, as well as to promote "elevated patriotism" (Negrón de Montilla 1990: 182). Against the background of the continuing efforts to "Americanize" and the political liberalization of the Jones Act, political ferment in the island continued. Support for independence, interpreted by U.S. officials as opposition to the United States, was suppressed. A high school student group was denied permission to name a school literary club in honor of the recently deceased independence spokesman José de Diego. When university students petitioned the U.S. House of Representatives for Puerto Rican independence, the education commissioner requested from the University of Puerto Rico a list of all of the petition's signers who were studying to become teachers. The commissioner declared that he would refer to the list to block anyone "whose loyalty to the United States of America is in doubt" from teaching in Puerto Rico (Negrón de Montilla 1975: 171).

The unofficial Puerto Rican flag that had been designed in 1895 was increasingly used by liberals and independence supporters as a symbol of their opposition to U.S. rule (Rosario Natal 1989: 60). Student independence supporters tangled with the commissioner of education over a student who waved the flag during a 1921 graduation ceremony in defiance of the commissioner's order (Negrón de Montilla 1975: 172).

The attitude that supporting Puerto Rican independence was akin to treason was fostered by E. Montgomery Reily, designated governor of the island in 1921. Reily refused to appoint to any post anyone who favored severing ties with the United States, stating in his inaugural address that in the mainland there was no expectation of, or sympathy for, Puerto Rican independence. "Neither, my friends," he continued, "is there any room on this island for any flag other than . . . the Stars and Stripes, and there never will be" (*La Democracia* 1921: 3).

Reily's untempered pro-Americanism and his opposition to Puerto Rican independence established the tone of his governorship. His public reference to the single-star Puerto Rican flag as "a dirty rag" (*Cong. Rec.* 1922a: 3303) was sufficiently offensive that the statement was alluded to, along with accusations of misconduct, corruption, and immorality, in a 1922 Puerto Rican Senate resolution calling for the U.S. president to remove him from office: "E. Montgomery Reily . . . in several speeches . . . expressed himself in the most insulting language against the Porto Rican flag, which is a symbol of local sentiment, and as such is consecrated and respected by the entire Porto Rican community" (*Cong. Rec.* 1922b). President Harding did not accede to the request to dismiss the governor.

Governor Reily appointed as commissioner of education Juan B. Huyke, the first Puerto Rican to hold that position. A leader of the pro-U.S. wing of the Unionist Party (Osuna 1949: 188–89), Huyke declared "Americanism is patriotism" and described the schools as "agencies of Americanism" (Negrón de Montilla 1975: 180–81). Huyke used his office to encourage such activities as singing patriotic songs, saluting the U.S. flag, and teaching American history. He aggressively promoted the use of English in schools, requiring that the Education Department be informed of any professor who could not or would not teach in English, that teachers and students use English even outside class, and that high school students pass an oral English examination in order to graduate (Negrón de Montilla 1975: 183, 189–91).

Huyke's support for statehood increasingly distanced him from his fellows in the Unionist Party, still the dominant political party in the island. In 1922, the party proposed a new variant of Puerto Rican autonomy as a solution to the problem of Puerto Rico's relationship with the United States. The Unionist Party Assembly approved a resolution advocating "the creation in Puerto Rico of a State, People or Community that is Free and that is Associated with the United States of America. . . . The creation of the 'Free Associated State' ('*Libre Estado Asociado*') of Puerto Rico is as of today the Program" of the Unionist Party. Commissioner Huyke did not vote on this resolution; finding himself and his policies vociferously opposed at every turn, he left the party meeting before the final voting took place (*La Democracia* 1922: 4–6).

Under Governor Reily and education commissioner Huyke, student unrest continued, with politics and public schools mixing in yet another way. The Education Department barred students from hanging the unofficial Puerto Rican flag during San Juan Central High School's 1922 graduation ceremony. Police intervention was required to enforce this order. In the towns of Caguas and Vega Alta, graduation ceremonies were suspended for the same reason, and in Fajardo the students agreed not to display the Puerto Rican flag only on the condition that the U.S. flag be removed (Negrón de Montilla 1990: 211–12).

In 1925 the Puerto Rican legislature asked a commission from Columbia University's International Institute of Teachers College to assess Puerto Rico's public school system. The commission found that the policy of using English as the language of instruction in all classes was not effective and recommended the use of Spanish through third grade, with English classes beginning in fourth grade. Even this expert recommendation did not sway the commissioner of education, who continued to insist that English be used in all classes in all grades (Rodríguez Bou 1966: 161–62; Negrón de Montilla 1975: 209–12).

The struggle for self-government did not abate. In 1928, resident commissioner Félix Córdova Dávila expressed his disappointment in actions of President Coolidge, including the appointment of "continental Americans" to various posts for which Córdova Dávila had recommended "distinguished Porto Ricans." With reference to the Puerto Rican governor, Córdova Dávila said, "Had the people of Porto Rico possessed the power of electing their governor, the selection of a man speaking a language not understood by our people should have never taken place." Language was not a marginal issue, Córdova Dávila continued:

> Language is a factor of unquestioned importance. The masses of the people of Porto Rico speak no other language but Spanish. The English language is known by some prominent men and by a number of young people educated in our secondary schools and higher institutions of learning. . . . In the heart of the country, in the mountains, Spanish alone is spoken. . . . The language of a people constitutes the voice of its soul, the means of expressing its feelings, and its personality. Love for the vernacular is ingrained in the individual. To deprive him of his native tongue would be heartless and cruel. . . .
>
> Spanish will never be driven out of use in Porto Rico. It is our language and we will speak it as long as Porto Rico exists. . . . If the disappearance of . . . Spanish be considered a requisite to the attainment of statehood, we wish to tell the American people frankly that we can not accept it at such a price. (*Cong. Rec.* 1928: 6329, 6332)

Related views had been expressed by Puerto Rican Senate president Antonio R. Barceló, addressing the General Assembly of the Teachers' Association in 1926. Barceló urged the teachers to practice "Puerto Ricanization" in education: "Have we been developing patriotism in our schools? If we wished to answer this question from the heart, we would have to hang our heads in shame, because in our schools, our regional symbols have been forgotten in favor of a false and unhealthy Americanism." At the same assembly, educator Juan J. Osuna, advocated "impart[ing] a personality to our Puerto Rican civilization, distinguishing it from others." Commissioner of Education Huyke pronounced these comments "unfriendly and disrespectful" and prohibited school supervisors and principals from further participation in the teachers' association. The teachers protested this ban and accusations flew on both sides until the Parent-Teacher Association negotiated an agreement (Negrón de Montilla 1975: 225–26; 1990: 238).

Ever seeking ways to communicate its desire for self-government, the island legislature used the 1928 stopover in Puerto Rico of renowned aviator Charles Lindbergh to "tell the United States that here are a people jealous of their origin and history, inflexibly defending their personality, and indeclinably defending their liberty and their rights" (*Cong. Rec.* 1928: 6348). In the ceremony welcoming Lindbergh, a message from the Puerto Rican legislature to the people of the United States was read in Spanish, then English: "Grant us the freedom that you enjoy, for which you struggled, which you worship, which we deserve, and you have promised us" (Hull 1928).

As the issue of political control of the island gained momentum, Victor S. Clark, the former education commissioner, directed a study of Puerto Rico for the Brookings Institution in 1928 and 1929. Clark commented that "[t]he case for autonomy seems to rest partly upon a sentimental appeal for political rights inspired by local pride, and perhaps in small part upon fear of control from Washington in the interests of large American taxpayers," and he suggested that the islanders needed guidance to learn the workings of democracy. The U.S. Congress should "give Porto Rico a Constitution," he proposed, keeping in mind "the fact that the temperament of the Porto Rican people justifies a concentration of power and responsibility in the hands of the executive greater than is usual in the States" (Clark et al. 1930: 104–5).

Puerto Rican politicians did not feel that their appeal for rights was sentimental, nor did they want to be "given" a constitution. Throughout this period of party divisions and realignments, all island political factions incessantly demanded self-government. Although it no longer used the term "Free Associated State," the Unionist Party continued to propose an autonomy arrangement with the United States that, without breaking ties, would allow Puerto Ricans "to rule their internal affairs in accordance with their own determination" (*La Democracia* 1929). In 1929 a breakaway faction of the Unionist Party discounted the idea of autonomy, declaring

> that the populace of Puerto Rico is by right and should be, free and sovereign, and that it aspires to obtain its liberty and sovereignty within a perfect intermixing of regard and interests with the people of the United States, as a State of the Union or as an Independent Republic. . . . And until our final status is resolved, the Unionist [Party] will work for the broadest reform of the current regime, that will permit us complete control over all our internal affairs. (Pagán 1959, vol. 1: 317–18)

Opposing this faction of the Unionist Party was the Alliance, a coalition of the remainder of the Unionist Party and the pro-statehood Republican Party. The Alliance accepted statehood or independence as feasible status options but also included as a third possible status alternative some sort of partial association with the United States through an "autonomous state":

> The supreme desire of the Puerto Rican people is to achieve and freely exercise sovereignty. We recognize that in Puerto Rico there exist three currents of opinion: one that favors the Statehood solution, another that aspires to Independence, and another that advocates an autonomous State. We recognize that it is up to the people of Puerto Rico to determine the preferred solution, and to the United States Congress to sanction whatever the people of Puerto Rico freely decide. (Pagán 1959, vol. 1: 319–20)

These party realignments and demands reflected the Puerto Rican frustration with U.S. rule, a frustration that intensified in the 1930s. In a formal act of self-assertion, the Puerto Rican legislature sought to redress the long-standing annoyance of the official mainland misspelling of the island's name. A unanimous resolution passed in 1930 charged that "immediately following the change of sovereignty . . . the Congress of the United States of America, without justifying reasons, officially gave the island the name of Porto Rico." The island legislature petitioned Congress "to restore to our island its true name of Puerto Rico in place of Porto Rico as it is now called because it is considered that full justice will thus be done to our history, our language, and our traditions" (U.S. Congress 1932: 2). This change would affect only English-language publications, since the U.S. spelling change had not been adopted in Spanish-language writings in the island. The U.S. Congress passed the bill in 1932. The same year, the Unionist Party changed its name to Liberal Party and changed its status choice from autonomy to independence (Wells 1969: 107). Puerto Rico's largest political organization had moved from advocating U.S. statehood in the early years, to proposing autonomy in 1922, to supporting independence ten years later.

EXPRESSIONS OF UNREST

The 1930s were marked by an increasingly self-conscious affirmation of Puerto Ricanness in literary and artistic production as well as in the use of political symbols. This affirmation was characterized in part by the search for defining elements of Puerto Rican culture (Ferrao 1993: 36–38, 45) and in part by manifestations of protest against the United States. Indicative of the attitude of Puerto Rican intellectuals was Antonio S. Pedreira's *Insularismo*, published in 1934. In this influential collection of essays on Puerto Rican society, Pedreira concluded that Puerto Rico had an identifiable culture: "In our [horseback] riding, in our walk, in dance, in behavior, in speaking, we are discovering unique modalities that define us. . . . We have an unmistakable way of being Puerto Ricans" (Pedreira [1936] 1957: 200, 207). But, he continued, that way of being was undermined by the omnipresent influence of the United States. The intense admiration of Puerto Rico's culture that was fostered during this period centered on its Spanish component (Ferrao 1993: 46). Pedreira exhorted Puerto Rican youth not to disregard their Hispanic heritage in the face of U.S. culture: "[I]f going backwards is impossible, it is certainly useless to go towards the future denying our heritage, and what is worse, lacking awareness of the current of history formed by the finest tributaries of our people" (211–12).

Supporters of independence saw U.S. colonial control as detrimental not only to their culture but also to the island's economy, which they felt was not being administered in Puerto Rico's interests. Political scientist Henry Wells (1969: 118) has noted that supporting independence also appeared to be a way to vent their ongoing "political frustration and resentment. Year after year Puerto Rican demands for a greater degree of self-government . . . had met with nothing but indifference and inaction on the part of Congress. Far from recognizing the dignity of the Puerto Rican people and the worth of their culture, American Senators and Representatives had seemed to be interested only in forcing Puerto Rican school children to learn English."

Throughout the 1930s, the language question continued to generate political sparks. José Padín, appointed commissioner of education in 1930 by President Hoover, approached the school language issue "critically and experimentally" (Rodríguez Bou 1966: 162). Padín differed from his predecessors not only because he attempted systematic analysis of the situation but also, according to Cebollero (1945: 23), because, rather than base his policies on the false assumption that Puerto Rico was a bilingual society, he started from "the frank recognition of English as a foreign language." In 1934, after, in Padín's own words, "five years of observation, testing, and experimenting," Padín ordered "the use of the Spanish language as the sole medium of instruction in the eight grades of the urban and rural elementary schools" (quoted in Osuna 1949: 366–67). According to Osuna (1949: 375), Padín's policy was "welcomed by an overwhelming majority" in Puerto Rico, "but apparently opposed by official Washington. The controversy over the language of instruction continued unabatedly and partisan political interests from all quarters took a very active part in the debate."

Agitation for independence continued to be expressed through political and intellectual channels and also in a series of incidents sparked by activities of the Nationalist Party, formed in 1922 to advocate independence. The Nationalists used as their insignia the single-star flag. In 1932, members of the party went to the Capitol building in San Juan to protest pending legislation to authorize officially the single-star flag for Puerto Rico. The Nationalists considered it an affront that Puerto Rico as a U.S. territory would adopt the flag that in their eyes stood for independence. The protest ended in the accidental deaths of two demonstrators (*El Día* 1932; Puerto Rico Constituent Assembly 1952: 2101). The single-star flag remained unofficial.

In 1936, two Nationalists assassinated the chief of the Puerto Rican police force, an appointee from the mainland. In response to the killing, U.S. senator Millard Tydings charged that "the American system is not functioning adequately in Puerto Rico" (*Cong. Rec.* 1936a: 5926) and proposed two bills for the island. An electoral reform bill met little objection, but a bill for a Puerto Rican plebiscite on independence was strongly criticized. Although independence had adherents in the island—including the Nationalists themselves—the Tydings bill was seen as harsh and punitive because it did not allow for a gradual transition to independence, if the voters were to choose that option. Independence advocate Antonio Barceló, of the Liberal Party, argued that the bill needed amending so that "the moral and material responsibilities assumed by the United States in its thirty-eight years of sovereignty over Puerto Rico are not discarded and thrown overboard with a cavalier washing of Pilate's hands." Barceló advocated "[a] period of economic readjustment as a transitional step between colony and sovereignty."

Barceló also objected that the plebiscite proposed by Tydings would not allow Puerto Rican voters the option of choosing statehood (*La Democracia* 1936). Puerto Rico's resident commissioner protested to Congress that Tydings had not consulted "proper and accredited representatives of the island" in drafting the legislation and, furthermore, that the Tydings proposal for independence had disregarded a request submitted to Congress by the Puerto Rican legislature for "complete self-government and final statehood" (*Cong. Rec.* 1936b: 8562). These exchanges did not temper the escalating tensions in the island, which culminated in the "Ponce massacre" of 1937, a confrontation between armed police and unarmed Nationalist Party demonstrators that left nineteen dead, including two policemen (Morales Carrión 1983: 238).

During this period of unrest, a significant event for Puerto Rico's political future occurred. In 1938, the independence wing of the Liberal Party split off and formed the Popular Democratic Party (Partido Popular Democrático, or PPD). Luis Muñoz Marín, the party's founder, took as the symbol for the party the straw hat worn by Puerto Rican peasants, representing Muñoz Marín's aim of incorporating the rural population into the island's political life (Muñoz Marín 1984: 93–95). The PPD soon dominated Puerto Rico's elective posts, and Muñoz Marín became president of the Senate in 1940.

As the number of qualified voters grew, and school enrollments increased in the island, the language issue continued to be a problem for both U.S. and Puerto Rican officials. U.S. policymakers were so dissatisfied with Commissioner of Education Padín's policy of Spanish instruction in primary grades that when he resigned in 1937 the issue of language became the most important factor in the search for his replacement. After nearly a year of candidate interviews focused on "the orthodoxy of the language doctrine" (Osuna 1949: 375), José M. Gallardo, a Puerto Rican with pedagogical experience in the mainland, was selected. In a letter to the new commissioner, President Franklin Roosevelt emphasized the importance of English instruction in Puerto Rico. This statement was taken as a favorable sign by those parties that advocated statehood and was interpreted by a rival of Muñoz Marín as a reaction against Muñoz Marín's "radical and extremist" agitation for independence (Pagán 1959, vol. 2: 121–22). Roosevelt's letter expressed publicly for the first time a U.S. position on language in Puerto Rico: "It is an indispensable part of American policy that the coming generation of American citizens in Puerto Rico grow up with complete facility in the English tongue. It is the language of our Nation. Only through the acquisition of this language will Puerto Rican Americans secure a better understanding of American ideals and principles" (quoted in Osuna 1949: 376–77).

Gallardo got the message. Upon taking office, he initiated a complex set of curricular changes aimed at strengthening English teaching. During his tenure, language policy specifics changed several times. Apparently, policy experimentation convinced Gallardo that Padín had been correct; by 1942 his policy resembled nothing so much as the discarded policy of his predecessor (Osuna 1949: 381; Brameld 1959: 244). In 1943 Gallardo testified before a U.S.

Senate subcommittee that absolute bilingualism was not achievable in the island because students' only exposure to English was in the classroom (Osuna 1949: 385–86). The extent of U.S. interest in the issue of school language in Puerto Rico was demonstrated by the reaction of U.S. interior secretary Harold L. Ickes, who accused Gallardo of disregarding President Roosevelt's instructions concerning English teaching. "I would not have recommended you to the President for this post," wrote Ickes, "if I had not been assured that you realized as much as I did the obligation to teach English in the Puerto Rican schools" (quoted in Rodríguez Bou 1966: 166). This charge led Gallardo to resign as secretary of education, evidently a stronger response than Ickes had intended. Ickes persuaded Gallardo to stay in the post, which he held for two more years.

The 1940s were a time of social and economic transformation for Puerto Rico. U.S. administration of the island had been transferred from the War Department to the Department of the Interior, considerable federal subsidies were extended to the island, and New Deal reforms were enacted (Lewis 1963: 124–25). A government campaign to attract investment and special tax breaks designed to encourage commercial development propelled rapid industrialization. "Operation Bootstrap," as this development drive came to be known, sparked the conversion of Puerto Rico's economic base from agriculture to industry; textile, clothing, and other manufacturing plants were established, contributing to economic growth and a rising standard of living (R. Anderson 1965: 5; Wells 1969: 150–53). This period also marked the beginning of the mass emigration of job-seeking Puerto Ricans to the U.S. mainland, particularly to New York and other East Coast cities.

The political realm was changing as well. When Muñoz Marín founded the Popular Democratic Party in 1938, he had taken with him many independence supporters from the Liberal Party. In the early 1940s he downplayed the status issue in favor of economic growth, the expansion of the franchise, and the reduction of political corruption. In 1943, his enthusiasm for independence waning, Muñoz Marín intimated that he might accept a status option that would be neither statehood nor independence but some combination of the two; by 1945 he had become convinced that the independence he had once sought would be economically devastating to Puerto Rico, which lagged far behind the United States in economic development (Wells 1969: 223, 226). He began to advocate finding a way to end Puerto Rico's colonial political relationship with the United States while retaining a beneficial economic relationship. During the next several years, Muñoz Marín explored the feasibility of an intermediate status that would combine internal political autonomy with continued economic, military, and other links with the United States. This change of heart concerned independence advocates in his Popular Democratic Party. In 1946 the independence wing split from the PDP and, joined by some Nationalist Party sympathizers, formed the Puerto Rican Independence Party, which favored promoting independence through the framework of the electoral system (R. Anderson 1965: 95–105; Pagán 1959, vol. 2: 260–61).

While Puerto Rican political parties were reconsidering their positions on the island's status, several bills concerning various aspects of self-government for Puerto Rico were proposed but not passed by the U.S. Congress. Unable to alter the island's relationship with the United States, the popularly elected Puerto Rican legislature turned yet again to a nagging symbol of U.S. domination. A bill restoring Spanish as the language of instruction in schools was passed in 1946. The bill was vetoed by the governor, who was still a U.S. appointee; the veto was overridden by the required two-thirds majority of both houses of the Puerto Rican legislature. Under the laws then in effect, any bill passed over the governor's veto went to the U.S. president for final decision. On the advice of the U.S. Department of the Interior, President Truman upheld the governor's veto, opting to defer the language issue pending determination of Puerto Rico's status (*La Prensa* 1946; Bhana 1975: 100). A commentary in the island newspaper *El Imparcial* expressed the depth of sentiment about this issue:

> In effect the most serious damage, the deepest wrong inflicted by the American government on the Puerto Rican people consists of the destruction in this people of its mother tongue. Perhaps the word destruction is excessive, excessive because it is premature; but let it be stated that the process of adulteration and decay that officially began forty-six years ago has intensified and been accentuated over time. . . . [O]ur local Legislature recently approved a law assigning our mother tongue in our public schools the logical, natural and divine function that corresponds to the mother tongue in all countries: and having sent the law to the President's desk for his consideration and action, what did the President do? God Almighty, the President vetoed it! . . . This is a vital problem: our vital problem *par excellence*. As vital to our souls as food is vital to our bodies. (Fernández Vanga 1946)

In protest of Truman's veto of the school language bill, 6,000 Puerto Rican university students staged a one-day strike (*New York Times* 1946). University students were active in island political life. In 1947 a group of students requested and received permission to raise the single-star flag on campus on the anniversary of the 1868 Grito de Lares independence uprising. Two months later, in honor of Nationalist Party leader Pedro Albizu Campos, students raised the flag without having received permission. University police took down the Puerto Rican flag and replaced it with the American flag; students again lowered the Stars and Stripes and raised the single-star flag. Island police were called in, and the American flag was raised on the campus. Three students were suspended; more than 5,000 signed petitions to readmit them (Acosta 1987: 50–51).

Along with the single-star flag, the school language issue remained a source of conflict. In 1947 President Truman named Puerto Rican educator Mariano Villaronga to the post of education commissioner of Puerto Rico. Villaronga's confirmation process stalled in the U.S. Senate, apparently because he did not support the official policy of English as the language of instruction in schools

(Rodríguez Bou 1966: 167–68; Brameld 1959: 244). At the same time, Congress was considering proposed legislation that, if passed, would fundamentally alter the island's relationship with the United States.

INTERNAL SELF-GOVERNMENT

In 1947 separate bills were introduced in the U.S. Congress, one providing for statehood, and another for independence for Puerto Rico (*Cong. Rec.* 1947: 658, 687). On 5 August, Congress instead took a middle road, approving an administration-sponsored bill that provided a significant measure of self-government through an amendment to the 1917 Jones Act. After some forty-nine years of lobbying, Puerto Ricans were granted permission to elect their own governor. The amendment also authorized the governor to appoint the commissioner of education and the attorney general, the only department heads that had remained under the direct control of the United States.

As the island prepared to change its position in the world, a smaller, perhaps representative, change was also afoot. Puerto Rico joined the International Olympic Committee and began fielding its own teams in international sports competitions.[3] A leading island newspaper reported in July 1948 that "[f]or the first time in its sports history, Puerto Rico marched yesterday . . . as a sovereign nation, in the Fourteenth Olympic Games." The principal mission of the Puerto Rican athletes, editorialized the paper, was "to sow affection and respect for Puerto Rico." In a last-minute arrangement, the Puerto Rican delegation carried the five-ring Olympic flag in the opening ceremony (*El Mundo* 1948a, 1948d, 1948e). This measure was taken because Puerto Rico did not have its own official flag. The single-star Puerto Rican flag had become so closely associated with the Nationalist and Independence parties that its public display in the island brought official disapprobation, leaving the U.S. flag to fly alone in the island.

The year 1948 marked significant changes in Puerto Rico's trajectory. Amid university student strikes sparked by demands for independence and the use of the single-star flag, preparations were under way for the first election in island history in which voters would select their own executive. A central issue of the gubernatorial campaign was the island's political status. Longtime political leader Luis Muñoz Marín promoted not only his own candidacy but also a revised model for United States–Puerto Rico relations. Muñoz Marín's model called for neither independence nor statehood but rather "one of the solutions that historically have been put forth" for Puerto Rico. Proposed for the island by Muñoz Marín's father, Luis Muñoz Rivera, in 1911 and intermittently by others thereafter, this arrangement coupled continued ties to the mainland with "maximum possible self-government." Muñoz Marín asserted that Puerto Rico needed time to industrialize and to strengthen its economy in order eventually to be able to pay U.S. federal taxes as a state, or import duties as an independent country. When a sufficient level of economic development had been attained, he said, the Puerto Rican people could decide which status they preferred (*El Mundo* 1948c).

Muñoz Marín faced two opponents in the 1948 gubernatorial election: Francisco M. Susoni of the Independence Party and Martín Travieso of the pro-statehood Coalition. Susoni's central campaign issue was advocacy of independence, as "the only solution to our political status that will allow us to resolve our economic and social problems." Travieso's campaign centered on fiscal reform (*El Mundo* 1948f).

Luis Muñoz Marín became the first elected governor in the history of Puerto Rico, winning 61.2 percent of the votes (R. Anderson 1988: 7). He was sworn in on the morning of 2 January 1949. That afternoon, he appointed as education commissioner Mariano Villaronga, the same man whose confirmation as education commissioner had been withheld by the U.S. Senate two years before. Within months, Villaronga declared Spanish the language of instruction in the Puerto Rican public school system. In this way, self-government, which for half a century had been Puerto Ricans' foremost political demand, brought with it the power to address the other principal demand—a return to Spanish as the school language.

The new policy ended a period of fifty years during which Puerto Rico's education system had been completely dominated by the controversy over the language of instruction. During the years that the Puerto Rican educational system was directed by U.S. appointees, the official policy on language of instruction had changed frequently as educators and administrators sought the best way to create a bilingual population. While most schoolchildren never advanced beyond fourth grade, some children were moving through the system and may have experienced several changes in it. Many observers have claimed that one of the principal effects of these shifting policies was to damage the schoolchildren (Coleman in Epstein 1970: 23; Cebollero 1945: 107–8), leaving "most pupils illiterate in both English and Spanish" (Wells 1969: 270). One educator from the University of Puerto Rico's English Institute had charged in 1948 that using English as the language of instruction for all subjects meant that English teachers spent most of their time "un-teaching the patois that the children learn in their other classes" rather than teaching English (*El Mundo* 1948b). The impact the language policies had on these students extended beyond their schooling; their attitudes toward the United States were shaped by their exposure to a system governed by U.S. rules (Osuna 1949: 365–66).

With a popularly elected governor, a locally appointed education commissioner, and the definitive return to Spanish as the language of instruction in schools, Puerto Rico entered a new phase of its history—home rule. The United States remained the island's sovereign power, but Puerto Ricans had gained a greater say in their own affairs than they had ever known before.

NOTES

1. Much of my description of U.S. actions in the Puerto Rican school system is drawn from Aida Negrón de Montilla's fine study *Americanization in Puerto Rico and the Public School System 1900–1930*. The book was first published in English in 1971 (reprinted 1975) and in Spanish in 1976 (2d ed. 1990). I have used both versions interchangeably. English-language originals are quoted here from the English version (1975). I have translated original Spanish-language documents from the Spanish version of Negrón de Montilla's book (1990).

2. The Socialist Party that existed from 1915-1954 was based in organized labor and favored Puerto Rican statehood. The present-day Socialist Party is Marxist in orientation and supports Puerto Rican independence (Anderson, R. 1988: 6, 14).

3. This was possible because the Olympic Charter allows the International Olympic Committee the discretion to recognize teams that do not represent sovereign countries. Thus, not only Puerto Rico but also, for example, Gibraltar, Hong Kong, and Guam compete in the Olympic Games (Serrano Geyls and Gorrín Peralta 1980: 14–15; Nafziger 1988: 90–91).

3

Commonwealth Status, 1949–1993

After the Puerto Ricans attained internal self-rule, the island's relationship with the United States remained on center stage in Puerto Rican politics. The efforts of Muñoz Marín and his Popular Democratic Party to achieve greater political autonomy while maintaining economic and political ties with the United States enjoyed considerable support in the island. This support, however, was not unanimous. Some feared that Puerto Rico was being drawn away from the option of independence. The small Nationalist Party, led by Pedro Albizu Campos, held that because the United States had taken and continued to maintain control over Puerto Rico by force, any form of resistance to U.S. rule was legitimate. In 1950, to draw international and United Nations attention to Puerto Rico, the Nationalist Party organized a violent uprising in several cities of the island and in Washington, D.C. (Rodríguez Fraticelli 1993: 123, 133). The attempted assassinations of Governor Muñoz Marín and President Harry Truman that were part of the uprising resulted in the deaths of several participants and guards. In 1954, four Nationalist Party sympathizers shouting "long live free Puerto Rico!" opened fire in the U.S. House of Representatives, wounding five congressmen.

The Nationalists' political beliefs and tactics were perceived as a threat to Puerto Rico's nascent political system as well as to the international image of the United States. To suppress the 1950 Nationalist uprising, Puerto Rican and U.S. law enforcement agencies together undertook a massive crackdown on advocates of Puerto Rican independence, whether they were members of the violent Nationalist Party or of the Independence Party, which was dedicated to achieving independence through the electoral process. For legal authority, officials invoked a "gag law" that had been passed in 1948 in reaction to a series of university student actions involving the single-star flag and students' thwarted efforts to have Albizu Campos speak at the University of Puerto Rico (Acosta 1987: 50–51). The law made it a felony to advocate violent action against the Puerto Rican government in speech or writing (*Laws of Puerto Rico* 1948: 170). Nicolás Nogueras, a member of the Civil Rights Commission that later investigated the reprisals following the "nationalist revolt" recalled in a 1991 interview:

> That event was one of the most incredible events in the life of any country. Blank arrest orders were issued, people were arrested at two o'clock and three o'clock in the morning—because they were *independentistas*, not because they were Nationalist [Party members]. [The police] broke down the doors of houses, burned books. . . . They held people under arrest for two or three days and then released them. All this was based on lists of people that were in City Halls and in [the seat of the Puerto Rican government] La Fortaleza. We passed through a period when the Nationalist movement was crushed, destroyed.

PUERTO RICAN CONSTITUTION

As the Nationalist movement was being crushed, Muñoz Marín's vision of a new relationship between Puerto Rico and the United States was being implemented in the drafting of a constitution for Puerto Rico. U.S. officials charged with overseeing Puerto Rican affairs had been generally impressed with the island's political and economic progress. They felt, in the words of one congressman, that Puerto Ricans were "capable of handling their affairs; and . . . if they are not it is time for us to find it out" (U.S. House Committee on Public Lands 1950: 43). They were not prepared, however, to give the Puerto Ricans carte blanche. In congressional discussions of a Puerto Rican constitution, one congressman advocated granting "the people of Puerto Rico the authority to organize a constitutional government of their own choosing within certain well-defined boundaries and limitations specified by Congress." This not only was the right thing to do, he maintained, but would also enhance the image of the United States during a period of worldwide pressure for decolonization: "[S]uch a practical demonstration of the principles of democracy will strengthen and elevate our position before the United Nations" (U.S. House Committee on Public Lands 1950: 38).

The 1952 constitution, Puerto Rico's first, provided a great degree of internal autonomy without challenging the continued sovereignty of the United States over the island. Under this unprecedented relationship, characterized by Muñoz Marín as a "political mutation" (1954: 541), Puerto Ricans would retain U.S. citizenship and continue to be exempt from federal taxes, elect their local officials but have no vote in federal elections, and continue to be represented in Congress by their resident commissioner, a nonvoting member of the House of Representatives. Puerto Rico and the United States would continue to share a monetary system and common market, and Puerto Rico would still be subject to U.S. tariffs and all federal legislation except federal tax laws.

The Puerto Rican Constitution was more than a set of rules of government.

"A constitution not only constitutes a structure of power and authority," posits Sheldon Wolin (1989: 9); "it constitutes a people in a certain way. It proposes a distinctive identity and envisions a form of politicalness for individuals in their new collective capacity." The Puerto Rican Constitution contained in its preamble this rendering of Puerto Rican collective identity: "We consider as determining factors in our life our citizenship of the United States of America and our aspiration continually to enrich our democratic heritage . . . [and] the coexistence in Puerto Rico of the two great cultures of the American Hemisphere" (Puerto Rico Constitutional Convention 1952: 31).

The idea of internal self-government with continued ties to the mainland, variously termed "autonomy," "dominion," "overseas state," or "unincorporated state," had been proposed periodically in Puerto Rico since the time of Spanish rule (Wells 1969: 221; Hunter 1966: 112; Trías Monge 1981, vol. 2: 140). When it was created in 1952, the new arrangement was termed "Estado Libre Asociado," which translates literally into English as "Associated Free State," or, as common usage has it, "Free Associated State." However, rather than use this phrase in English, the word *commonwealth* was chosen as the English denomination for the revamped relationship. This word is imprecise, generally referring to some self-governing group of people but also, according to Webster's Dictionary, "loosely, to any state of the United States" and "strictly," to several states, such as Virginia and Pennsylvania, that were historically so designated. The application of the term to Puerto Rico requires a separate dictionary entry: "the official designation of Puerto Rico in its special status under the U.S. government" (Guralnik 1970: 287). U.S. historian Robert Hunter (1966: 112) notes that in bilateral United States-Puerto Rico discussions as early as 1943 Muñoz Marín had used the English word "commonwealth" to describe the proposed relationship. Puerto Rican historian Arturo Morales Carrión (1983: 278) maintains that the purpose of this word choice was "to allay fears that Puerto Rico was asking for statehood."

The Puerto Rican Constitution was drafted by a popularly elected constituent assembly between September 1951 and February 1952. Ratified by Puerto Rican voters in a referendum held 3 March 1952, the constitution was then sent to Washington. President Truman quickly approved it and sent it to Congress, which conditioned approval on three changes: the addition of a clause stating that future amendments must be consistent with the U.S. Constitution and applicable U.S. and Puerto Rican laws; a clarification of the wording of one section of the Bill of Rights; and the elimination of Section 20 of the Bill of Rights. Based on the United Nations Universal Declaration of Human Rights, Section 20 recognized, but did not guarantee, among other things, the right to an education and the right to obtain work (Puerto Rico Constitutional Convention 1952: 49).

Amid protestations in the island that U.S. authorities had not accepted the Puerto Rican Constitution as it was written, the elimination of Section 20 of the Bill of Rights generated the greatest reaction. Jaime Benítez, rector of the University of Puerto Rico and member of the constituent assembly, preferred to accept the changes rather than lose the momentum of the constitutional process.

"Fortunately, the elimination of Section 20 has no practical effects of any sort in terms of diminishing the authority of the People of Puerto Rico to legislate for human rights," said Benítez. "I recommend accepting the Constitution of the Commonwealth of Puerto Rico. May the principles that we unanimously set down in Section 20 of the Bill of Rights endure in our spirit and in our will as an unwritten part of the Constitution of Puerto Rico" (*El Mundo* 1952a).

The Puerto Rican constituent assembly accepted the required changes pending popular ratification, which came later that year by a margin of seven-to-one (Hunter 1966: 124). The constitution replaced sections of the Amended Jones Act of 1917 concerning the U.S. role in Puerto Rico, including the U.S. government's prerogative to overrule Puerto Rican legislation. Ultimate sovereignty over the island remained with the United States, as evidenced by the provision that Puerto Rican laws conform to the requirements of the U.S. Constitution and specified statutes.

With the new Puerto Rican Constitution, most U.S. laws concerning the governance of Puerto Rico were rescinded. The constitutional convention declared, "We have arrived at the goal of full self-government, leaving behind . . . all vestiges of colonialism, and we are entering into a period of new developments in democratic civilization" (quoted in Muñoz Marín 1980: 110). "This is a great day in our history," proclaimed Resident Commissioner Antonio Fernós Isern when the constitution received U.S. Senate approval (Baymont 1952: 16). For their part, U.S. officials believed that they were "doing what the people of Puerto Rico would like to have us do for them" (U.S. House Committee on Public Lands 1950: 48). Furthermore, the change in Puerto Rico's status had symbolic value in the international arena. Before the Puerto Rican Constitution was written, the U.S. assistant secretary of state for inter-American affairs had stated in its support: "In view of the importance of 'colonialism' and 'imperialism' in anti-American propaganda, the Department of State feels that [the constitution] would have great value as a symbol of the basic freedom enjoyed by Puerto Rico, within the larger framework of the United States of America" (U.S. House Committee on Public Lands 1950: 46).

The first law passed in Puerto Rico under the new constitution adopted the single-star flag, identified in the statute as the flag "traditionally known heretofore as the Puerto Rican Flag," for the island (*Laws of Puerto Rico Annotated* 1982: 371). Once a proscribed symbol of independence groups, the flag became an official representation of the Commonwealth of Puerto Rico. The new commonwealth's second law adopted "La Borinqueña" as the island's anthem (*Laws of Puerto Rico Annotated* 1982: 374). It was not by chance that the first two laws of the Commonwealth of Puerto Rico created official symbols to represent the island. Arturo Morales Carrión notes the "profound psychological change that took place in 1952 when Puerto Ricans established a right to their own anthem and flag. It was a great emotional experience when Muñoz symbolically raised the Puerto Rican flag," which would thereafter fly "officially and symbolically side by side with the American flag" (1983: 279, 281).

The official adoption of "the old separatist flag" has been interpreted by some as a ploy by Muñoz Marín to "neutralize the *independentistas* in his own party" (Carr 1984: 80). The Independence Party itself, with which the flag had been associated, accused the Puerto Rican government of "corrupting beloved symbols" and ordered that the flag be flown at half-mast for two days at party offices in protest of the new commonwealth arrangement and the "captive" flag (Carlo 1952). Certainly, a new flag for Puerto Rico could have been designed at this juncture. But, as the statement in the law that the flag was "traditionally known" as the Puerto Rican flag suggests, the flag had gained acceptance well beyond independence circles. When he raised the Puerto Rican flag for the first time, Muñoz Marín declared to the thousands of spectators:

> The Puerto Rican flag does not belong to narrow nationalism nor does it proscribe love and respect . . . for the other peoples of the earth. It belongs to all Puerto Ricans. It belongs to those who used terrorism in the past and to those who raised it as an insignia of peace and valor in the present. In rescuing it for Puerto Rico we do it for the very people who wanted to reduce it to a sign of division. We are rescuing it for the unity that, within a diversity of free opinions, should govern the affairs of all good peoples. We see reflected in the flag, not mistrust of others, but trust in ourselves and fraternal respect for everyone. (*El Mundo* 1952c)

In a commentary headlined "At Last Puerto Rico Has Ceased to be a People without a Flag!" an editor of *El Mundo*, a leading island newspaper, crowed:

> From now on there will be no fear of raising the single-star flag as Puerto Rico's official flag. In the future our athletes abroad will not have to face the incomprehension of other peoples when our country's representatives attend competitions with fellow countries. Tomorrow Puerto Ricans who excel in all walks of life will be able to attend meetings and conventions with satisfaction and their hearts overflowing with pride under the same flag that unofficially was accepted by all Puerto Ricans and by all the countries of the world as the Puerto Rican flag. . . . The entire Puerto Rican people would never have forgiven the adoption of a national symbol other than the one that has been recognized since that historic December 22nd of the year 1895. (Galvez Maturana 1952)

The symbolism surrounding the political change emphasized Puerto Rico as both distinct from, and connected to, the United States. It was not an accident that the date chosen to inaugurate the Puerto Rican Constitution was 25 July 1952, the fifty-fourth anniversary of the U.S. invasion of Puerto Rico. Moreover, at the same time that the single-star Puerto Rican flag was officially displayed for the first time, the Stars and Stripes were used to represent the jubilation that many felt at the establishment of the island's new relationship with the mainland. Page after page of newspaper advertisements featured illustrations of the U.S. flag with accompanying felicitations from island businesses. Typical was the large display ad for Moscoso Pharmacy in *El Mundo* (1952b):

> With great joy we congratulate the people and officials of Puerto Rico on the occasion of celebrating today Constitution Day in the Free Associated State of Puerto Rico. To all those who worked for this liberating achievement and especially to the Honorable Luis Muñoz Marín, whose vision has made this Puerto Rican dream a reality, goes this message of recognition, of support, and of respect.

The message of a liquor distributor in the same newspaper was somewhat less disinterested: below an illustration of the U.S. flag and text expressing "happiness for the coming of the Free Associated State of Puerto Rico" were an illustration of a bottle and text suggesting White Horse Whiskey for the celebration (*El Mundo* 1952b).

At the time of the change to commonwealth status, Muñoz Marín noted that the new status would not necessarily be permanent; rather, it could constitute a stopover on the way to an eventual status—either statehood or independence—which the Puerto Rican people would determine. Thus, this new arrangement did not resolve the perpetual question of Puerto Rico's ultimate political fate. Although no status option had been officially ruled out, advocating independence continued to be suspect. The "gag law" remained in effect until 1957, succeeding, according to a Puerto Rican scholar who has studied the law and its effects, not only in destroying the Nationalist Party but also in greatly reducing the electoral strength of the Puerto Rican Independence Party (Acosta 1987: 236–37).

In the years following the establishment of the commonwealth, Puerto Rican politics jelled into a three-party system, each party advocating one of the status options: commonwealth, statehood, or independence. The relationship of these parties to the U.S. Democratic and Republican parties has been based on historic ties and mutual convenience, rather than ideological affinity. Puerto Rican politicians endeavor to maintain good relationships with both Democrats and Republicans in order to have maximum leverage within the U.S. political system, and island affiliates of U.S. political organizations generally have goals related to the influence of the United States over Puerto Rican politics. This pattern was exemplified in the comments of a statehood party interviewee who explained that the Puerto Rican branch of the Young Republicans had been founded

> because of a concern of young professional Puerto Ricans to put pressure and have a political presence in the United States in terms of a plebiscite and eventual statehood for Puerto Rico . . . and we understood that the Young Republicans in the United States had a lot of political strength . . . so we became part of the organization in

order to be able to exercise political pressure through them in Congress.

This affiliation reflects the long-standing alignment of the Puerto Rican statehood party with the U.S. Republican Party (although there have been prominent statehood-party Democrats). The commonwealth party has maintained an association with the Democratic Party. Puerto Rican politicians see these alignments as channels of communication to U.S. officialdom. The communication also functions in the reverse direction, particularly during presidential primary season. Although Puerto Ricans do not vote in federal elections, presidential primaries have been held in the island since 1980, and Puerto Rico sends delegates to the conventions of both parties. The primary process brings U.S. presidential candidates to the island and makes Puerto Rican issues visible to mainland politicians, if only fleetingly.

Within Puerto Rico, the commonwealth party has dominated Puerto Rican politics since 1949, holding the governorship for eight terms to the statehood party's four terms. Support for the statehood party has steadily increased, from 14 percent in the 1948 gubernatorial election, to 34.7 percent in 1964, to 50 percent in 1992 (Wells 1969: 277; Comisión Estatal de Elecciones 1992). The independence party share of votes has declined, due, in part, to the repression connected with the "gag law" (Acosta 1987: 236–37), from a high of 18.9 percent in 1952 to a low of 2.6 percent in 1964 (R. Anderson 1988: 17). In 1992, the independence party gubernatorial candidate garnered 4.2 percent of the vote (Comisión Estatal de Elecciones 1992).

For more than twenty years, the distribution of party support has remained relatively constant, the independence party claiming less than 7 percent and the commonwealth and statehood parties splitting the remaining 90-plus percent of the votes in gubernatorial elections. Occasionally, an independence party candidate garners a higher total, as was the case in 1984, when the party's candidate for an islandwide at-large seat in the Puerto Rican Senate won 12.5 percent of the vote. Nonetheless, the dominance of the commonwealth and statehood parties and their near-equal division of voter support indicate that the Puerto Rican political system has become, as described by political analyst Robert W. Anderson (1988: 12), "in effect, an evenly-balanced two-party system." The parties and the issues do not match those of the mainland United States: "[S]tateside and Puerto Rican political organizations are two independent spheres which touch only tangentially" (R. Anderson 1988: 35).

That the political parties of island and mainland are, at most, loosely connected does not imply the absence of a connection between island and mainland political systems. U.S. involvement with the island was reduced, but not eliminated, with self-rule. Puerto Rico's continuing economic ties with the United States, its strategic Caribbean location and proximity to the mainland, and the visible Puerto Rican minority in the continental United States have kept the island on the congressional agenda. Above all, the sense that Puerto Rico's status is unresolved has contributed to an ambiguous relationship in which, legal definitions notwithstanding, the lines of authority are disputed.

LANGUAGE ISSUES RESURFACE

Even after the institution of self-rule, control over school language has been used repeatedly by Puerto Rican and U.S. policymakers as an assertion of decision-making power. When the Puerto Rican public educational system returned to Spanish as the language of instruction, a constituency for English instruction in schools remained. At that time there was an increase in the number of Catholic schools run by U.S. religious orders, most of which used English in the classroom (Beirne 1975: 29). This led to accusations that the Catholic schools were acting as Americanizing agents. In 1962 Puerto Rican secretary of education Cándido Oliveras expressed concern that more than half of Puerto Rico's private Catholic schools were using English as the language of instruction. In response to reporters' extensive hypothetical questioning, Secretary Oliveras stated that English-language schools were acceptable in several situations, such as for students from the mainland and for students whose parents wanted them to have full-time English instruction. But, the secretary continued, should the Catholic school system as a whole move to institutionalize the use of English as the language of instruction—he noted that he had seen no evidence of such a move—he would take steps against it. Referring to "the quite distant past," when schools were used "as a means of Americanization of Puerto Rico," the secretary stated his opposition to "any attempt to use the school for any purpose that is not purely pedagogical" (Oliveras 1962: 107–12).

Reaction to these statements was immediate both in the island and on the mainland. An editorial published the following day in Puerto Rico's English-language newspaper, the *San Juan Star*, accused Oliveras of attempting to "curb the spread of English through the island's private schools." Congressman James Roosevelt of California cited the editorial on the floor of the U.S. House and sought support from his colleagues to "explore possibilities for bringing about a change in this unfortunate policy." Roosevelt found Oliveras's nonpolicy "unfortunate" because he believed Puerto Ricans would benefit from exposure to English, given the island's "close ties with the United States through its Commonwealth status." His reaction exemplified the ongoing conflict and confusion generated by the unresolved status question. The English language was seen as necessary for interaction with the United States, and, although Roosevelt professed "a desire for noninterference in Puerto Rico's internal affairs," he feared that the island was "embark[ing] on a path that will needlessly handicap its own citizens and drive completely the wedge of a language barrier between our peoples" (*Cong. Rec.* 1962: 13175).

The language issue arose again in 1965, this time in the judicial branch of government. The island's Supreme Court rejected a petition from an attorney (presumably from the mainland) practicing in Puerto Rico who sought permission to argue a case in English because he did not have command of Spanish. "It is a fact not subject to historical rectification that the vehicle of expression, the language of the Puerto Rican people—integral part of our origin and of our hispanic culture—has been and continues to be Spanish," stated the court. "The means of expression of our people is Spanish, and that is a reality that cannot be changed by any law" (Puerto Rico Supreme Court 1965: 588–89).

While there was an unqualified commitment to Spanish, Puerto Rican leaders consistently pointed out the importance of learning English. In 1963, Muñoz Marín urged the populace to study English not only because of Puerto Rico's association with the United States and because English was an international language but also to have access to literature in the English language (Muñoz Marín 1980: 310). Statehood party governor Luis A. Ferré said in his 1969 Annual Message that public schools should continue to use Spanish as the language of instruction, "but it is essential that all students gain a more effective command of English" (Ferré 1969: 84).

STATUS PLEBISCITE, 1967

Since the implementation of the commonwealth arrangement, discussion had centered on what Puerto Rico's eventual status was to be. The admission of Alaska and Hawaii as the forty-ninth and fiftieth states of the Union in 1959 bolstered support for statehood in Puerto Rico (Partido Estadista Republicano 1959; Padilla 1959), and an official commission was convened in 1964 to investigate status alternatives for the island. After two years of study, the commission concluded that all three status options were valid and that "[i]nsofar as the questions of ideology and of culture and language are involved in arriving at a consensus regarding their future political status, it is the people of Puerto Rico themselves who must resolve these questions" (United States-Puerto Rico Commission on the Status of Puerto Rico 1966: 7). The commission suggested a plebiscite as a means of reaching such a decision. The commonwealth party majority in the Puerto Rican legislature passed a plebiscite bill in December 1966 over the objections of statehood and independence supporters, who argued that commonwealth was not a legitimate status and should not appear on the ballot. A partial boycott of the polls by opponents of commonwealth status resulted in a turnout in the plebiscite of 65.8 percent of registered voters. Although commonwealth status won 60.5 percent of the vote, the abstention rate of 34 percent, which was high by Puerto Rican standards, allowed each party to claim victory for its strategy (Wells 1969: 258–61).

AGITATION AGAINST THE STATUS QUO

The Vietnam War had repercussions in Puerto Rico, as, like their mainland counterparts, students protested obligatory service in the U.S. military. The University of Puerto Rico Reserve Officers' Training Corps (ROTC) building was the focus of demonstrations and counterdemonstrations involving fights, rock throwing, and Molotov cocktails, and in 1969 it was ransacked and burned (*New York Times* 1969a, 1969b). The outrage that many students felt at being subject to the draft was framed differently in Puerto Rico than it was on the mainland, as is indicated by the assertion of a speaker at an antidraft demonstration: "This is the time to decide; either you're a Yanqui or you're a Puerto Rican" (*New York Times* 1969c).

Protest against the draft and the war was often linked to independence supporters. Even after the repeal of the "gag law," advocating independence was considered subversive, and repression of independence supporters continued (Acosta 1987: 236). In the 1960s and 1970s, for example, the U.S. Federal Bureau of Investigation (FBI) threatened island radio stations, which were under the jurisdiction of the U.S. Federal Communications Commission, with loss of license if they broadcast too much pro-independence programming (Subervi-Vélez, Hernández-López, and Frambes-Buxeda 1990: 158).

The FBI's campaign against perceived subversion played a key role in a significant event in recent Puerto Rican history. In 1978 Puerto Rican police shot and killed two independence supporters who were allegedly about to sabotage a television tower at Cerro Maravilla, a mountain in the center of the island. It later emerged that the two were set up by an undercover FBI informer and that Puerto Rican police had not been entirely forthcoming in investigations of the killings. Ten policemen were ultimately convicted on charges of murder, perjury, and obstruction of justice, but the Cerro Maravilla case has not yet been fully resolved. Public hearings on the case were held in the Puerto Rican Senate in 1983–1984 and again in 1992.

The Cerro Maravilla killings were, in part, a reaction to a series of sporadic terrorist actions both in the island and on the mainland by groups advocating Puerto Rican independence. Throughout the 1970s and early 1980s, the Puerto Rican Armed Forces of National Liberation (Fuerzas Armadas de Liberación Nacional, or FALN) claimed credit for more than 100 bombings at mainland train stations, airports, and multinational corporations. In Puerto Rico, FALN targets were U.S. Navy, National Guard, and postal facilities. The group also planted symbolic "scare bombs"—harmless devices that looked like bombs (Smolowe 1980; Andelman 1980). In 1980, as the U.S. Republican and Democratic parties held presidential primaries in the island for the first time, the FALN raided the mainland offices of presidential candidates. "This is a political action," said one raider, whose motive was apparently to express displeasure with candidate George Bush's endorsement of statehood for Puerto Rico (Andelman 1980).

Another violent pro-independence group called Los Macheteros (the Machete

Wielders) formed in 1976. In 1978 the group carried out its first action—kidnapping one Puerto Rican policeman and killing another—in retaliation for the Cerro Maravilla killings. The FALN, Los Macheteros, and other organizations collaborated in terrorist activities through the mid-1980s (Fernández 1987: 57, 259–61).

During this period of unrest, a controversy centered on two key symbols of Puerto Rican identity was triggered by the Pan American Games of 1979. Puerto Rico was to be the host of this quadrennial sporting competition of the Americas and the Caribbean. Governor Carlos Romero Barceló, leader of the statehood party, insisted that the anthems of both Puerto Rico and the United States be played at the opening ceremony of the games. The Puerto Rican Olympic Committee argued that only the Puerto Rican anthem should be played. Consulted about the legalities of the situation, the Puerto Rican Justice Department ruled that it would be illegal *not* to include the U.S. anthem and flag in the ceremonies. The Pan American Sports Organization countered that these ceremonies were "ruled by their own supranational protocol, removed from local regulations," and threatened to move the games to another site if the situation was not resolved. Finally, after intense debate within Puerto Rico on the meaning of using one or both anthems and flags, a two-part opening ceremony was devised. One part would be official, with both flags and anthems; the other part, at which only the Puerto Rican symbols would be displayed, would be solely a sports ceremony (Morales 1979).

At the ceremony itself, the raising of the U.S. flag and the governor's opening remarks were met with boos and jeers from antistatehood spectators (Amdur 1979; MacAloon 1984: 339–40). During one part of the ceremony, however, there was no partisan disagreement. A *New York Times* reporter noted the "tumultuous" enthusiasm shown for the Puerto Rican athletes: "There may be division on the island over statehood, but there is no doubt how residents feel about Puerto Rico's participation in international sports" (Amdur 1979).

PLEBISCITE PROPOSAL, REFERENDUM, PLEBISCITE, 1989–1993

Sports representation united Puerto Ricans of all status preferences, but the status issue continued to divide them. Political violence subsided in the 1980s, particularly after the arrest of sixteen members and alleged sympathizers of Los Macheteros accused of participating in the 1983 robbery of 7 million dollars from a Wells Fargo Bank armored car depot in Connecticut (Fernández 1987: 222–27, 234–37). But political debate over Puerto Rico's relationship with the United States did not ebb. The notion of a popular vote to gauge citizen sentiment was taken up again in early 1989. The three leading Puerto Rican political parties together agreed to ask the U.S. Congress to enact plebiscite legislation. Although a local plebiscite could have been held without congressional action, it was felt that since the power to enact any change in Puerto Rican status rests with

Congress, a local plebiscite would be little more than a glorified opinion poll. Therefore, the three parties requested that the plebiscite results be binding—that Congress "guarantee that the will of the people, once expressed, be implemented" (quoted in Rodríguez Orellana 1991: 3). The parties put enormous resources into lobbying in the United States for a plebiscite bill and in Puerto Rico for support for their respective status options. But after wandering the labyrinth of the U.S. Congress for two years, the proposed plebiscite bill died in Senate committee in early 1991. Puerto Ricans had followed the process closely and were disappointed by this outcome. Many felt betrayed or teased by Congress. Exemplifying this attitude, in a letter to the editor published in the *San Juan Star*, one Puerto Rican accused "a few tight-fisted Senators" of "denying Puerto Rico the right to free determination" (González Bracero Jr. 1991). It was widely held that Congress was not willing to open the door to possible Puerto Rican statehood (Hernández Colón 1991a: 3; Rodríguez Orellana 1991: 5–11). Even Puerto Ricans who did not favor statehood felt insulted. Political analyst Juan Manuel García Passalacqua commented on "the brutal attack on statehood" in the Senate hearings: "I said it a long time ago. They don't want us. Yesterday, with utter bluntness, the American said it" (García Passalacqua 1991a).

The plebiscite bill was a tangible piece of legislation that would have had broad consequences for the island if it had passed. The failure of Congress to enact a plebiscite bill reinforced Puerto Rican leaders' frustration over the island's unresolved political status. In response, they took recourse to actions that did not require the cooperation of U.S. authorities.

In April 1991 the Puerto Rican legislature passed a law that had vast symbolic implications. In order "to abolish an anachronism and reaffirm our historic condition as a Spanish-speaking people," the new law designated Spanish as the official language of Puerto Rico, while retaining English as a mandatory subject in schools (Estado Libre Asociado 1991). This law, which overturned the 1902 statute permitting either English or Spanish to be used in government dealings in the island, did not simply burst into existence as a response to the plebiscite process. It had been making its way through the Puerto Rican legislative process for nearly a year. Statehood supporters claimed that the visibility of the language bill contributed to some U.S. senators' opposition to a Puerto Rican plebiscite (Luciano 1991a). Senator Daniel Patrick Moynihan (1993: 73) has confirmed this view, stating that "Congressional resistance arises largely from the question of whether the island should have the option to choose statehood whilst retaining Spanish as an official language." The possible interplay of symbolic communication is intricate, as the Puerto Rican language law and the U.S. plebiscite bill were being considered during the same period by their respective legislative bodies. Whether by accident or design, less than two months after the plebiscite bill died in the U.S. Senate committee, the language bill was signed into law in Puerto Rico.

The law had little impact on the daily lives of most Puerto Ricans. Both socially and officially, Puerto Ricans communicate with one another in Spanish.

In the 1990 census, 52 percent of Puerto Ricans reported that they spoke just Spanish and could speak no English at all, and another 24 percent reported that they could speak English only with difficulty (Covas Quevedo 1993). Surveys have confirmed that the overwhelming majority of Puerto Ricans—95 percent in a 1993 poll—prefer the Spanish language (Estrada Resto 1993a). The controversy generated by the Spanish-language law was not about problems in implementation or compliance, although some difficulties did arise, but about allegiances to Puerto Rican political parties and the status options they represent. The bill had been proposed and passed by the commonwealth majority in the Puerto Rican legislature, with support of the independence party. Statehood advocates had opposed the language law, favoring the preservation of English as an officially sanctioned language in Puerto Rico.

The positions taken on the language law and the terms used to debate it echoed those of partisans in precommonwealth times. A supporter of the bill criticized the statehood party in barely veiled terms when he described the law as "the culmination of an almost century-long struggle carried out by Puerto Ricans who are proud of being Puerto Ricans and of their culture . . . against those who have advocated Americanization since 1898, and who desire political and cultural assimilation with the United States" (Covas Quevedo 1991). Statehood supporters, in turn, termed the law a "separatist project promoted by a minority that is attempting to weaken ties of union with the United States" (Estrada Resto 1991a). They opposed the law in the Puerto Rican legislature, protested it publicly in the island, and challenged it in federal court on constitutional grounds (Estrada Resto 1991a).

Statehood supporters were not arguing for the adoption of English. Years before, statehood party leader Carlos Romero Barceló had declared, "[O]ur language and our culture are *not* negotiable" (1978: 9). During discussion of the proposed law, statehood party leader Pedro Rosselló observed that "[t]he reality is that [the law] would not change in any way the situation that has existed since the 1949–50 school year when Spanish was established as the language of instruction in Puerto Rican schools." Rosselló argued that legislation to make Spanish official was unnecessary because Spanish was already "the principal medium of official and everyday communication" (Rosselló 1991). Statehood advocates opposed the Spanish-language law not because they had practical objections to it but because they felt it removed English "from its proper place as a symbol of our loyal association with the United States" (Ferré 1991).

Just as opposition to the law was based on the power of language as a political symbol, expressions of support relied on the symbolic attributes of language. The law's supporters saw it as an "event of national definition" (García Passalacqua 1991c). "The language law," asserted one supporter, though a "timid measure," carried "enormous symbolism. . . . By valuing, defending, and fostering its language, Puerto Rico remains true to itself" (Castro Pereda 1991a). The bill's symbolic communication extended beyond the island. A supporter explained that it would send a message to the U.S. Congress that "they have to respect the fact that the Government of Puerto Rico conducts its work in Spanish . . . the message is that neither our culture nor our language is negotiable" (Luciano 1990).

The lavish and emotional ceremony signing the bill into law was attended by invited dignitaries from Spain and Latin America and was televised live (WIPR 1991). The remarks of commonwealth party leader and governor Rafael Hernández Colón inaugurating the law were keenly received. "With this law," said Hernández Colón, "we declare our mother tongue to be the most precious sign of our identity" (Estrada Resto 1991b). He referred specifically to the failed plebiscite bill: "[T]he negative outcome of the plebiscite in the United States Congress caused by Senate resistance to statehood demonstrates the recognition that we are a culturally differentiated people. . . . Our identity comes not from citizenship, but from forming part of the people of Puerto Rico, a human collectivity with common blood, land, history, will, culture, and destiny" (Hernández Colón 1991a: 1, 4).

While trumpeting this law in the island, the governor apparently suspected that more explanation would be needed in Washington. In a letter sent to all members of Congress and in quarter-page English-language advertisements placed in the *New York Times* and *Washington Post*, Hernández Colón emphasized the importance to Puerto Ricans of both the Spanish language and their ties to the U.S. mainland: "As we reaffirm our Spanish language and culture today, we also reaffirm our unity with the United States" (Hernández Colón 1991b).

This preemptive gesture did not forestall immediate congressional repercussions. Republicans on the House Committee of the Interior and Insular Affairs, which oversees issues relating to Puerto Rico, maintained that the language bill itself could be considered a referendum on United States-Puerto Rico relations, as it had the effect of distancing Puerto Rico from the United States. Nebraska congressman Doug Bereuter, a proponent of declaring English the official language of the federal government, expressed alarm at Puerto Rico's move in the other direction. Congressman David Schulze of Pennsylvania was so displeased with the language law that he submitted to Congress a measure to eliminate the special tax exemption for U.S. industries operating in Puerto Rico (Galib Bras 1991a, 1991b).

The next round of this indirect dialogue began with discussions within Puerto Rican political parties concerning life after the failed status plebiscite bill. A series of meetings in the summer of 1991 led to a preliminary agreement to work together to define those matters that the three major Puerto Rican parties agreed would not be negotiable under any status formula. This tripartite consensus quickly broke down. The statehood party withdrew its support after being thwarted in an attempt to include a clause preserving the right to use both Spanish and English, as well as the flags and anthems of both the United States and Puerto Rico, in the island. The commonwealth party's legislative majority prevailed, with support from the independence party, and the list of nonnegotiable points became the foundation of a proposed referendum, dubbed the "Law of Democratic

Rights of the People of Puerto Rico."

The six-point referendum delineated conditions for any future status plebiscite, asserted the right under any status alternative to retain U.S. citizenship, and dealt directly with symbols of Puerto Rican identity, affirming "the right that any consultation about status would guarantee, under any alternative, our culture, language and our own identity, which includes our international sports representation." The referendum bill also stipulated that the results would be translated and sent to the U.S. president and every member of Congress (Comisión Estatal de Elecciones 1991).

This referendum represented an attempt by Puerto Rican political leaders to communicate with the United States symbolically after their attempts to address Puerto Rico's situation directly through the U.S. Congress had failed. Puerto Rican senator Marco A. Rigau, of the commonwealth party, said the purpose of the referendum was "to send Congress a message" about the First Amendment right to redress grievances. His independence party colleague Fernando Martín concurred, noting before the vote that, although the results would have "no legal consequences," defeat of the referendum would send an undesirable message to Congress "that Puerto Ricans are not interested in their political status" (Luciano 1991c).

The message that referendum supporters were sending within the island was that a "yes" vote approving the referendum was a vote for "Puerto Ricanness." A newspaper advertisement placed by the independence party read, "Say 'I do' to what you love the most. To your Puerto Rican nation. To your culture. . . . To your right to express your sentiments and aspirations in the language that your parents bequeathed to you" (Partido Independentista Puertorriqueño 1991). Statehood supporters urged voters to reject the referendum, among other reasons, "because a 'yes' vote will be interpreted in Congress and the United States press as a vote against the United States" (Luciano 1991b). A television advertisement for the "no" campaign repeated the statehood party slogan "vote 'no' to separation" over an audio background of the U.S. national anthem and a video background of a gently waving U.S. flag.

The December 1991 referendum was defeated by a 53 percent vote to reject the referendum, to 45 percent to approve it, surprising almost everyone (Bauza 1991). Puerto Rican analysts attributed this result to a combination of factors, including the abstention of commonwealth party voters in response to internal party divisions; confusion generated by a complex ballot; rising support for statehood and the fear of losing U.S. patronage; and displeasure with Rafael Hernández Colón, the sitting commonwealth party governor, who had pushed the referendum (Castro Pereda 1991b; Nuevo Día 1991b).

Voter dissatisfaction with the commonwealth party was again evident in the 1992 Puerto Rico gubernatorial election. The statehood party, listing among its priorities social goals such as crime control, as well as overturning the Spanish-language law and holding a status plebiscite, swept the elections. For only the second time since 1948, the statehood party won both the governorship and control of the two houses of the Puerto Rican legislature.

The first bill submitted to the newly elected legislature called for rescinding the 1991 language law and reinstating the 1902 law that had allowed the indiscriminate use of English and Spanish for official business in the island. During legislative and public discussions of the law, each side accused the other of using the law only for political ends. A commonwealth party opponent of the bill said the purpose of the bill was simply to "help pave the rocky road to statehood" by showing the U.S. government that "English is an official language in Puerto Rico" (Luciano 1993a). A statehood party leader, in turn, accused the commonwealth party of opposing the law solely out of "political motivations directed at trying to impose barriers to permanent union and the harmonious coexistence of Puerto Rico with the United States" (P. García 1993). But commonwealth party spokespersons explained their opposition to the bill by linking language, culture, and the school language issue that had dominated Puerto Rican politics for the first half of the century: "[T]he new law constitutes a threat to Puerto Rican culture, as it would allow the eventual substitution of English for Spanish as the instrument of instruction in schools" (Estrada Resto 1993b). Pedro Rosselló, the newly elected governor, defended the law reinstating English as an official language in the island with the same argument he had used to oppose the Spanish-language law of the previous administration: that the law would not affect daily life. "The language in which the people communicate is and will continue to be principally Spanish, regardless of any language laws that may be passed," said Rosselló. His reason for supporting the law, he continued, was indeed political: "In submitting this law we are reaffirming our . . . desire to live in permanent union with the United States" (Martínez 1993). The language law was passed in January 1993.

Acting on another campaign promise, Rosselló and the statehood party-led legislature put together a status plebiscite for November 1993. In contrast to the failed plebiscite attempt of 1989, the 1993 vote was organized and conducted internally, with no U.S. involvement. Since the U.S. Congress is vested with ultimate authority in determining Puerto Rico's legal status, the plebiscite results were necessarily "nonbinding": the vote did not carry automatic implementation. Instead, the results were to be submitted to Congress as evidence of the will of the Puerto Rican people concerning the island's status.

The plebiscite was intensely contested. The statehood party based its campaign on the claim that statehood would bring political and economic equality with the rest of the United States, ending Puerto Ricans' condition as "second-class citizens" and increasing the island's share of federal monies (Rivera 1993). The commonwealth party billed its status as a known quantity that represented the "best of both worlds." The independence party urged voters to cast their ballots "for sovereignty and against statehood" by choosing the independence option. With the low level of support for independence, the contest was effectively between the statehood and commonwealth options, but a vote for independence, the party asserted, would decisively reject statehood and prevent either statehood or commonwealth from receiving an absolute majority (Berríos Martínez 1993).

The central issues of the plebiscite campaign fell into three major categories: citizenship, economics, and culture. Citizenship became the center of attention with the release of a U.S. Congressional Research Service report saying that Puerto Ricans' U.S. citizenship was subject to congressional revocation. This study was quickly countered by Puerto Rican and U.S. officials who cited another study and a U.S. Supreme Court decision, both of which had determined that U.S. citizenship, once conferred, could not be revoked (Mulero 1993; Luciano 1993c). In official campaign statements, each party guaranteed that U.S. citizenship would be protected under the status it promoted. The independence party offered, in addition to Puerto Rican citizenship, "United States citizenship for those who desire to retain it." The commonwealth party listed "irrevocable American citizenship" among its guarantees. The statehood party pressed its advantage on this issue, stressing that statehood carried "the permanent guarantee of American citizenship" (Comisión Estatal de Elecciones 1993).

Economic arguments concerned changes in financial arrangements that were predicted to come about with statehood.[1] Statehood party claims that federal benefits would increase if Puerto Rico became a state were met by commonwealth party claims that statehood would bring higher income and sales taxes. Statehood advocates maintained that tourism would increase under statehood, filling Puerto Rico's coffers. Commonwealth supporters said that under statehood, retirees' pensions would be subject to federal taxes, from which they were exempt under the commonwealth, and that Puerto Rico's coffee industry would no longer qualify for protective import duties (Partido Popular Democrático 1993b; *Nuevo Día* 1993). The security offered by statehood would lead to the creation of "new and better jobs," contended statehood supporters (Rivera 1993); commonwealth advocates countered with a Congressional Budget Office study concluding that jobs would be lost under statehood (Hernández Agosto 1993). The independence party chimed in with the assertion that independent countries smaller than Puerto Rico had higher earnings than the island and that, with independence, Puerto Rico would be able to attract foreign capital and to protect economically its agriculture and industry (Berríos Martínez 1993).

Cultural claims centered around the Spanish language and Puerto Rican identity, with ritual invocation of flag, anthem, and Olympic representation. Although Puerto Rican culture was one of several campaign themes, the director of the commonwealth party's campaign went so far as to state: "We are a people with our own language, our own culture. This plebiscite is about preserving that identity" (Barrett 1993). The commonwealth party listed among its guarantees the "full development of our cultural identity." It stressed the importance of the Puerto Rican Olympic Committee and "our own international sports representation" (Comisión Estatal de Elecciones 1993). Commonwealth party television advertisements played on fears that statehood would mean the loss of Olympic representation. One ad featured a winning athlete having his Puerto Rican uniform and flag stripped away; another showed a tearful young woman

competitor recalling the raising of the Puerto Rican flag after an athletic victory
(I. García 1993). The independence party asserted that a sovereign government
would "affirm our nationality and language" (Comisión Estatal de Elecciones
1993). "Value our only flag, our only Homeland, our only Nation" read an
advertisement for the independence option (Partido Independentista Puertorriqueño
1993). The statehood party program guaranteed "our two languages, anthems, and
flags" (Comisión Estatal de Elecciones 1993). Statehood party leaders simply
ridiculed the charge that Puerto Rico would lose its culture as a state. Senator
Rolando Silva (1993) wrote in a newspaper opinion piece that commonwealth
campaigners "suffer from an inferiority complex that prevents them from trusting
our own Puerto Ricanness." Another statehood party leader, former governor
Carlos Romero Barceló, accused commonwealth supporters of "want[ing] us to
believe that under statehood snow is going to fall here, and all the children from
now on will be born with blue eyes and that mothers are going to stop singing
their children to sleep in Spanish" (Reguero 1993). Statehood supporters offered
various responses to opposition contentions that Puerto Rico would lose its
international sports participation if it became a state. One reaction was dismissal
of the significance of sporting events compared to such gains as voting for
president; another was to request Germán Rieckehoff Sampayo, honorary member
of the International Olympic Committee and former president of Puerto Rico's
Olympic Committee, to lobby for continued Olympic representation in the case of
Puerto Rican statehood (Reguero 1993; Estrada Resto 1993c).

Language received considerable attention throughout the plebiscite campaign.
Among the claims of the independence party was that independence was the best
way to protect the Spanish language. The commonwealth party charged that
statehood would entail losing the Spanish language and culture. Former
commonwealth party governor Rafael Hernández Colón said: "If all of Puerto
Rico's official life has to be carried out in a language that is not its own,
eventually the same thing will happen to us as happened to the Spanish speakers
of New Mexico or Texas or California, who have become English speakers of
Hispanic descent. They ceased being what they were to adopt a new identity:
American" (Partido Popular Democrático 1993a). The statehood party countered
that the benefits of statehood would include the legal ability to protect the Spanish
language. Said Governor Rosselló, "Statehood, in fact, gives more instruments
and more legal power to the Puerto Rican people to guarantee Spanish as an
official language, than does commonwealth, which is a territory and doesn't have
any such power" (Martínez 1993).

The commonwealth and statehood campaigns both featured U.S. politicians in
their advertisements. Former U.S. presidents Gerald Ford, Ronald Reagan, and
George Bush appeared in television advertisements in support of the statehood
option. Two Republican congressional supporters of "English only" legislation
in the United States appeared in commonwealth party commercials to corroborate
the argument that under statehood Puerto Rico would lose the Spanish language
(Rohter 1993). In addition, the U.S. organization English First placed a Spanish-

language newspaper advertisement headlined "Electoral Advisory! Statehood Means ENGLISH as First Language" (English First 1993).

The status plebiscite was held on 14 November 1993. With voter participation at 73.5 percent, the commonwealth option won 48.6 percent of the votes to statehood's 46.3 percent; 4.4 percent of the ballots were cast for independence. Statehood party founder Luis A. Ferré promptly called for another status plebiscite to be held after the 1996 gubernatorial elections (Carrasco 1993). Statehood party senator Nicolás Nogueras, asserting that the plebiscite's results were inconclusive because no status option had garnered an absolute majority, filed a bill in the Puerto Rican Senate for an internal status plebiscite to be held in 1995 (Bauza 1993).

NOTE

1. Although by Latin American standards the island is highly advanced in most social and economic indicators, Puerto Rico's per capita income is less than half of that of Mississippi, the poorest state of the United States. Puerto Rico's 1992 per capita income was $6,360 to Mississippi's $14,088. This disparity is due, in part, to Puerto Rico's high unemployment rate of approximately 15 percent.

Part II

Identity in Contemporary Puerto Rico

4

Symbols of Identity: What Is Puerto Rico?

> A group of miscellaneous colors don't make a painting, but when you combine them they make a painting. A group of miscellaneous components don't make a meal, but together they can make a casserole, or something else, like a clock. Puerto Rico has a combination of elements ... and it is the result of all those influences.
>
> —Commonwealth party leader

Puerto Rico's history in the century of U.S. sovereignty has been characterized by persistent resistance to Americanization. Leaders of political parties favoring independence or some form of autonomy have vigilantly demonstrated their unwillingness to acquiesce to the island's becoming "essentially American" in its language and customs. Over time, however, an increasing proportion of islanders has expressed the desire to integrate into the United States as a state, with statehood party support among voters reaching a high of 50 percent in the 1992 gubernatorial election. Since different preferences for Puerto Rico's fate would seem either to stem from, or to lead to, different conceptions of Puerto Ricanness, the notions of Puerto Rican identity held by advocates of different status options merit exploration.

In 1990 I set out to discover the attitudes of Puerto Rican political leaders about their own identity as Puerto Ricans. I conducted in-depth interviews with fourteen Puerto Rican politicians—including legislators, mayors, and internal party officials—and group interviews ("focus groups") with eleven groups of young political activists. Excerpts from these interviews, which explored the ways members and future members of the island's political elite think about Puerto Rico, are presented in the chapters that follow. Excerpts from five shorter interviews are also cited, but the shorter interviews, which were too brief to address all of the questions and therefore are not entirely comparable, are not included in categorizations of the interviews as a body. Interviewees are identified by political party as they are cited in the text. Although none of the interviewees declined to be cited by name (perhaps expressing the majority viewpoint, one joked, "You're asking a politician whether he wants to be quoted?"), because of the frankness of the responses and the turbulence of Puerto Rican politics, I have presented interviewee responses anonymously. In addition to two independence party officials, five statehood party leaders, and six commonwealth party leaders, I interviewed representatives of two other political organizations—the Puerto Rican Socialist Party, which favors independence, and Puerto Ricans in Civic Action, a nonpartisan group that advocates statehood. For continuity of reference, each interviewee has been assigned a number preceded by "i" for "interviewee," which appears in parentheses following each interview excerpt.

Focus groups are similarly identified, with numbers preceded by the letter "g" for "group." Individual focus group participants have been assigned pseudonyms when they are quoted. Four focus groups each were conducted with members of statehood party and commonwealth party youth organizations, and two with independence party youth. In addition to the ten political party focus groups, one focus group was conducted with members of a nonpartisan University of Puerto Rico organization called Students United for Peace. In contrast to the single-party focus groups, the large (seven participants) campus focus group included several unaffiliated participants as well as individuals who favored each of the three status options. This focus group is referred to as University of Puerto Rico focus group. A tabulation of interview and focus group responses appears in Figures 1 and 2, pp. 71–72. All of the in-depth interviewees and thirty-six of the forty-three focus group participants also filled out a brief, written questionnaire, selected results of which are tabulated in Table 1, pp. 99–100. (The questionnaire and a discussion of methodological issues appear in the Appendix.)

Substantively, the responses of the interviewees of each party and the focus group participants of the same party were congruent. Focus group participants' analyses and explanations may have been less sophisticated at times, but even that generalization is difficult to sustain, as many focus group participants provided articulate explanations for their views, while interviewees at times responded viscerally. The most notable difference was that the views of some focus group participants on some issues were less fixed than those of their political leaders. The focus group process yielded interesting exchanges as participants worked through unformed or conflicting opinions.

Overall, the interviews and questionnaires reveal substantial agreement on many points among the majority of respondents across party affiliation, geography, and other variables. These points of consensus included pride in Puerto Rico, a sense that Puerto Rico was a nation, the customs and traditions that were identified as quintessentially Puerto Rican, and the strength of U.S. influence on the island. Within these broad areas of consensus, there were differences in responses. Agreements and disagreements are explored here.

Figure 1. What Is Puerto Ricanness? In-Depth Interviewees

unprompted responses	Commonwealth						Statehood					Indep.		SP*
	i1	i2	i3	i4	i5	i6	i7	i8	i9	i10	i11	i12	i13	i14
nation/nationality				x	x	x		x		x		x	x	x
3 cultures						x						x		x
3 cultures + U.S.				x			x		x					
history				x		x	x			x		x		x
world view					x		x	x		x		x	x	
lifestyle	x	x					x	x						
celebrations		x		x			x	x						
traditions/customs	x	x	x	x			x	x	x		x	x		
Spanish language	x	x	x	x	x	x	x	x	x	x	x	x	x	x
P. R. dialect		x		x			x		x					
"music"/name type				x	x	x	x	x	x	x			x	x
"food"/name type	x	x	x	x	x	x	x	x	x				x	x
hospitable/generous		x	x		x	x	x	x				x		
religious values					x			x		x				
Latin elements		x				x	x		x	x		x		
Olympics/sports	x	x	x	x	x		x		x					
Miss Universe	x			x										
historical P.Rican		x	x	x	x	x				x		x		
contemporary P.R'n	x	x	x	x					x					
flag	x												x	
anthem	x													
pride	x	x		x		x	x	x	x			x	x	x

* Socialist Party

PRIDE IN PUERTO RICO

> We have one thing that unifies us a lot and that is that we can say
> that all Puerto Ricans are proud of being Puerto Rican (g3).

While perhaps not all Puerto Ricans would agree with the above statement of a commonwealth party focus group participant, interview and focus group respondents were remarkably consistent in communicating their feelings that Puerto Rico was a great place and being Puerto Rican was a great thing. Devotion to the island was taken as a given by interviewees and focus group participants across all status preferences.

These respondents might be expected to be particularly devoted for two reasons.

Figure 2.   What Is Puerto Ricanness?
Focus Groups—Political Party Youth Groups

unprompted responses	Commonwealth				Statehood				Indep.		UPR*
	g1	g2	g3	g4	g5	g6	g7	g8	g9	g10	g11
nation/nationality	x		x						x		
3 cultures	x	x	x			x					
3 cultures + U.S.		x			x						
history	x	x	x	x					x		
world view							x				
lifestyle	x				x	x		x			x
celebrations		x	x	x	x	x		x			x
traditions/customs	x		x	x	x	x					x
Spanish language	x	x	x	x	x	x	x	x	x	x	x
P.R. dialect		x		x							x
"music"/name type	x	x	x	x	x	x	x	x	x	x	
"food"/name type		x	x		x	x	x		x		x
hospitable/generous		x	x	x		x	x				
religious values			x	x							x
Latin elements		x	x						x		
Olympics/sports	x	x	x	x		x		x	x	x	x
Miss Universe		x									
historical P.Rican	x	x	x		x	x		x	x	x	x
contemporary P.R'n		x			x		x		x		
flag		x	x	x	x		x		x	x	
anthem		x		x	x				x		
pride		x	x	x	x	x	x		x	x	

* University of Puerto Rico

First, they have chosen to reside in Puerto Rico, although as U.S. citizens they could easily move to the mainland, as have more than 2 million of their fellows. Second, they are active in island politics, an avocation that often entails a sense of belonging and commitment.   What is notable is that this sentiment emerged unsolicited in nearly all of the interviews and focus groups. The backdrop for this examination of Puerto Ricans' views, therefore, is the respondents' underlying pleasure and pride in being Puerto Rican. This is not unusual; it is commonplace for people to express pride in their country or region. It merits mention, nonetheless, for two reasons: first, to note that this pride is consistent with the conclusions of social psychologists that members of social groups seek to create positive evaluations for their groups (Turner 1982: 33–36) and, second, to point out that such pride is not a necessary concomitant to residence in a particular place.

While respondents of all views expressed positive feelings toward Puerto Rico, there was variation along party lines. Independence advocates made fewer generalized statements attesting to their pride in Puerto Rico than did other respondents. This may be because inherent in their commitment to establishing Puerto Rico as an independent country is a sense of valuing the island. "Nobody can accuse us of being anti-Puerto Rican," said an independence party interviewee; "nobody questions that in us" (i13). Independence party leaders' pride in Puerto Rico surfaced explicitly in these interviews chiefly through recognition of the achievements of Puerto Ricans:

> *Independence party interviewee:*
> We have produced so many painters, so many singers, so many sculptors . . . intellectuals, essayists, philosophers. There is rich cultural and intellectual production here. And it keeps growing (i13).

> *Independence party interviewee:*
> We should feel proud to have been born in this land. . . . We have made great contributions. . . . When the Americans were hunting buffalo and killing Indians, at the end of the nineteenth century, we had an institution of higher education in Puerto Rico. . . . We had produced philosophers, . . . painters, . . . we had produced men and women of great quality (i12).

Independence party youth group members spoke in more general terms.

> *Independence party focus group:*
> I'm very proud to speak Spanish, very proud to be Latin American, very proud to be Puerto Rican (g10).

> *Independence party focus group:*
> I have not found any places that are prettier than this piece of earth (g9).

Several commonwealth party members, like independence supporters, lauded the achievements of Puerto Ricans.

> *Commonwealth party interviewee:*
> In spite of being a small country it has many luminaries. Many, in different realms. For example we have in art, in music, Rafael Hernández. . . . In medicine you know that the [then] Surgeon General [of the United States] is Puerto Rican. . . . Mr. Méndez Grado who used to be Secretary of Health here in Puerto Rico holds an important post in the United States. . . . Puerto Rico is a quarry of great luminaries. I think here everyone is a luminary; what

happens is that some are a little better known and others less known
(i2).

Commonwealth party interviewee:
Puerto Rico has a whole culture, in art, in music it has its notables.
We have some Puerto Rican painters and writers who were especially
outstanding in the last century. . . . In politics there have been
persons of stature . . . in every ideological sector (i6).

Commonwealth party focus group:
We have realized that in every important event in the world, there's
always a Puerto Rican there. Yes! (g4).

Generalized feelings of pride were also freely expressed by commonwealth
interviewees and focus group participants.

Commonwealth party interviewee:
[I] feel proud of what we have. . . . I feel so proud of my country
that when I have a vacation, I take it here (i2).

Commonwealth party focus group:
Puerto Rico is a paradise—the best there is (g2).

Commonwealth party focus group:
I don't know where you're from, . . . but it makes me proud that we
would attract the attention of someone and that they would come and
see how we live here in Puerto Rico (g3).

Statehood supporters, too, demonstrated appreciation for Puerto Rico. They did
not view their wish to become a state as inconsistent with fervent allegiance to the
island. Joining their fellows of other political parties, members of one statehood
party focus group noted the contributions of Puerto Ricans in the world:

In sports as well as in writing and intellectuals Puerto Rico has
produced a number of very important people in society and in
history (g6).

But statehood supporters' pride in Puerto Rico was more often expressed in general
terms.

Statehood party interviewee:
I'm very proud of being Puerto Rican, wherever I may be (i8).

Statehood party interviewee:
We're very proud of [the] cultures [that make up Puerto Rico]. I can
tell you, we're very, but *very* proud of all of them. And each

characteristic of these cultures is unique, exclusively in Puerto Rico (i7).

Statehood party focus group:
To me having been born in this special land with a culture so distinct from other countries in the world is very important. I feel very proud to be Puerto Rican.... I think my island is the most beautiful in the world (g5).

Statehood party focus group:
Jaime: We always feel proud of our origins, of our language, of our culture....
Guillermo: Basically we carry [Puerto Rico] inside of us. The Puerto Rican carries it wherever he is and says "I'm Puerto Rican" with pride....
Susana: It's so nice to say "I'm Caribbean, I'm from Puerto Rico" because I'm sure that many people from other countries would want to be Puerto Rican, because they say: "I would like to be Puerto Rican, I would like to go to that famous island," ... and really it's something you feel in your heart, a feeling of joy and happiness (g6).

These excerpts from members of all political parties illustrate the attachment to the island that was repeatedly expressed in interviews and focus groups. The contrasting views of two interviewees merit mention. The first was a commonwealth party interviewee whose fealty to Puerto Rico took a more tempered tone:

Leaders can transmit to the people ... that peoples, with their limitations, should try to be the best they can. And not fool ourselves, not believe that ours is the best place in the world, as you hear all the politicians here say, and that this is the most beautiful country in the world, and we are the best people in the world. You go to the Dominican Republic and they say the same thing and you go to France and they say the same thing. Those are shortsighted views. I'm not really concerned whether Puerto Rico is the best or the worst; it's my country (i4).

The only other exception to the majority sentiment was put forth by a statehood party interviewee. Saying that "geographic nationalism is out of date," he decried what he perceived as the decline of tradition and civility in Puerto Rican society and anticipated moving to the U.S. mainland some day:

When you move you miss your home, the street, and if you don't have the same pillow you miss the pillow, the symbols of the things you grew up with, sure you miss them. But really this defines you in one place in particular.... I don't believe that....

When I move . . . I'll look back at Puerto Rico with affection and great nostalgia and from there I'll remember when I was in the Capitol, I'll remember when I studied at the University of Puerto Rico, my alma mater. . . . And when they ask me after a few years, "would you like to go back?" I'll answer, . . . "I found civilization. I love it. I'll never go back" (i11).

PUERTO RICO AS A NATION

The pride that respondents described was explicitly tied to Puerto Rico as a separate and unique entity. Many interviewees, across all status preferences, contended that Puerto Rico was itself a nation, defining the term with references to Puerto Rico's distinct history and culture. Some respondents further clarified their terminology by explaining that the island was a "sociological nation," as distinguished from a political nation or nation-state.

It is not surprising that advocates of independence would make this claim. Their political goal and reason for being are based on Puerto Rico's becoming an independent state, as alluded to by an independence party interviewee:

What does the independence [movement] pursue? The normal course of historical events of a nationality (i13).

A colleague echoed this position:

Independence party interviewee:
We are a nation. . . . The aspiration of the Puerto Ricans, what we want, is to maintain ourselves as a nation, as what we are, and the only thing we lack is sovereignty. We have all the other characteristics (i12).

The Puerto Rican Socialist Party interviewee explained:

We are a nation with the fundamentals, with a history, with a culture, with a music, with a heritage, with collective experiences of the people, of a nation (i14).

Independence party youth group members had similar, if less focused, ideas:

Independence party focus group:
[It's important to me] to be able to say that we're a country, that we're Puerto Rico, we have our own things, our money, our culture, language, that we're a nation (g10).

Independence party focus group:
Even my father, who is a statehooder, calls Americans "*gringo*." He

has a sense of nationality (g10).

Commonwealth supporters also explicitly termed Puerto Rico a nation, without an accompanying call for political independence.

Commonwealth party interviewee:
Puerto Rico is a nation. It is a people with a history and its own idiosyncrasy (i6).

Commonwealth party interviewee:
Being Puerto Rican is feeling an identification with a nationality that excludes other nationalities (i5).

Commonwealth party focus group:
Being Puerto Rican is being part of a group, a country, a nation in sociological terms, since Puerto Ricans have ... a language in common, colloquialisms in common, some basic customs in common, a history that defines us as a group separated from the others (g1).

But not only independence and commonwealth advocates specifically termed Puerto Rico a nation. Some statehood advocates also made this claim.

Statehood party interviewee:
Puerto Rico is a nation because it has a cultural identity (i8).

Statehood party interviewee:
Basically what we're saying is that sociologically, Puerto Rico has a distinct culture and to a certain extent a distinct sociological nationhood. In terms that you have a distinct people, in a distinct geographic locality, with a distinct language, distinct dialect within that language, with its own literature, its own music, its own everything. And in that sense, sociologically speaking we are a nation (i10).

The respondents who expressly termed Puerto Rico a nation were all based in San Juan, breathing the charged political air of the capital. Other respondents did not put forward this academic interpretation of Puerto Rican nationhood but did make comments that revealed similar underlying assumptions. In some cases, such comments suggest the position of commonwealth supporters who may favor independence but feel that it is not a practical choice because of its low level of popular support. This position was made explicit by a commonwealth party interviewee who explained why he did not support independence:

Independence is not the status that the majority of the people want. It might be a principle of mine, to be free. But one can't go against the majority (i3).

Other respondents were less explicit but alluded to the inherent dignity of independence or the naturalness of the desire to be independent, with the concomitant, implicit recognition of nationhood.

> *Commonwealth party focus group:*
> I would like to see our nationality recognized some day, by the United Nations, by the world (g3).

> *University of Puerto Rico focus group:*
> We Puerto Ricans are a distinct culture that is well defined. That is, the Puerto Rican is Puerto Rican (g11).

> *Commonwealth party interviewee:*
> Here they say that if the Puerto Rican people drank four beers when it was time to go vote, everyone would vote for independence. Even the [commonwealth party] governor. Yes, because when we think it through, we say: "I'm Puerto Rican and I want to be free" (i1).

> *Commonwealth party interviewee:*
> I don't have any problem [with independence] because liberty is a natural thing in peoples and in men (i3).

> *Commonwealth party focus group:*
> I understand that eventually every country . . . should aspire to be an independent country to achieve full development. . . . And at some point we will go towards independence (g4).

> *Statehood party interviewee:*
> At heart I'm for independence, but in the end I'm a statehooder because when I exercise reason I see that the most logical form of independence for my country is statehood (i8).

PUERTO RICANNESS

Respondents unequivocally identified themselves as Puerto Rican, believed that Puerto Rico was a uniquely recognizable entity, and felt positively toward that entity. To explore what that meant to them—how they conceptualized Puerto Rico, how they distinguished it from everywhere else, and what generated their pride and sense of belonging—I posed a question that was broad enough to allow various interpretations in response: "To you, what is Puerto Ricanness; what does it mean to be Puerto Rican?"

Some respondents did not have a ready answer to this question. In many cases the first reaction was quite general: the essence of Puerto Rico was "its people" (i3, i7, g3, g7, g8) or simply a feeling that was difficult to define. The remarks of George McDougall, who was born and raised on the U.S. mainland, but who has lived in Puerto Rico since 1971 and has been a statehood party member of the San Juan City Council since 1981, exemplified this attitude:

> How can you define an essence when obviously it has to do with an affection and allegiance to the island? Beyond that, I think it would be very hard to pin down.

Respondents of all status positions expressed the same reservation:

> *Statehood party focus group:*
> Sometimes it's hard for us to describe what we are (g7).
>
> *Commonwealth party interviewee:*
> These are concepts that at times are difficult to explain because they're sort of spiritual. They aren't seen, but rather they're felt, and what is felt is sometimes difficult to express (i1).
>
> *Commonwealth party interviewee:*
> Look, there's no definition for this country. It's difficult to describe it. . . . There's no composer who hasn't written [a song] for this country (i2).
>
> *Independence party interviewee:*
> That might be a bit like the definition of obscenity given by a Supreme Court Justice: "I don't know what it is, but I know it when I see it" (i13).
>
> *Puerto Rican Socialist Party interviewee:*
> I think there aren't exact definitions . . . of many things, and of some feelings. . . . It's hard to say what is Puerto Rican, so many things. But it's a very special sentiment (i14).

These respondents began haltingly. Others provided vague overarching terms, and still others launched unhesitatingly into a description of Puerto Rican history or traditions. The response of an independence party interviewee to the first question illustrated each of these tendencies in turn. He began by suggesting that Puerto Ricanness was an elusive quantity, then put forward a general characterization, and then moved to more specific elements, all without any interruption or prompting:

> I don't think you can apply any scientific parameter, it seems to me, because we are talking about a category that is fundamentally emotional. . . . I think that it's more important than ever to try to arrive at a definition of that thing that's called Puerto Ricanness. I

think that it's a community of interests, a community of sentiments, a spiritual community, a community of traditions, of language, that in a specific territory and with a specific historical trajectory, produce what we know as the Puerto Rican. Which is a mixture of the Spaniard, the African, the Indian, that have coexisted. . . . So Puerto Ricanness is that totality of spiritual, historical communities, of language, of experience that defines us as a people (i12).

Puerto Rican Traits

When asked for specifics, respondents often said that Puerto Ricanness was the product of a mixture of characteristic elements such as customs, traditions, history, and language. None concurred with the disaffected statehood party interviewee who claimed that "there's no longer any typical Puerto Rican characteristic at all" (i11). A commonwealth party interviewee summed up the comments of many respondents, stating that Puerto Ricanness comprises a "series of elements and ingredients, none of which by itself makes Puerto Ricanness, but the combination of all of them does" (i4). This affirmation was echoed by Felisa Rincón de Gautier, mayor of San Juan for the commonwealth party from 1947 to 1968, who defined the essence of Puerto Ricanness as "the totality of our personality. Not just one thing, all of them: our music, our dance, our food, our behavior, our lifestyle."

Many interviewees provided general lists of these elements.

Commonwealth party interviewee:
Puerto Rico is its people. Puerto Rico is our customs, Puerto Rico is the way we greet one another (i3).

Statehood party interviewee:
To me, being Puerto Rican is having lived the experiences of this generation that was born and raised in Puerto Rico . . . that means that I as a Puerto Rican participate in some common experiences with other Puerto Ricans. . . . It has to do with a multitude of factors. For example, a culture that we share, a history that we share, to a certain extent a vision of the future that we share (i16).

Independence party interviewee:
Food, music, speech, all those things together with a worldview (i13).

Independence party interviewee:
Specific elements, we could say, that are transmitted from generation to generation through the same lullabies, the same attitudes, the same habits, the same patterns of behavior. Like

attitudes toward life (i12).

Focus group participants, too, often began to answer the question, What is Puerto Ricanness? with lists of generalities.

> *Statehood party focus group:*
> For me, Puerto Ricanness is everything that represents a Puerto Rican ... our language, our culture, our typical food, our music (g7).

> *Commonwealth party focus group:*
> What is ours, our customs, our traditions, our way of thinking and living and speaking (g3).

> *University of Puerto Rico focus group:*
> Raúl: We have our own language, our own characteristics, ... our own type of food ...
> María: —typical customs—
> Rosa: —music—
> Luis: —social, religious customs (g11).

After each respondent's first response, whether it had been brief or extended, I probed for more. If a respondent had mentioned general terms such as culture or customs, I asked what that meant. This often opened the floodgates. A commonwealth party interviewee spoke first of the "identification with this land, with our cultural traits, our own way of being, of saying things, of speaking with the whole body, with our hands." When asked what he meant by "cultural traits," he replied with this concise synopsis:

> Okay, we speak Spanish. ... Our Spanish has a certain pronunciation and characteristics. ... We have a music that doesn't exist in any other part of the world. ... Our food is similar in certain ways to the cooking in other tropical and Latin American countries but even so ... rice and beans ... identifies us. Another cultural trait of ours is our celebrations. ... We enjoy festivities. The Puerto Rican is hospitable (i5).

With this list, the interviewee neatly summarized the elements that emerged as respondents were pushed beyond generalities to detail the specifics of their Puerto Ricanness. Describing elements that they perceived as being identifiably Puerto Rican, at times they distinguished between personal preferences and recognition that these elements were associated with Puerto Rico. In the words of a commonwealth party interviewee:

> One does not necessarily prefer his country's food to another country's, but one accepts that that is his culture. As [Cuban poet

José] Martí said: "It's our wine. It's bitter, but it's ours" (i4).

Language. The most consistently cited element of Puerto Ricanness was the Spanish language, which was mentioned in every focus group and by all interviewees. On the questionnaire, eleven of the thirteen interviewees ranked Spanish as "extremely important" to their conception of Puerto Rico; the remaining two, statehooders both, ranked it "of medium importance." Of the thirty-six focus group respondents, twenty-eight ranked it "extremely important," with the dissenters being four statehood supporters, three unaffiliated respondents from the University of Puerto Rico group, and one independence supporter. In interviews and focus groups, many respondents termed the Spanish language "fundamental" or "basic" to their own conceptions of what Puerto Ricanness is.

Ongoing political events in Puerto Rico provided context for respondents' comments. During the period of these interviews, the law making Spanish the official language of government was debated and passed by the Puerto Rican legislature. The elation that this event evoked in commonwealth and independence advocates and the corresponding aggravation provoked in statehood advocates were reflected in these discussions.

Although statehood party members were the least likely of the respondents to rank Spanish as an element of highest importance to their conception of Puerto Rico, neither did they dismiss the language. A statehood party leader stressed that he valued the ability to use both English and Spanish and would not want to be limited to Spanish only. Asked about Puerto Ricanness, however, he immediately responded:

> As a Puerto Rican I participate in some common experiences with other Puerto Ricans, such as the vernacular, the language that defines me and characterizes me as Puerto Rican (i16).

Other statehood supporters confirmed the importance of Spanish, even in an environment in which they were defending the use of English in Puerto Rico.

> *Statehood party interviewee:*
> We are not going to renounce our Spanish for anything in the world, ever (i8).

> *Statehood party interviewee:*
> First of all language. First and foremost language. We . . . believe that Puerto Rico should retain the two official languages. . . . We think there is no reason to . . . eliminate English as an official language, because official languages have nothing to do with the vernacular. And it doesn't necessarily have anything to do with the language of instruction in the schools. We believe that Spanish should continue being the main language of instruction in the schools. . . . [T]he biggest trait of all is the Spanish language (i10).

Commonwealth and independence supporters were unreservedly adamant about the importance of the Spanish language. So strong was their assumption of the centrality of Spanish that references to the language threaded through their comments on most issues. The following selections have been chosen because they refer to language in an excerptable way.

> *Commonwealth party interviewee:*
> No doubt the principal expression of our culture is our language, our Spanish language (i6).

> *Commonwealth party focus group:*
> [The language] is the essence of the Puerto Rican (g4).

> *Independence party focus group:*
> Ricardo: There's something fundamental, which is our language.
> Jorge: That comes first of all (g9).

Jorge then parroted a statehood party phrase that has been adopted across the Puerto Rican political spectrum: "Spanish is not negotiable" (g9).

> *University of Puerto Rico focus group:*
> The language is primordial, because that is what identifies us (g11).

> *Commonwealth party focus group:*
> Our language, Spanish, is a thing that distinguishes us. . . . We couldn't be Puerto Ricans speaking American—that is, speaking English (g2).

As that focus group participant noted, the Spanish language is a significant differentiator between Puerto Rico and the United States. But Spanish is spoken in many countries. Several respondents distinguished Puerto Rican Spanish from that spoken elsewhere.

> *Statehood party interviewee:*
> The vocabulary is different; our Puerto Rican vocabulary is unique in the world (i8).

> *Commonwealth party interviewee:*
> We speak Spanish, but it is not the Spanish that the Argentines speak. Nor the Spanish that the Cubans speak. Nor that the Dominicans speak. Nor the Spanish that is spoken in South America, nor that is spoken in Spain. Our Spanish has a certain pronunciation and it has certain characteristics that identify us as Puerto Ricans (i5).

Commonwealth party focus group:
The way we talk ... we have our own tone of voice, our own way of talking that distinguishes us even among Latin Americans. You can take a Cuban, a Dominican, and you can tell if there's a Puerto Rican among them. That is identity. You don't have to say "I'm Puerto Rican" to distinguish yourself (g2).

University of Puerto Rico focus group:
Luis: Our own way of speaking here diverges from Spanish.
Raúl: The language as well as colloquialisms.
María: The Spanish from here is not the same as that of Spain, of Santo Domingo, of Cuba (g11).

A particular phonological characteristic of Puerto Rican Spanish was mentioned in one statehood party focus group as an identifier:

Don't you see how we talk? ... We mix up the "l" and the "r" (g8).

Another prominent characteristic of Puerto Rican pronunciation—the tendency to replace what would be a rolled or trilled "r" in standard Spanish with the velar "r" sound characteristic of French—was noted by a commonwealth party interviewee (i3), who was unsure whether this generalized characteristic of Puerto Rican Spanish (Dalbor 1969: 129) was limited to his town or heard throughout the island.

History. Another commonly cited element that respondents felt defined Puerto Rico and set it apart was the island's history, particularly 400 years of Spanish colonialism, 100 years of U.S. sovereignty, and the blend of the cultures of the indigenous Taíno Indians, Spanish colonizers, and African slaves. Interviewees of all parties named one or a combination of these historical landmarks as significant to Puerto Ricanness.

Statehood party interviewee:
A defined country like ours, which has five hundred years of history (i7).

Commonwealth party focus group:
Here there are four centuries of history, of a development of ideas .... Before the relationship [with the United States] there was something here and there were processes and there was a defined country (g1).

Puerto Rican Socialist Party interviewee:
We are products of Indians, Africans, and Spanish. We have a little of all of that (i14).

Independence party interviewee:
The Puerto Rican is a mixture of the Spaniard, the African, the Indian (i12).

Commonwealth party interviewee:
Puerto Rico ... is a people with a history, with its own idiosyncrasy.... I don't think we are a random assortment of people that are cohabiting on the one hundred by thirty-five miles which is the size of our island. I think we're more than that. I think we're a nation that has a history that was established from the time before colonization. First there were natives on our island who were the aborigines, the Taíno indians. Then came the era of Spanish colonization. Then comes the importation of slaves, which brings the African element also. That is, we are a national composition of three distinct types of extractions. First the Taíno people, then the Spanish and the African, which produces a Puerto Rican being.... And that's where we are.... We are the sum of those three (i6).

Several statehood and commonwealth party respondents included in their interpretation of Puerto Rican history the addition of the U.S. culture as a fourth element of Puerto Rico's makeup.

Statehood party interviewee:
I would say that [Puerto Rico] is a mixture of many things.... In the first place is the influence of its roots, its native roots of the Indians ... all that mixture of the indigenous culture with the European culture during colonization made the creole[1] component of Puerto Rico which exists today.... And the African part ... the mixture with the African race that was brought here from Africa to replace the Indians as they disappeared.... And also Anglo-Saxon blood has been added to this mixture, from the United States, which has governed us, or has been influencing our culture since 1898.... All of this mixture, each one had its culture, right? They have been incorporated and have been making the Puerto Rican, who is neither European, nor Spanish, nor Taíno, nor black, nor Anglo-Saxon. He's Puerto Rican (i9).

Statehood party interviewee:
As you know, Puerto Rico has five hundred years of history. Columbus arrived in our land in 1493.... And that historical baggage that has been accumulating identifies us as Puerto Ricans ... with an amalgam of cultures. Our indigenous culture.... and then comes the colonization, Spain brings its culture, and this cultural baggage is augmented by the African who is brought as a slave.... In 1898, with the North American invasion, Spain cedes Puerto Rico to the United States ... and in these ninety-some years of contact with the United States ... the North

American culture has been added (i7).

Commonwealth party interviewee:
Puerto Rico ... has within itself a combination of Spanish
elements, of African elements, and of some autochthonous elements
that remain ... and North American influence, and European
influence.... Puerto Rico is a nationality that is the result of all
those influences through five hundred years of history (i4).

Commonwealth party focus group:
Our cultural roots ... [have been] enhanced by the African, Taíno,
and Spanish tendencies. And now the American influence which
also joins our culture (g2).

Customs and traditions. Elements of the island's multiple cultures have
developed over time into a set of generally shared traditions. Respondents of all
positions and status preferences mentioned Puerto Rican customs in general and
specifically—particularly holiday celebrations, food, music, and combinations of
these—as contributing to Puerto Rico's particular character.

Statehood party focus group:
We're a small people but very special, and with deeply rooted
customs (g5).

Commonwealth party interviewee:
Another cultural characteristic of ours is our celebrations. One
celebrates the Christmas period in a certain way (i5).

Commonwealth party focus group:
We defend our culture, our way of being.... We like the parties
that we have at Christmas, we go out on *trullas*, [2] we celebrate
Mother's Day, we celebrate Valentine's Day (g2).

Statehood party interviewee:
We have made our own traditions. For example, the celebration of
Three Kings Day is unique in Puerto Rico. And our typical
Christmas food (i7).

Commonwealth party focus group:
One of our characteristics is the religious celebrations of Christmas.
We celebrate it very differently than other countries. The tradition
of the Three Kings, although it is foreign, has become ours. The
Puerto Rican peasant carved the images of the Three Kings in wood
but he didn't put them on camels, he put them on horses. It's
different, you see? He gave it characteristics from here, ours (g3).

Statehood party interviewee:
The tendency to celebrate fiestas and certain dates, holidays. We could be in Russia, in China, and the Three Kings Day—which is only Puerto Rican, hardly anywhere in the world is it celebrated— but the Puerto Rican, wherever he is, celebrates Three Kings Day (i8).

Statehood party focus group:
At Christmas we eat rice and pigeon peas, with *pasteles*,[3] with pork, because that's the custom and that comes from the culture perhaps of our parents, our grandparents, something from way back that perhaps originated in Puerto Rico as a country (g6).

University of Puerto Rico focus group:
Roast pig, which is typical in our Christmas, is very important (g11).

Puerto Ricans in Civic Action interviewee:
Food is so important to the people of Puerto Rico, the typical food of Puerto Rico, that when I lived in France my mother made sure that she could get the ingredients to make our food. . . . And we used to do it in New Jersey. And if we go to Japan, we'll do it in Japan. And my daughter lives in California and I mail stuff for her. . . . And that doesn't mean that it's anything particularly dramatic or special (i15).

Statehood party interviewee:
The Puerto Rican is used to eating rice and beans, which is very different from eating mashed potatoes. . . . The Puerto Rican was the one who ate rice, beans, fish, right? All those things, in terms of culinary arts, differentiate. . . . Fried codfish is ours, the *pastel* (i9).

Commonwealth party interviewee:
Rice and beans, *pasteles*, that's Puerto Rico (i3).

Commonwealth party interviewee:
Rice and beans, and chicken. That is Puerto Rican food (i1).

Commonwealth party interviewee:
We have some very special foods. Here rice and beans is the national dish, and *alcapurrias* [fried stuffed yucca], tripe, fried codfish (i6).

Commonwealth party focus group:
The majority of Puerto Ricans like to eat the same food, we value traditional food . . . roast pig, rice and pigeon peas, *pasteles* are

popular with Puerto Ricans everywhere.... We have certain characteristic foods (g3).

Commonwealth party interviewee:
If you ask any Puerto Rican from here "what do you like most?" he'll tell you that it's rice and beans. This identifies us. I don't know if that is because it's good—and to me it's good—or if it's because being a country that has been rising up from poverty, rice and beans are the cheapest.... But what's clear is that even after having emerged from that extreme poverty, in the best restaurants you can always get rice and beans.... Upon returning from being away from Puerto Rico for a while, one of the first things that a Puerto Rican says is, "I'm dying to eat rice and beans" (i5).

This interviewee then recounted an experience crossing the border between the United States and Mexico. U.S. citizens are allowed to travel to Mexico without passports. The interviewee did not have his passport, but he was able to demonstrate that he was Puerto Rican and thus a U.S. citizen by describing *tostones*, a typical Puerto Rican snack.

They asked me where I was from. I was from Puerto Rico, American citizen. And then:
  —"But from where?"
  —"I'm from Puerto Rico."
And my "passport" was being able to explain to the official there on the border what *tostones* are. He asked me:
  —"And what are *tostones*?"
And I answered that they use the plantain when it is more or less green, you take off the peel, you cut it in pieces like this, you boil it, then you flatten it, you put it back in, you toast it, that is what *tostones* are. He said:
  —"You can [enter]."
Even in those circumstances that identifies us (i5).

Another defining element of Puerto Rican culture, mentioned in nine of the fourteen interviews and ten of the eleven focus groups, was music. Some respondents specified Spanish-Caribbean salsa music; others, traditional Puerto Rican rhythms: *bomba*, *plena*, and *danza*.

Statehood party interviewee:
We have our distinct music which obviously has the infusion of the African sounds ... other Caribbean sounds and all that, but we have, for example, our autochthonous *danza*, which is a type of music that is not found anywhere else (i10).

Statehood party focus group:
Miguel: We feel the attachment for the music when they play a

bomba which is the traditional music of these regions here in Puerto Rico . . . although I personally don't identify with it.
Camilo: Everybody identifies with the *plena*!
Miguel: Me, more than anything with *plena* and *danza* (g5).

Commonwealth party interviewee:
What is from here, the *bomba* and the *plena*. That is our cultural creation, our contribution (i4).

Commonwealth party interviewee:
We have a music that doesn't exist anywhere [else] in the world. Our *décima*, our *seis chorreao*, our *aguinaldo* [country ballad]. . . . There may be similar musical expressions. But not even the Cuban *punto*, not even Venezuelan typical music or from those countries, they aren't like our peasant music (i5).

Commonwealth party focus group:
Angela: Here everyone, I think even the littlest one, when the *plena* starts, and everyone hears it, and . . . even though we're young and we also like *merengue,* salsa, rap, and whatever, we hear our music and we get more enthusiastic—
Roberto: —and even at parties—
Angela: Exactly. . . . There's a festival . . . and groups come to play music from the interior of Puerto Rico and . . . although we're young and we . . . don't really identify with folklore, . . . everyone is Puerto Rican at that moment.
Juan: The *plena* band comes and everyone sings and—
Angela: —the *güiro* [musical instrument] and the maracas at Christmas—
Roberto: —and always the Christmas singing (g4).

University of Puerto Rico focus group:
Salsa isn't Puerto Rican as such but it's music in Spanish, that's sung in Spanish, and we identify with it (g11).

Independence respondents waxed less poetic about food and music than did commonwealth and statehood party respondents. They acknowledged both as identifiable Puerto Rican elements, mentioning them in their preliminary lists of Puerto Ricanness. One participant in an independence party focus group referred affectionately to Puerto Rico as "this plate of rice and beans" (g9). But independence supporters did not provide the heartfelt emotional descriptions of culinary and musical traditions that their counterparts of other status preferences did. To the contrary, while mentioning food and music as part of Puerto Ricanness, they asserted that to reduce Puerto Ricanness to that level was to diminish it.

Independence party interviewee:
I think that in the long run, colonialism is taking us toward [a weakened sense of identity] ... so that Puerto Ricanness will become fried codfish, rice and beans, *tostones* and roast pork, *pasteles* and blood sausage. But they eat that in Africa too, they eat that in Santo Domingo too. And they also eat that in Cincinnati, Ohio. That by itself will not keep us defined as Puerto Ricans (i13).

Independence party interviewee:
For a commonwealth party member Puerto Rican identity is folklore: *güiros*, maracas, artistic expressions. But the root of cultural expression is the freedom to create, to be what one wants to be with one's mind, hands, the capacity to create without restriction, which is culture. Commonwealth supporters lose the essence of culture with their concept of cultural identity that limits it strictly to folklore. It's not that folklore is not important. I think it is important, but it's not the totality, it's part of the culture. For us culture is the total capacity to create without conditions, that a man or woman has to have in any society (i12).

Personality. Beyond noting general societal characteristics, most interviewees expressed some sense of what a person from Puerto Rico is like. This nonpartisan stereotyping of the "Puerto Rican personality" included such traits as warmth, gregariousness, generosity, expressiveness, and, especially, hospitality.

Commonwealth party focus group:
In Puerto Rico you are always treated with cordiality, with friendliness. Sometimes you go somewhere else and the people are sort of cold (g3).

Statehood party focus group:
Here in Puerto Rico we still have that unity between neighbor and brother, that human warmth. ... It's not like—there are countries in which nobody cares what happens to their neighbor or anything. Here people are close, friendly (g6).

Statehood party interviewee:
We are very expressive, very spontaneous, we talk loudly, we make our presence known, we're not very reserved, more extroverted than, for example, the Anglo-Saxon (i8).

Independence party interviewee:
We are a culture of men and women who are sensitive. And sensual, in the broad sense of the word. ... In oral expression, in songs, ... in poetry, you note all that sensuality that I don't see in such notable form in other cultures. And always in Puerto Rican

culture there has been compassion (i12).

Puerto Rican Socialist Party interviewee:
The Puerto Rican is very gregarious (i14).

University of Puerto Rico focus group:
The Puerto Rican is very expressive and very communicative (g11).

Commonwealth party interviewee:
My country, my people, have not lost that hospitality. And we
have problems like everyone has, all the countries of the world. But
anyone who comes here feels immediately part of Puerto Rico, and I
think that's the best description that can be given of my country
(i2).

Commonwealth party interviewee:
This is a hospitable people (i3).

Statehood party interviewee:
The immense majority of the people are nice, they're people who
help you if you're lost . . . they invite you to have a cup of coffee
(i7).

Commonwealth party interviewee:
The Puerto Rican is hospitable. We love people. . . . The Puerto
Rican has always been open to helping others (i6).

Commonwealth party focus group:
The Puerto Rican is very hospitable, generous, kind (g2).

Statehood party focus group:
Human warmth, that's what makes us Puerto Ricans (g7).

Commonwealth party focus group:
Roberto: The hospitality of the Puerto Rican distinguishes him,
        doesn't it? I would say the humility, the sense of being a
        human being, of helping—
Adrián: —Of helping—
Roberto: —that identifies us—
Angela: —of helping one another. . . . We always cooperate with
        each other.
Juan: Another thing, we feel close to one another. . . . North
        Americans keep their distance—
Roberto: We're more affectionate—
Juan: —more open—
Roberto: —more expressive . . . I'd say that is in nearly all Latin
        Americans, but I think we stand out a bit more in that (g4).

Commonwealth party interviewee:
The Puerto Rican is hospitable. . . . One of the things that I have
seen here since I was little is when you visit a Puerto Rican home,
it's hard to get out of there without eating. It's like if you don't eat,
you didn't visit. And the Puerto Rican really goes all out: "But eat
something!" And you say: "Look, I just had lunch," and they say:
"But just a little, try some." And you have to eat! (i5).

Statehood party focus group:
Here in Puerto Rico there's still that unity between neighbor and
brother, that human warmth. . . . It's not like in some countries
where nobody cares what happens to their neighbors. Here people
are united, very friendly (g7).

One respondent did not share this feeling. A disillusioned statehood party
interviewee felt that typical Puerto Rican characteristics were being lost with rapid
social change:

In trying to define the Puerto Rican in terms of a person who is
easygoing, straightforward, pleasant—that's been lost . . . in this
whole process of survival, of conflict, and of loss of
leadership. . . . What other characteristics are being lost? The
sense of helping others in need. Why is it being lost? Because you
learn that if you help someone you'll have a hundred problems. Here
they attack someone in the street and in the past, ten people came
out to help. Now they close the door, close the window . . . so now
there's no typical Puerto Rican characteristic at all (i11).

International Sports Representation

A latecomer to Puerto Rico's cluster of important symbols is the island's
Olympic team and international sports representation in general. Puerto Rico has
been a member of the International Olympic Committee since 1948, fielding a
team under its own flag in the Olympic Games and other international sporting
events such as the Pan American Games and Central American Games. The
fortunes of the Puerto Rican Olympic team and Olympic Committee are covered
extensively by island media, receiving far more coverage than does the U.S.
Olympic Committee in mainland nonspecialist press.

Respondents frequently pointed to the existence of the Puerto Rican Olympic
team as an important part of their perception of their own Puerto Ricanness. The
Olympic team and committee were mentioned in seven of fourteen interviews and
eight of eleven focus groups. There was a distinct partisan tilt to this
phenomenon. The importance of international sports participation was
emphasized by almost all commonwealth party respondents, compared to about
half of statehood party respondents. Independence party respondents divided by

position: politicians did not mention sports; youth group participants did. Questionnaire results reflected these positions. Commonwealth party respondents unanimously rated the Olympic team as of the highest importance. Statehood interviewees ranked it of medium importance; statehood focus group participants' rankings were distributed across all possibilities from unimportant to extremely important. Independence party politicians ranked the Olympic team as of medium importance; youth group members ranked it highly. (See Table 1, p. 99.)

This party-based variation in responses may be due to the nature of international sports as projecting a representation of the country (in most cases) or community that the team is from. It stands to reason that those Puerto Ricans who most identify with Puerto Rico as it is now—the Puerto Rico that the team represents—feel most strongly about the importance of the team. Statehood and independence supporters may be ambivalent about a team that, regardless of the individual affiliations of its members, officially represents "the Commonwealth of Puerto Rico." Even with this qualification, however, the enthusiasm for Puerto Rican international sports representation by interviewees of all status preferences was remarkable.

For the same reason that sports competition is so important, international beauty contests are regarded by some Puerto Ricans as a chance to shine. As the following excerpts attest, sports and, secondarily, beauty competitions also provide the opportunity to showcase other valued symbols such as the flag and anthem.

> *Statehood party interviewee:*
> There's one aspect of culture, which is sports, which in many communities is not an important element of culture. In Puerto Rico it is. And we have our distinct sports identity because we have our own Olympic team (i10).

> *Commonwealth party interviewee:*
> We are really proud, especially when our national team plays. Everyone has the Puerto Rican flag. . . . When one of our boxers fights and wins . . . Puerto Ricans are proud. When a big league ballplayer becomes famous like Roberto Clemente and now Bobby Bonilla of the [Pittsburgh] Pirates, who is Puerto Rican, we feel proud that he's Puerto Rican (i1).

> *Commonwealth party focus group:*
> In the [1990] Central American Games we won the marathon and a huge number of gold medals, as Puerto Ricans, showing our symbol, our flag, and they played our anthem when a Puerto Rican won. . . . [And] Puerto Rico has had two Miss Universes! (g2).

> *Commonwealth party focus group:*
> We're now a power in basketball. And all that is part of our culture (g4).

Independence party focus group:
Everybody's proud when we win international sports competitions
(g10).

Independence party focus group:
Here in Puerto Rico it's really important, the Puerto Rican
population is very sports oriented, and sports is rooted in the
people's nationalism (g9).

University of Puerto Rico focus group:
Everyone is a nationalist during the Pan American Games, during the
Olympics; everyone is Puerto Rican when Puerto Rico plays,
especially basketball (g11).

Respondents did not distinguish between international participation and other traits of Puerto Ricanness such as typical food. But international competition is different because there is nothing historically or identifiably Puerto Rican about the Olympic Games or beauty pageants. Rather, these activities are a way of celebrating the sense of belonging to a distinct group and the pride in that group that Puerto Ricans feel.

The importance of international competition seems to derive from two factors: the equal status of competing teams and the overt partisanship of sports. The first factor is important for many Puerto Ricans. The sense that Puerto Rico is unknown or not respected in the world is a source of disgruntlement. A specialist in international sporting events has pointed out that "the ritual appearance of Puerto Rico as a nation" in the Olympic Games is particularly important because "Puerto Rico is a full and independent member of no other international organization of any significance" (MacAloon 1984: 330). Respondents alluded to this importance in general terms.

Commonwealth party focus group:
With sports Puerto Ricans have gotten so famous that we're
international (g3).

Commonwealth party interviewee:
Some twelve, fifteen, twenty years ago, other cultures were not
aware of Puerto Rico. . . . In the last twenty years . . . a principal
way that we've become known has been through sports (i2).

In a newspaper interview, a Puerto Rican Olympic team official expressed this sentiment directly. "Everybody starts to cry" when Puerto Rico appears in Olympic Games ceremonies, he said. "We suddenly see ourselves on the same level with all the other countries of the world" (Marquis 1991).

In terms of partisanship, in athletic contests, unlike government negotiations, cheering for one's own side is not only allowed, but expected. In the words of Donald Horne, "[O]ne of the main social consequences of sport" is that "it can provide exemplary displays of superiority" and an outlet for "a gut national chauvinism" (1986: 115). Sociologist Paavo Seppänen has summed up this factor concisely: "Sport is the only activity in which the measuring and comparison of national achievements is made in an indisputable manner" (1984: 117). Commonwealth party respondents, in particular, exhibited this tendency:

> *Commonwealth party interviewee:*
> We play against Cuba, against Spain, against Mexico, against those great powers, even in basketball. Beating the United States is a source of pride for us (i1).

> *Commonwealth party focus group:*
> [It's great] to see our team participate and be one of the best, not just here in Latin America and in Central America but in the world (g4).

> *Commonwealth party focus group:*
> The Puerto Rican Olympic team has won many medals and sometimes we even beat the national team of the United States of America. A little island! (g3).

> *Commonwealth party interviewee:*
> In the Miss Universe contests, we send our girl there to compete, and we've had two or three [winners], above all the others (i5).

> *Commonwealth party focus group:*
> In the [1990] Central American Games we won the marathon and a huge number of gold medals, as Puerto Ricans (g2).

Demonstrating the perceived importance of international competition to the island, as well as the sweetness of symbolic victory, when Puerto Rico's basketball team defeated the U.S. team for the championship in the Pan American Games of August 1991, the major Puerto Rican newspaper carried this news as its front-page banner headline (*Nuevo Día* 1991a).

SENSE OF BELONGING

This review of respondents' views on Puerto Ricanness has shown broad agreement that Puerto Rico has certain distinctive elements. That Puerto Rican politicians and young people of all political persuasions spoke similarly about their language, history, customs, traditions, and pride indicates that for these leaders, at least, there exists a shared sense of being part of a group.

There was not total agreement on which elements defined Puerto Ricanness. Elements proffered by just one or two respondents included cockfighting, the island's vegetation, and Puerto Rico's style of house construction. Moreover, respondents sometimes offered differing interpretations of the meaning and importance of some elements of Puerto Ricanness. Some of these differences were systematically related to party positions. But there was no respondent who did not mention and elaborate on at least some of the elements discussed in this chapter as collectively held representations of Puerto Ricanness. The table of selected questionnaire responses on pages 99–100 indicates the low importance of style of dress across political parties; the predictable variation by party on the importance of Santa Claus, a symbol clearly associated with the United States; and the high level of importance placed by members of all political parties on the recognized Puerto Rican symbols of the Three Kings, language, flag, anthem, traditional music, and Puerto Rican food.

These respondents share a sense of belonging to a group that is defined and recognizable through its symbols. This sense of belonging was explicitly mentioned by several respondents. On the written questionnaire, respondents were given a blank space in which to write any additional item that they thought important to Puerto Ricanness. Of the thirteen respondents who took the time to add anything, three wrote in items referring to a feeling of belonging. A commonwealth party interviewee added "friendship" and "sense of belonging"; a commonwealth party focus group member added "the importance of union among all Puerto Ricans"; and a participant in the University of Puerto Rico focus group wrote "sense of brotherhood from afar even among people who don't know each other." In interviews and focus groups, the idea of belonging was expressed as well.

> *Statehood party focus group:*
> I would say it's an attitude. Because just like you dance here, you can dance somewhere else. Just like you have a party or speak your language here, you speak it anywhere. But being here, sharing with people, you say "ours" because . . . when you're in a group . . . the people interact. And . . . it's like the group keeps growing. Well, Puerto Rico is one big group (g8).

> *Independence party focus group:*
> [Being Puerto Rican] is a feeling of belonging (g10).

> *Commonwealth party interviewee:*
> You come here and you immediately feel part of Puerto Rico, and I think that's the best description there is of Puerto Rico (i2).

THE PERCEPTION OF UNIQUENESS

This sense of being a group, of "us" as opposed to "them," is based on recognition of which traits are generally shared by the group and which are not. Most respondents not only mentioned elements of Puerto Ricanness that were shared by many other respondents but also expressed a clear sense of Puerto Rico as having a defined culture, distinguishable from others by specific traits. This perception is demonstrated in the following excerpts, most of them culled from this chapter.

> *Commonwealth party interviewee:*
> Being Puerto Rican is feeling an identification with a nationality that excludes other nationalities (i5).

> *Commonwealth party focus group:*
> [We have] a history that defines us as a group separated from the others (g1).

> *University of Puerto Rico focus group:*
> We Puerto Ricans are a distinct culture that is well defined (g11).

> *Statehood party interviewee:*
> A defined country like ours which has five hundred years of history (i7).

> *Commonwealth party interviewee:*
> Puerto Rico . . . [has] its own idiosyncrasy (i6).

> *Independence party focus group:*
> We're different, we're a distinct entity. Our personal relationships, our daily social routine, we're different (g9).

> *Statehood party focus group:*
> There's something that unquestionably separates us from everything. That's the famous Puerto Rican *coquí*. It doesn't exist anywhere else (g6).

As the last excerpt indicates, respondents felt that many traits that they mentioned not only defined Puerto Rico as an entity but also were unique to the island. This is true in the case of the *coquí*, a tiny frog that is found only in Puerto Rico. Some of the other traits mentioned were not, in fact, unique to Puerto Rico. The issue, however, is not whether it is objectively true that the traits identified are unique but that respondents perceived them to be.

> *Statehood party interviewee:*
> [E]ach characteristic of these cultures is unique, exclusively in Puerto Rico (i7).

> *Statehood party focus group:*
> [T]his special land with a culture so distinct from other countries (g5).

Statehood party interviewee:
Our Puerto Rican vocabulary is unique in the world (i8).

Statehood party interviewee:
Three Kings Day . . . is only Puerto Rican, hardly anywhere in the
world is it celebrated (i8).

Statehood party interviewee:
We have . . . our autochthonous *danza*, which is a type of music
that is not found anywhere else (i10).

Commonwealth party interviewee:
We have a music that doesn't exist anywhere [else] in the world (i5).

Independence party interviewee:
In oral expression, in songs, . . . in poetry, you note all that
sensuality that I don't see in such notable form in other cultures
(i12).

Across political parties, respondents identified shared elements that they
believed distinguished Puerto Ricans from others. In addition to the broadly
recognized symbols, some respondents referred to symbols that resonated with
meaning for them but were not generally shared by others. Style of dressing, for
example, was mentioned by just one statehood party interviewee. Its average rank
on the questionnaire was below medium importance, but to that interviewee it was
sufficiently important to be mentioned without prompting when he was cataloging
elements of Puerto Ricanness. Other aspects of Puerto Rico were touched upon
by small numbers of respondents as significant to their personal conception of the
island. There was no discernible pattern to occasional references to the *coquí* or to
a sole respondent's identification of the island's flora as symbols of Puerto
Ricanness. This is not surprising; individuals anywhere may have specific
idiosyncratic associations with their groups. But for these nineteen interviewees
and forty-three focus group members as a whole, the most important symbols—
language, food, music, holiday celebrations, Olympic team—were widely agreed
upon. The respondents' sense of Puerto Ricanness was based on the recognition
and valuing of the symbols and traits that they felt uniquely defined Puerto Rico.

Table 1.   Selected Questionnaire Responses

The following words and phrases have been mentioned by some people as things that they associate with Puerto Rico. Please indicate the importance of each of these words and phrases to your personal conception of what it means to be Puerto Rican, using a scale of 1 to 7, from lesser to greater importance.

1=unimportant   4=somewhat important   7=extremely important

	Mean response by political party	
questionnaire item	focus group participants (N=36)	in-depth interviewees (N=13)
Olympic team		
Commonwealth	7.0	7.0
Statehood	4.7	3.3
Independence*	5.8	5.3
Univ. of P.R.	5.6	
The Three Kings		
Commonwealth	6.8	6.2
Statehood	6.5	5.5
Independence*	5.6	5.0
Univ. of P.R.	5.4	
Santa Claus		
Commonwealth	1.7	2.5
Statehood	4.4	4.8
Independence*	1.3	1.0
Univ. of P.R.	1.8	
bomba and *plena* (traditional Puerto Rican musical rhythms)		
Commonwealth	6.9	5.7
Statehood	6.1	3.3
Independence*	5.9	4.7
Univ. of P.R.	5.0	

Table 1 (continued)

questionnaire item	focus group participants	in-depth interviewees
food		
Commonwealth	6.1	5.5
Statehood	5.7	5.0
Independence*	5.3	3.7
Univ. of P.R.	4.4	
style of dressing		
Commonwealth	4.6	3.7
Statehood	3.8	3.5
Independence*	3.8	3.7
Univ. of P.R.	3.2	
the Spanish language		
Commonwealth	7.0	7.0
Statehood	6.4	5.5
Independence*	6.8	7.0
Univ. of P.R.	5.2	
Puerto Rican flag		
Commonwealth	7.0	7.0
Statehood	6.6	6.0
Independence*	6.8	6.3
Univ. of P.R.	6.2	
Puerto Rican anthem		
Commonwealth	7.0	6.7
Statehood	6.4	5.5
Independence*	6.4	6.3
Univ. of P.R.	5.6	

* The Socialist Party interviewee's responses are included with independence party interviewees' responses.

NOTES

1. The term "creole" (*criollo*) was used in sixteenth- through nineteenth-century colonial Latin America to describe a person born in the New World of Spanish parents. In Puerto Rico, the word carries the connotation "of the island," or simply "Puerto Rican."

2. *Trulla* is a Puerto Rican Christmas tradition of house-to-house caroling. The *trulla* begins late at night and lasts until dawn, with the caroling group growing as residents of each house visited invite the group in for a drink and then join in for the duration.

3. *Pasteles* are a typical Puerto Rican Christmas treat, made of boiled stuffed plantain (tropical banana) wrapped in plantain leaves.

5

Self-Identity: What Am I?

"I'm Puerto Rican-American; I'm a United States citizen of Puerto Rico" (i15).

"*Estadounidense*? Never! We're two different things" (i14).

These two comments represent the extremes of opinion on the continuum of respondents' sense of identification with the United States. The general agreement that respondents had exhibited on the key symbols that represent Puerto Rico did not carry through to categories of geographical personal self-identification beyond that of being Puerto Rican.

Geographic identities are generally amenable to being "nested" within one another, with larger units encompassing smaller ones. A person is a resident of an apartment building, a street, and a neighborhood, with these fairly straightforward subunits expanding outward to city, region, country, and so on. This concept of "nested identities" (Feldman 1979) neatly captures the set of concentric categories that can answer the question, "Where are you from?" The salience of each category depends on the context of an interaction.

For Puerto Ricans, however, the nested geographic subunits are complex. The island is physically in the Caribbean, closer to the northern coast of South America than to North America, and historically and culturally related to Latin America. But perhaps because of its relationship with the United States and the ongoing political struggle concerning that relationship, Puerto Rican respondents did not share a set of nested identities. To explore self-identities, interviewees and focus group participants were asked a series of five self-identification questions: "Do you feel Latin American?" "Do you feel Caribbean?" "Do you feel Hispanic?" "Do you feel *estadounidense*?" and "Do you feel Puerto Rican?" The corresponding item on the questionnaire was the following:

> *Put the following words in order of relative importance in terms of how you define yourself, beginning with the most important (1), and ending with the least important (5).*

> *1=the most important   5=the least important*

> _____ *Caribbean*
> _____ *Hispanic*
> _____ *Latin American*
> _____ *North American/estadounidense*
> _____ *Puerto Rican*

PUERTO RICAN

Respondents' strong sense of being Puerto Rican was unmistakable in their questionnaire responses. Puerto Rico was listed last in the alphabetized list of terms, but the thirteen interviewees who filled out the questionnaire all ranked it first in terms of importance to their sense of self-identity. The only deviation was one statehood mayor who ranked both Puerto Rican and North American/ *estadounidense* equally in first place, although in the interview, when asked if he felt North American, he responded, "I feel Puerto Rican" (i7). The fourteenth interviewee, also a statehood supporter, refused to do the ranking, saying, " 'How do you define yourself?' All of the above" (i11).

Of the thirty-six focus group participants who filled out the questionnaire, thirty-two ranked Puerto Rican first, one statehood supporter ranking Puerto Rican equally with North American/*estadounidense* at first; three respondents ranked Puerto Rican second, after Caribbean or Latin American; and one respondent ranked Puerto Rican last, which may possibly have been a misinterpretation of the ranking task (see Table 2 for rankings of self-identity).

In interviews and focus groups, the question "Do you feel Puerto Rican?" was asked last, after the other self-identifications. Respondents often answered earlier self-identification questions by saying they felt Puerto Rican.

> *Independence party interviewee:*
> Q: Do you feel Caribbean?
> A: Less than Puerto Rican. . . . I have always felt Puerto Rican (i13).

> *Commonwealth party interviewee:*
> Q: Do you feel Latin American?
> A: No, I feel Puerto Rican. I don't feel Spanish either; I feel Puerto Rican (i19).

Table 2.   Self-Identifications

*Put the following words in order of relative importance in terms of how
you define yourself, beginning with the most important (1), and ending
with the least important (5).*

1=the most important   *5=the least important*

_____ *Caribbean*
_____ *Hispanic*
_____ *Latin American*
_____ *North American/estadounidense*
_____ *Puerto Rican*

Mean Questionnaire Responses

In-depth interviewees N=13

	C'wealth	Statehood	Indep*		Total
Caribbean	2.2	3.3	2.4		2.5
Hispanic	2.8	2.5	4.0		3.0
Latin American	3.0	4.5	2.3		2.9
North American	4.8	1.8	5.1**		4.1
Puerto Rican	1.0	1.0	1.0		1.0

Focus group participants N=36

	C'wealth	Statehood	Indep	UPR	Total
Caribbean	3.2	3.2	2.5	2.8	2.6
Hispanic	3.0	3.6	3.5	3.8	3.4
Latin American	3.1	3.2	2.1	2.0	2.7
North American	4.2**	3.8	5.1**	4.4	4.4
Puerto Rican	1.0	1.1	1.1	2.0	1.1

*Includes Socialist Party respondent.

**Four respondents (one independence party focus group participant, one
commonwealth party focus group participant, and both independence party
interviewees) refused to include North American in their rankings. In those cases, a
value of 6 was assigned to North American, to indicate the respondents' complete
rejection of the category as a component of their self-identification.

Commonwealth party interviewee:
Q: Do you feel Caribbean?
A: Look, I feel Puerto Rican above all (i2).

Statehood party interviewee:
To be frank, very frank, I don't have an awareness of being Caribbean per se. . . . Nor Latin American either. I feel Puerto Rican (i8).

Commonwealth party focus group:
Q: Do you feel North American?
A: North American, no. I feel Puerto Rican above all (g3).

Respondents emphatically considered themselves Puerto Rican first and foremost. Asked, "Do you feel Puerto Rican?" many laughed at the obviousness of the answer as they replied "definitely"(g2, g3, g4, g8) or "one hundred percent" (i6, g2, g3, g4) and elaborated on the strength of their sense of being Puerto Rican.

Independence party interviewee:
I really feel Puerto Rican. . . . Puerto Rican first (i12).

Independence party interviewee:
I have always felt Puerto Rican (i13).

Commonwealth party interviewee:
First Puerto Rican, above all else Puerto Rican. That is, first Puerto Rican, second Puerto Rican, third Puerto Rican, and if anything's left over, Puerto Rican also (i6).

Commonwealth party interviewee:
First Puerto Rican, of course. First Puerto Rican, that's a given (i5).

Commonwealth party interviewee:
[laughing]. Oh, beyond any doubt. That is how it is; that is not negotiable (i2).

Commonwealth party interviewee:
Q: And the last one, Puerto Rican.
A: The first or the last?
Q: Well, the last one on this list that I'm asking you, Puerto Rican.
A: Puerto Rican is first and last for me (i3).

Commonwealth party focus group:
I'm a fanatic about being Puerto Rican (g2).

> *Statehood party interviewee:*
> I continue to feel strongly Puerto Rican (i8).

> *Statehood party focus group:*
> Arturo: Above all.
> Elena: Very Puerto Rican (g7).

While all respondents felt Puerto Rican, statehood supporters often qualified this self-identification to some degree, in conformity with their status preference.

> *Statehood party focus group:*
> I consider myself Puerto Rican and Puerto Rican I would be wherever I might be. Being Puerto Rican is not contrary to being American (g5).

> *Statehood party interviewee:*
> I feel Puerto Rican. But I have great ties of friendship with North America (i7).

> *Statehood party interviewee:*
> We are Puerto Rican first, we are Americans second, just like many people in Texas (i10).

Even the statehood party interviewee who refused to fill out the questionnaire maintained:

> I feel Puerto Rican who is permanently identified and who shares many features of his life with the American nation. And I feel comfortable in a relationship that I don't have to define (i11).

A statehood party interviewee said he wouldn't trade Puerto Rico for any place on the mainland, but:

> I feel Puerto Rican. In the same way that someone from New York feels New Yorker. He's a New Yorker of the North American nation. I would be a Puerto Rican of the North American nation. There's no difference (i9).

NORTH AMERICAN

Respondents' sense of identification with the United States followed patterns that varied across party lines. Not surprisingly, independence and commonwealth supporters exhibited the absence or outright rejection of identification with the United States. More surprisingly, perhaps, the responses of statehood advocates ranged from the assertion of equal self-identity as both Puerto Rican and *estadounidense* to the complete absence of identification with the United States. Of the thirteen interviewees who responded to the survey, six ranked *estadounidense* last of the five self-identifications, two invented their own category indicating that they would not rank it at all, and one ranked it second-to-last. One statehood party interviewee ranked the United States as first together with Puerto Rican, and the remaining three respondents, all statehood party members, ranked it third. Focus group participants showed a similar pattern.

When asked in the interview "Do you feel *estadounidense?*" interviewees, with a few exceptions among statehood supporters, emphatically considered themselves *not* to be *estadounidenses*. The strongest exceptions were expressed by the interviewee from the statehood advocacy group Puerto Ricans in Civic Action and by a statehood party focus group member who was also a member of Young Republicans of Puerto Rico. Both of these respondents maintained that there was no difference between being Puerto Rican and *estadounidense*:

> *Puerto Ricans in Civic Action interviewee:*
> Q: Do you consider yourself *estadounidense?*
> A: Yes, I do.
> Q: Do you consider yourself Puerto Rican?
> A: I do.
> Q: Can you rank those?
> A: Well, I don't know who "dis-ranked" them. I mean, whoever "dis-ranked" them wants to create the sensation that we're two different things, and they were never disassociated in my mind (i15).

> *Statehood party focus group:*
> I feel completely *estadounidense*, I feel comfortable and I completely admire the United States. There was no problem at all when I was [in the United States] feeling *estadounidense* and feeling Puerto Rican. . . . There has been no internal conflict between one feeling and the other. . . . But I'm in the minority, well in the minority, within the party (g5).

The observation that he was in the minority was borne out by other statehood party respondents, who expressed varying degrees of distance from U.S. identification.

> *Statehood party focus group:*
> It's not that I'm American-American, nor would I want to be. . . . but in a certain way, yes. Because of the relationship that we have. Here there's a lot of influence, in clothing, in music, in food. But to say that I feel more American than Latin American, no (g8).

> *Statehood party focus group:*
> I'm not American because I was born in Puerto Rico and I'm Puerto Rican and I will always be Puerto Rican (g6).

Statehood party interviewee:
When I fight for [statehood], I'm not fighting to feel
estadounidense.... I feel Puerto Rican although I look only
northward when the time comes to think about development and
progress ... but, no, I still feel strongly Puerto Rican. I don't feel
North American (i8).

The lack of identification with the United States was more forcefully expressed
by independence party youth leaders.

Independence party focus group:
Puerto Rican, we're Puerto Rican. We're in Latin America, we're
Latin Americans. We're in the Caribbean, we're Caribbean. The
only thing we're not is North American (g9).

Commonwealth party respondents also expressed an unambiguous lack of
identification with the United States but, congruent with their status preference,
acceptance of the mainland.

Commonwealth party interviewee:
I've learned a lot from the Americans.
Q: But do you feel *estadounidense,* do you feel North American?
A: [laughing] Well, the thing is you can't feel Latin American and
feel North American too (i2).

Commonwealth party focus group:
I feel like a partner of North Americans, I feel like a friend of the
North Americans, I feel related to the North Americans in some
way.... We see [the United States] as allies, partners, friends,
culturally distinct. The North Americans have their culture: apple
pie, baseball, that sort of thing. We have ours (g3).

Commonwealth party interviewee:
We don't feel *estadounidense.* It's strange, isn't it? It's like
negotiating, seeing that that nation has grown, that it's a friend,
that it receives us well, it provides many people opportunities.... But nonetheless, I feel Puerto Rican, I don't feel
North American. We're not Americans ... the *estadounidense*
... came from England, pilgrims that left Europe. And they're the
prototype of a tall person, large, blue eyes. They speak another
language.... We're different (i1).

Commonwealth party interviewee:
I don't have anything against the United States; I have a good time
in the United States, I don't have any problem being an ally of the
United States, but I'm Puerto Rican (i4).

Many commonwealth party respondents separated their personal identification from their U.S. citizenship. Although public opinion polls and political behavior indicate that U.S. citizenship is valued by Puerto Ricans, the distinction made by many respondents suggests that the issue that generated resistance nearly eighty years ago remains cognitively problematic.

> *Commonwealth party interviewee:*
> Q: Do you feel estadounidense?
> A: No. United States citizenship is a legal concept (i19).

> *Commonwealth party interviewee:*
> I recognize that I am a North American citizen, but there is a history of the North American nation that I did not experience, that I respect, but really within my Puerto Rican self, I feel that it is not mine (i6).

> *Commonwealth party interviewee:*
> Q: Do you feel estadounidense?
> A: Um, well, part of the Americas.
> Q: But North American itself.
> A: No. Well, there's the citizenship, but my heart and my will are here in the Caribbean (i3).

> *Commonwealth party focus group:*
> Enrique: We're American citizens, but not *estadounidenses.*
> Fernando: Puerto Ricans (g2).

> *Commonwealth party focus group:*
> The passport is more like a legal element. It's a legal card that is not tied to sentiment (g3).

> *Commonwealth party focus group:*
> [Citizenship] has given us security. Several generations have grown up under North American citizenship without ever having to give up our own identity (g2).

> *Commonwealth party interviewee:*
> No, no I feel Puerto Rican. But American citizenship—when I go to another country and I show my passport, I'm not embarrassed, I don't feel bad, being Puerto Rican and showing an American passport. But when they ask me who I am, where I'm from, I don't say from the United States. I'm from Puerto Rico. It's like we have separated in our minds being Puerto Rican from being American citizens (i5).

An independence party interviewee did not share this acceptance of the U.S. passport:

I don't like having a United States passport. I personally feel very
badly when I go on a trip. [The problem] is not that I have the
United States passport—it would be OK to have that too—it's that I
don't have a Puerto Rican passport (i13).

Other independence supporters had varying views of their citizenship.

Independence party interviewee:
Q: Do you feel estadounidense?
A: No, I don't. I feel really Puerto Rican, Caribbean, Latin
American, and I'm a North American citizen, which is a legal
concept. But I don't feel that I share North American values. I'm
not anti-American because I believe that the North American
populace is a populace like all the peoples of the world, with its
virtues and its failings, but I don't feel American, I feel Puerto
Rican, Latin American (i12).

Independence party focus group:
For us, if Puerto Rico becomes independent, tomorrow we'd
renounce our American citizenship. We can see that the rest of the
people think that American citizenship is their lungs and without it
they'll suffocate . . . but I think after ten years people will see that
American citizenship isn't important, what's important is Puerto
Rican citizenship (g10).

Puerto Rican Socialist Party interviewee:
There's nothing good about United States citizenship. It's just for
getting the money. Here American citizenship means going to the
Persian Gulf [War], and giving our lives in Vietnam and Korea. Here
it means being subject to the federal courts, trials in English and
with fewer guarantees and rights than in the Puerto Rican
Constitution (i14).

An extended discussion in the University of Puerto Rico focus group illustrates
several positions on the issues of U.S. citizenship and identification with the
United States.

Raúl: For me citizenship is indispensable—a person has to have a
nation that will back him. But the United States nationality
isn't important, it could be Japanese, which is one of the big
powers right now. . . . That is, I'm not stuck thinking just
about the United States. But a citizenship, yes, I think that is
important, it could be Puerto Rican—that is in the sense that I
need a nation that will back me up so if something happens to
me or something happens in the world, somewhere to turn,
that will back me up, that will defend my interests.
Carla: For me, having American citizenship is degrading; for me

it's an embarrassment. First, because I never asked for it. Second, because it is embarrassing to belong to such a bellicose nation as the United States. To me citizenship is important if it's my country. And if I feel that my citizenship is something that I helped to build, you know? That I have forged my country. But a country that doesn't give me participation, a country that tells me what I have to do without even asking me ... I don't have any reason to have the "honor" of being a United States citizen. And to me ... American citizenship [is just] having a blue passport, [it's] not thinking that I will have support because they are going to come with twenty tanks and a hundred machine guns and so anyone has support....

Pablo: I have a lot of conflicts about that within myself. Because it's a fact that it's incredibly convenient to have American citizenship, everyone wants to be American citizens. You do what you want, you enter, you travel, you leave, you can do what you want all over the world. But ... to me it doesn't represent any political value, it doesn't represent any type of value. That is, I am burdened with something I don't like. And that's where the conflict comes in.

Rosa: For me citizenship is something, well, it's there. In order to work and for other things if I don't have citizenship I can't do it. But if I could exchange it for another, that would be fine with me, there's no problem. I don't know, I'm just indifferent to it, to me it doesn't mean anything, it has no personal significance or anything.

Luis: The majority of this country, we are in favor of having American citizenship.

[Other group participants: derisive laughter]

Luis: I am sure that the majority of the people are very proud of their American citizenship.... Look, I understand that a group of people do not agree with the American lifestyle, that they don't agree with the image of the United States, I know that, but here in this country there are many people, many people ... who favor their American citizenship and who would defend it to the end. Right now, there are some forty thousand or fifty thousand Puerto Ricans in [the U.S. Army in the Gulf War in] Saudi Arabia. Those people are there to defend their American citizenship and to defend it with everything.... They are there because they believe in American citizenship.

Carla: That Puerto Rican is in the reserves or in the Army because he needs money (g11).

Although the participants erupted in laughter when Luis stated that U.S. citizenship was important to "the majority of the people," surveys and political party manifestos support his assertion. Students' opinions on citizenship may indicate their college idealism as contrasted with their parents' pragmatism. What this discussion clearly shows is these students' lack of identification with the United States.

If interviewees and focus group participants generally agreed they felt Puerto Rican and did not feel *estadounidense*, the rough consensus broke down after that; respondents exhibited considerable variation in self-identity as Caribbean and Latin American and differing interpretations of the meaning of the term Hispanic.

CARIBBEAN

Puerto Rico's northern coast faces the Atlantic Ocean; the western and southern coasts face the Caribbean. Variation in feeling Caribbean varied with status preference, place of residence in the island, and, apparently, age, in a complex three-way interrelationship. Asked, "Do you feel Caribbean?" independence and commonwealth supporters generally, but not unanimously, answered that they did; statehood party interviewees generally, but not unanimously, answered that they did not. Focus group participants, regardless of party or place of residence, were more likely to express Caribbean identity than were interviewees. Participants in nine of the eleven focus groups said they did feel Caribbean; members of one commonwealth party group and one statehood party group said they did not. Residents of Caribbean coastal towns, regardless of party and age, were more likely to identify with the Caribbean.

In the capital city of San Juan, which faces the Atlantic Ocean on the island's northern shore, statehood supporters did not perceive themselves as part of another geopolitical entity, be it the Caribbean or Latin America. One statehood party interviewee voiced this notion starkly: "I feel Puerto Rican as if Puerto Rico didn't have any specific location" (i8). Another, asked "Do you feel Caribbean?" replied, "Not so much. . . . Puerto Rican has certain elements of Caribbean in it, but . . . I would never say "I'm from the Caribbean" (i10). In contrast, commonwealth and independence supporters based in San Juan shared a sense of Puerto Rico as both Caribbean and Latin American.

> *Commonwealth party interviewee (San Juan):*
> Yes, I'm Caribbean. Puerto Ricans are a Caribbean people (i4).

> *Commonwealth party focus group (San Juan):*
> The countries that are closest to us [in terms of commonalities] are those of Latin America and within that, the Caribbean countries. Santo Domingo. Cuba, with all of its differences in terms of political arrangements, is very close to us in cultural terms (g1).

> *Independence party interviewee (San Juan):*
> Q: Do you feel Caribbean?
> A: Yes, of course (i12).

Outside San Juan, however, regional identity was less associated with status preference and apparently more related to geography. Respondents from the Caribbean side of Puerto Rico expressed a stronger Caribbean identity than did those from the Atlantic side or the interior of the island. A statehood party focus group participant from the interior explained his view of what it meant to be Caribbean:

> If you analyze what is Caribbean . . . you have a culture that is centered on the beach. Fishing, the heat, all that. But I, for example, live in a town where there's no beach. . . . We in the center of the island don't share that (g8).

Other focus group participants from various areas outside San Juan tended to express a Caribbean identification.

> *Independence party focus group (mixed provenance):*
> We're Caribbean, period (g10).

> *Commonwealth party focus group (Ponce):*
> I identify myself as Caribbean because of the geographic position of the island in the Caribbean (g3).

> *Statehood party focus group (mixed, central Puerto Rico):*
> Víctor: Yes, I feel Caribbean.
> Pedro: Me too. Naturally: I'm from here; I live in the Caribbean (g6).

> *Statehood party focus group (mixed, not San Juan):*
> Yes, I feel Caribbean, I feel Latin, I feel Puerto Rican (g7).

The notable exception to the pattern of Caribbean identification on the part of respondents from outside the capital city was the interviewee from the statehood advocacy group Puerto Ricans in Civic Action, who lives in a Caribbean coastal city but whose identification is elsewhere:

> No, I don't think I've ever thought about being Caribbean (i15).

Statehood supporters tended to believe that their absence of Caribbean identity was shared throughout the island. A statehood party interviewee maintained that Caribbean identity throughout Puerto Rico matched his own in being "minimal, infinitesimal, infinitesimal" (i8). Others felt themselves to be Caribbean but believed this sense was not shared across Puerto Rican society. A commonwealth party interviewee noted that Puerto Rico "is a Caribbean people but the populace hasn't realized it, they're not aware of this" (i4). An independence party leader remarked:

> We've been isolated from the Caribbean. This comes from the mentality of the colonized nationality—our eyes have been directed northward.... We are realizing that we have more affinity with a Jamaican than with an American from Cincinnati ... But Puerto Rico has to rediscover the Caribbean to rediscover itself (i13).

Still others felt that Caribbean identity was developing in the island. An independence party interviewee's comments may explain why party youth group members had more consistent views of themselves as Caribbean than did their older generation leaders:

> In school when I was little, they oriented me towards the United States, not within the Caribbean context. But little by little I acquired it. Now this has changed, now in the schools they are teaching the kids the importance of our Caribbean location.... The sense of belonging to the Caribbean, and belonging to Latin America, is improving bit by bit (i12).

This shift in orientation was also perceived by a commonwealth party interviewee, who attributed it to the work of his party:

> It seems to me that in the last two administrations of Governor Hernández Colón, there were some initiatives for development of the Caribbean Basin. He has made our people aware that we are very much part of the Caribbean (i6).

LATIN AMERICAN

In the course of answering if they felt Caribbean, many commonwealth and independence supporters anticipated the next question, volunteering that they also felt Latin American.

> *Commonwealth party interviewee:*
> Q: Do you feel Caribbean?
> A: Yes, and Latin American (i6).

> *Commonwealth party focus group:*
> Roberto: I, personally, don't feel Caribbean. I feel Latin American.
> Angela and Juan in unison: Me too (g4).

Latin American identity followed the same pattern as the Caribbean identification: independence and commonwealth party interviewees expressed identification with Latin America; statehood party interviewees, while recognizing their Latin American roots, were reluctant to identify with Latin America; and focus group participants of all parties felt Latin American to some degree.

Commonwealth party focus group:
I think Puerto Rico is part of Latin America, and not of North America (g3).

Commonwealth party interviewee:
The majority of Puerto Ricans, although we might wish to say otherwise, identify with Latin America. That's the way it is (i2).

Commonwealth party focus group:
For many Puerto Ricans, speaking of Latin America, it's like they don't understand. That's a connection that is hard to comprehend. Yes, we're Puerto Ricans and we're American citizens, but Latin American? That sounds like South America and that's far away. But when you talk about Latin America, people with the same roots; same ancestors; same language, in most cases; . . . our cultures are very similar (g2).

Statehood party interviewee:
Q: Do you consider yourself Latin American?
A: To the extent that a Puerto Rican is Latin American, yes. But if you offer me the choice between being American or Latin American, I will put down "American." . . . We share certain things with the rest of Latin America but we're not strictly speaking Latin American (i10).

The difficulty in disentangling Puerto Rican from Latin American elements was demonstrated by the comments of a statehood party interviewee who explained that when traveling in South America

I felt Hispano-American, because of the language. And the religious issue, I'm Catholic, there's a lot of Catholicism, a lot of religion, the language, certain tendencies, similar ways of being. . . . But apart from that identification I do not feel Latin American at all, and less so in terms of politics (i8).

But a different view surfaced in a statehood party focus group:

Gloria: The Mexican can say "Yes, I'm Latin American" but they're very different from us. Different from the Chileans, the Argentines, and they are all Latin American. I feel Latin American. . . . Once I got very angry at the founder of our party because he said that we were not Latin Americans. And our leaders should be respected, but when they don't tell the truth, or they make a mistake, they should be told. And he said that we weren't Latin Americans. I think that [statehood party leader] Mr. Luis Ferré was mistaken, because we are definitely Latin Americans.

> Ramón: To me, I feel Latin American but I don't think of it in a
> cultural sense. To me it's more like a title. It's as if you were
> to say "chicken." Well you have Cocorico [brand] chicken,
> Cooking Good chicken, you have Picú chicken, and they're all
> chicken although they're different. Well that's what I see.
> We're very different but we have something that makes us all
> Latin Americans (g8).

Many respondents identified with Latin American culture and with Puerto
Rico's shared history as a Spanish colony. But the political difficulties in many
Latin American countries seemed to be a significant reason for rejecting Latin
American identification.

> *Statehood party interviewee:*
> We have certain things that separate us a bit from Latin America.
> We have to accept that we are within that cluster of nations. But
> Puerto Rico departs somewhat from that Latin American pattern. We
> don't like coups d'etat. If you've noted Puerto Rican history, there
> haven't been coups. . . . Here we don't overthrow the government
> for fun. What goes on in those other nations doesn't happen here,
> and that differentiates us markedly from our other Latin American
> friends, *compañeros* (i7).

> *Independence party interviewee:*
> I have traveled in Latin America and it's truly unfortunate that those
> places haven't developed as they should. The problem is that the
> underdevelopment that you see in many Latin American countries is
> not due to them being independent, which is what some would have
> us believe. It's because they've had bad government, lots of
> corruption, bad administrations. . . . I recognize our Latin
> American heritage although I don't see Latin America as a
> development model for Puerto Rico. That isn't the model I want for
> this country, because they're models of bad governments (i12).

A different view was expressed in an independence party focus group:

> They teach us that the Caribbean is behind, way behind even Central
> America and all those countries: Argentina, Venezuela, Mexico. So
> we don't want to be involved with those [Caribbean] people and we
> identify, if at all, with Venezuela, Argentina, Mexico (g10).

From the nineteenth-century Latin American independence wars to the present,
Puerto Rico has taken in many refugees from Latin America and the Caribbean.
Respondents attributed various and contrary identifications to the influence of these
exiles.

Commonwealth party focus group:
Culturally, we have a lot of influence from Spain. At one point
intellectuals, professors, came here from Venezuela, Costa Rica,
wherever. They took this as their second home. And that influence
is pronounced, and we feel Latin American like all the others (g4).

Puerto Rican Socialist Party interviewee:
We have a lot of Cubans and Dominicans here, Caribbeans, you
know? And I think those Cubans and Dominicans have Carib-
beanized Puerto Rico quite a bit, their presence has been felt. In
restaurants, in food, in music (i14).

These were responses to direct questions about Caribbean and Latin American
self-identity. In another context, respondents did not seem to find it troublesome
to feel Latin American. When discussing aspects of "the Puerto Rican
personality," several traits were characterized simply as "Latin."

Statehood party interviewee:
Here we don't feel at all concerned about being late . . . you know
two o'clock means between two-ish and three-ish. And in that sense
we're very Latin (i10).

Independence party interviewee:
I don't know if it's the Latin heritage, the tardiness; we're not very
strict about time. . . . I think the Puerto Rican is not punctual like
any Latin is not punctual (i12).

Statehood party interviewee:
[In the past] the typical crime was one of passion, of anger,
fighting, that Latin character, violent (i11).

Statehood party interviewee:
[We have] a high degree of religiousness in our culture, that is,
religion is fundamental in Latin culture. We're extremely Latin (i8).

Commonwealth party interviewee:
Puerto Rico fits with everything that is Latin (i2).

Commonwealth party focus group:
We're very passionate, that's more like part of the Latin American
race. . . . It's hard for us to be calm and tranquil like the North
Americans. We try and try to control our emotions but in difficult
moments . . . the Latin American in us comes out (g3).

Independence party focus group:
Family is important to us. That's part of being Puerto Rican and of
being Latin American (g10).

University of Puerto Rico focus group:
The Puerto Rican is full of life and Latin spark (g11).

HISPANIC

Asked if they felt Hispanic, none of the interviewees answered negatively, but there were different interpretations of the meaning of the term. These interpretations generally followed party lines.

Statehood supporters took Hispanic to mean Spanish-speaking.

Statehood party interviewee:
Yes, from Hispano-America because I speak Spanish (i8).

Statehood party interviewee:
Yes, my main language is Spanish (i10).

Statehood party interviewee:
Hispanic, Hispanic. Because we speak Spanish. But we speak English too (i9).

Statehood party focus group:
Arturo: Yes, I feel Hispanic. I feel Hispanic and I will always feel
       Hispanic. Even if I were in Siberia, I would feel Hispanic.
Héctor: Yes, it's a feeling of language, of culture (g7).

Commonwealth party leaders took the term to refer to cultural roots from Spain:

Commonwealth party interviewee:
Yes, we come from Spain, our culture is Spanish, that is my history, rather than that of George Washington, etc. (i6).

Commonwealth party interviewee:
Yes. [Hispanic means] peoples that have roots in Spain (i4).

Commonwealth party focus group:
To me being Hispanic is belonging to the Spanish culture, having signs of the Spanish. . . . Last names, my last name is García; hers is Méndez. That is, we don't have German or English last names (g3).

Commonwealth party focus group:
Roberto: Hispanic. Hispano-America. I define Hispanic because we
       share a language, and we have the same origin: Spain,
       Hispano-America.

> Adrián: That's what I understand as Hispanic. Hispanic-American
> . . . our origins are there. Here we say the mother country is
> Spain, and we all come from there, or most of us (g4).

Independence leaders identified themselves as Hispanic and then added that they perceived Hispanic to be a catchall term used mostly in the United States. The Puerto Rican Socialist Party interviewee said, "I think in the United States they call everyone Hispanic who speaks Spanish" (i14). An independence party interviewee said he felt Hispanic, but

> The term Hispanic here is sort of extraneous. . . . Hispanic as
> compared to what? Among Latin Americans why am I going to feel
> Hispanic? It's a term that takes on meaning in the United States
> (i13).

One participant in an independence party focus group stated that the term Hispanic was not used in Puerto Rico. Another added, "More like for the language. Hispanic as opposed to Anglo Saxon." The label Hispanic as used in the United States was a concern in two commonwealth focus groups.

> Enrique: Definitely. Even in the United States they term us
> Hispanics.
> Violeta: Yes, but that's like the *mancha de plátano.*[1]
> Fernando: Denying being Hispanic is like, I don't know. Non-
> Hispanic, what's that? Is it American? (g2).

> Adrián: Maybe Americans have a bit of—
> Roberto: —Rejection of the Hispanic.
> Adrián: Rejection, yes, rejection.
> Roberto: Like: "They are second class people and we are first."
> Adrián: Yes. Once you say "Hispanic," you're marked.
> Roberto: You have a label, and you're a second class person.
> Adrián: You can say that you're Puerto Rican . . . but if you say
> Hispanic—
> Angela: And not even Puerto Rican, because you get there and [they
> say]: "They are Latinos," and [you might as well] forget it!
> (g4).

REGIONAL IDENTIFICATION

The interview and questionnaire asked about five predetermined self-identifications. But another, clearly nested, subsidiary identity emerged in the course of the interviews. Puerto Ricans outside San Juan demonstrated regional identification within the island.

Commonwealth party focus group:
Each town has its tradition, its saint, something that identifies it, distinguishes it (g4).

Statehood party focus group:
Gloria: For me Bayamón is, oh! the city of the *chicharrón*, cowboys. But in reality, *cowboys* in Bayamón? But here everyone identifies [with their town], and you see it lots, lots in [local] sports.

Bobby: In my case I see it more in the cultural things of my town, Las Piedras. Because maybe Las Piedras doesn't have a good basketball team . . . but since I was little I have always liked my town, the old structures, the places where they have found indigenous sites that are still being studied. What I always say is that you have to start in your own house. I can't say "I love Puerto Rico, I defend the Puerto Rican flag" if I don't know my own town of Las Piedras, the flag of Las Piedras, what its coat of arms represents. From there I can go on to say "I love Puerto Rico." But . . . it would be hypocritical to say "I love Puerto Rico very much" without being familiar with my own area.

Gloria: Bayamón was one of the most important sugar refining centers, and the best organized slave revolts originated in Bayamón. . . . And the father of statehood is from Bayamón.

Bobby: I always reaffirm that first I'm *pedreño* [from Las Piedras], and then Puerto Rican (g8).

Commonwealth party interviewee:
The person from Cabo Rojo can be away from Cabo Rojo but he always looks for Cabo Rojoans to be with. For example, the only club in the [San Juan] metropolitan area of people from another town is the Cabo Rojo Club. In New York there's a Cabo Rojo Club, in Ponce there's a Cabo Rojo Club. We're regionalists in that.
Q: What is the distinction between Cabo Rojo and Puerto Rico?
A: I set Cabo Rojo apart. Because no other town in the country has had the luck that Dr. Ramón Emeterio Betances, . . . who is called the father of the country, was born here. He was born and raised here. Cabo Rojo produced, to mention the other side, the only [Puerto Rican] pirate that's known: Cofré the pirate. Cabo Rojo produced the first historian in the country, Dr. Salvador Brau, who was the first to write the history of Puerto Rico. And we are proud to say we are Cabo Rojoans because that stock, that root we have, of those like Betances who initiated the famous Grito de Lares [revolt], the man who fought for the abolition of slavery, the man who was a doctor and fought against cholera in the past century, a man who wrote fabulous books, he wrote verse, he wrote opera, he excelled in medicine, in literature, he was a political revolutionary. And now, the governor of Puerto Rico, his father is from Cabo Rojo. Yes!

Q: So there's Cabo Rojo itself, and then Puerto Rico?
A: Yes. We see Cabo Rojo as part of Puerto Rico but Puerto Rico without Cabo Rojo is not Puerto Rico (i3).

Statehood party interviewee:
Every Puerto Rican is proud to belong to his town. I'm proud to be from Loíza. And I wouldn't trade Loíza for San Juan or Ponce or Humacao or Mayagüez. I wouldn't trade. In fact, I've never wanted to live outside my town (i9).

Commonwealth party focus group:
Ponce has some very special characteristics and the principal characteristic is that we're very regionalist. We are very proud of the city that we have and of the things we have in the city, of the customs. And it's normal and natural to hear a *ponceño* [person from Ponce] say "I'm from Ponce" but with a proud, bombastic tone. "*I'm* from *Ponce!*" you know? Every *ponceño* speaks exaggeratedly well of Ponce. I have been surprised myself, hearing some *ponceño* from a distance and I say "*caramba*! he's just like me!" And I don't know him. I haven't said anything to him and he hasn't said anything to me and he thinks the same way. We're very proud of the city, the city is three hundred years old, it bears the name of Juan Ponce de León, the first Spanish governor, a mythical figure. . . . It's prettier than San Juan [laughs]. I have fights with people from San Juan. When I say something about Ponce, they get furious. They're lazy; they talk a lot.
Q: How does the pride in Ponce relate to the pride you feel as a Puerto Rican?
A: I think we see Ponce as a country with all its characteristics, but small, in miniature. Because we have our own cathedral. We have our fruits, our music. All from the city. That is, we wouldn't need anything from the island. The majority of the governors of Puerto Rico are from Ponce. [Then-Governor] Rafael Hernández Colón, *ponceño*. Mr. Luis A. Ferré, he's from the [statehood] party, opposed to my own, but he is well beloved by all, and more, in my case, because he's from Ponce.
Q: I'm trying to understand the relationship of this regionalism and Puerto Rico.
A: I would say that first we're *ponceños* and then Puerto Ricans (g3).

These Puerto Ricans seemingly assert their strong regional loyalties only inside Puerto Rico; respondents across the political spectrum expressed the certainty that if two Puerto Ricans were to meet outside Puerto Rico, they would experience an instantaneous affinity that would transcend their individual political views or regional rivalries. A statehood party focus group participant noted the positive response "when we see another Puerto Rican, [it's] our natural reaction" (g8).

Statehood party focus group:
When we're in Puerto Rico we distinguish ourselves, we identify as the *ponceño*, the Guayanillan, the Vega Bajan, but when we're outside of Puerto Rico, we're all Puerto Ricans. . . . We're one (g7).

Puerto Rican Socialist Party interviewee:
I don't know if this happens with other nationalities but one Puerto Rican meets another that he has never seen, never met . . . and they feel like they have known each other all their lives because they're both from Puerto Rico. And maybe one is annexionist and the other *independentista* but there that is not an issue (i14).

An independence party interviewee suggested that this phenomenon had to do with the ease of communication with group members:

If I run into another Puerto Rican, say, in France . . . there's an immediate connection. There are some things that are taken for granted, some unarticulated premises in communication that don't have to be discussed, and we can communicate at those levels. . . . Even if I run into [statehood party president] Pedro Rosselló. This doesn't have anything to do with party affiliation (i13).

This affinity can be more easily felt, according to some respondents, because there is something recognizably Puerto Rican that can be perceived by other members of the group.

Commonwealth party interviewee:
Anywhere in the world you can find a Puerto Rican in a group of people and it is not difficult to identify him. That's the way it is (i5).

Commonwealth party focus group:
Sometimes we can be identified by our way of being. You can be in Europe and you see a cheerful person with a flowered shirt and it turns out to be a Puerto Rican (g3).

Commonwealth party focus group:
Fernando: You can tell a Puerto Rican anywhere . . . by his way of being, his cheerfulness.
Violeta: Very cheerful.
Fernando: A cheerful person, he likes noise, he likes—
Violeta: —parties—
Fernando: —parties.
Enrique: You go in an airplane and if there's a group of Puerto Ricans you can tell because they're all talking loudly, joking, laughing, happy (g2).

Commonwealth party interviewee:
There's something in the Puerto Rican that you can tell right away
in a crowd who is Puerto Rican and who is not.
Q: How can you tell?
A: How should I know? You feel it. I know right away who's Puerto
Rican, even in the way we greet each other (i3).

Independence party interviewee:
It's a world view that identifies us anywhere in the world and makes
us recognize each other (i13).

NUYORICANS

The talk about affinity and recognizing one another runs up against a sore point
in Puerto Rican society and a factor that complicates "us and them" judgments:
resentment of Puerto Ricans who move to New York, commonly called
Nuyoricans ["New York-Ricans"]. Many of these migrants later return to Puerto
Rico, where they may encounter trouble fitting in.

Commonwealth party focus group:
Angela: Nuyoricans . . . watch cable TV all day. And you see the
        difference. You are here your whole life and there comes a
        moment when you say, "I wouldn't trade what I have . . .
        because my identification as a Puerto Rican is first."
Roberto: We feel that they're completely different cultures . . . and
        the Nuyorican is a subculture of the United States, it's not a
        culture that belongs to the United States. But even so we don't
        interact [with them].
Angela: It's hard . . . they're people who you've known, and they
        go there and come back here . . . and they speak English,
        and—hey, what's happening? You're in Puerto Rico! Speak
        Spanish, because you're Puerto Rican! (g4).

Commonwealth party interviewee:
Here in my town the so-called Nuyoricans are arriving. This is a
type of guy who comes with a certain haircut, talking . . . about
some things and they don't even know how to speak English well,
nor to speak Spanish well. With completely different customs, and
they say they don't adapt [in the mainland], that the Puerto Ricans
don't adapt. Here they don't adapt either when they return (i1).

Statehood party interviewee:
The Puerto Rican from there is very different from the Puerto Rican
from here. . . . The Spanish is different; the vocabulary is
different. The Puerto Rican in New York is different. He has a
strange mixture that we can't say is Puerto Rican because that's not

> the real Puerto Rican. . . . They're so different that even when they
> return to Puerto Rico . . . they seek each other out and they go live
> [in the same area]. . . . It's because they're different, and they feel
> different. And we perceive that (i8).

The rejection of Nuyoricans is based on perceptible differences in characteristics that are identified as Puerto Rican, notably language. This illustrates the role that these characteristics play in establishing the difference between "us" and "them"— between who is considered to be in the group and who is not. But there were contradictory comments as well. A member of an independence party focus group argued for self-definition:

> If a person comes from elsewhere and lives here a while and feels
> Puerto Rican, I would say he or she is. And if someone from here
> goes to New York and lives for many years but still feels Puerto
> Rican, he or she is (g10).

Another independence party respondent put forward a contrary argument:

> I have a dear friend . . . she's American, and she's been here years
> and years and years. If anyone has given something in this country
> in the struggle for social justice with talent and dedication . . . she
> has done it. And nevertheless I just said she is American. . . . The
> father of [another interviewee] is American. He has been here thirty-
> nine years! And I just said he's American!
> Q: How do you tell?
> A: I don't know his father. But since he was born there, he's
> American. Nonetheless, the daughter of [a friend] was born in
> Boston. My daughter was born in Boston. But his daughter is
> Puerto Rican, my daughter is Puerto Rican . . . there are extremely
> subjective aspects. And arbitrary. But the thing is, there's a
> consensus about that arbitrariness (i13).

These interview excerpts indicate that while there is considerable agreement, there is not complete "consensus about that arbitrariness" of who is in the group and who is not. Taken as a whole, the views of Puerto Rican political leaders about their identity were nearly uniform at one level and widely divergent at another. All interviewees professed a remarkable consistency and depth of fidelity to Puerto Rico. Almost as consistent was the absence of identification with the United States. Not surprisingly, the few interviewees who felt some U.S. identity all favored statehood for the island. More surprising was that most statehood supporters interviewed attested that they did not feel any U.S. identification at all. Considering that these are political leaders whose working lives center around achieving Puerto Rican statehood, their lack of identification with the United States is notable.

Overlying the common base of strong Puerto Rican identity and near-unanimous absence of identification with the United States were divergent views concerning the specifics of group membership and other regional identities. There was no clear pattern of identification with the Caribbean or Latin America. Puerto Rico's relationship with these areas is complicated by the island's political situation, and the messages about Puerto Rico's relationship with the rest of the region change with changing political conditions outside and inside the island.

This review of Puerto Rican politicians and youth leaders' descriptions of their own identities—their sense of which groups they are part of—has shown a pattern of concordance and difference similar to the pattern that emerged when they attempted to define what constituted Puerto Ricanness. Just as there was clear agreement that the Spanish language and certain traditions were central to Puerto Ricanness, there was agreement that the most important category of self-identification was Puerto Rican, and there was a generalized lack of identification with the United States. Just as there were disagreements about the relative importance of some elements of Puerto Ricanness, there was disagreement over who may claim membership in the group that calls itself "Puerto Ricans" and about regional identifications. Some of the differences of opinion followed the lines of status preference, some seemed to be geographically based, and some manifested no discernible pattern.

This exploration of Puerto Ricans' self-identifications has considered only one set of geographically based categories. For any Puerto Rican, multiple layers of other identities—class, race, gender, sexuality, and more—coexist with these tiers of geopolitical designations. All of these identities inflect one another in different ways at different times, investing identity with great variety and dynamism. In part because of this mutability, identities are resilient, as demonstrated by the variation as well as the conformity expressed in the interview excerpts presented here. Mutability and resilience contribute to the complexity of collective identities, to their strength, and to their perpetuation.

NOTE

1. *Mancha de plátano* literally means "plantain stain." The phrase is used in Puerto Rico to indicate Puerto Ricanness that cannot be hidden or disguised.

Part III

Identity Under Challenge

6

The Challenge to Puerto Rican Identity

> The most Puerto Rican thing that exists is the name. The customs and all the things from before, from my parents' time, don't exist anymore. Everything is Americanized.
>
> —Puerto Rican taxi driver

Puerto Rican leaders have clear ideas of what constitutes Puerto Ricanness, and they feel emphatically Puerto Rican. In the "us and them" equation that lies at the heart of collective identity, Puerto Rico is "us," and the United States is "them." This is the case despite deliberate U.S. attempts in the early twentieth century to implant its institutions and to make Puerto Ricans "American in spirit, American in hope, American in sentiment" (Hunt 1903: 322).

Transforming Puerto Ricans is no longer a professed U.S. policy objective, and heavy-handed political coercion is no longer exerted by the United States. But U.S. influence is readily evident in the island, through the partial integration formalized in the commonwealth arrangement. The U.S. government retains ultimate political sovereignty over the island; federal institutions such as the Post Office, Park Service, court system, and military are conspicuous in Puerto Rico; and U.S. businesses continue to exercise considerable economic power there. These are visible, concrete manifestations of the United States' relationship with the island. The effects of the U.S. presence on less tangible aspects of Puerto Rican culture and identity are more difficult, if not impossible, to ascertain. What can be examined are Puerto Rican leaders' perceptions of the effects of nearly a century of external pressure on Puerto Rican culture and the attitudes of these leaders toward these perceived effects. These perceptions and attitudes are relevant not just because they are a window to attitudes that may be more widely shared on the island but also because they inform the actions, strategies, and symbolic communication of Puerto Rico's political elites.

CONSENSUS: EXISTENCE OF U.S. INFLUENCE

Interviewees shared the view that nearly a century of U.S. presence in Puerto Rico has had an obvious effect on island culture. Many noted this influence in general terms.

> *Commonwealth party interviewee:*
> Ninety-three years don't pass unnoticed and here there is a tie to the North American nation. And that has been maintained and we are North American citizens and something has taken root in us (i3).

> *Puerto Ricans in Civic Action interviewee:*
> You take a Puerto Rican right now and you ask him to move to a state of the union and he'll move there and he'll adapt better than if you take that Puerto Rican and move him to Peru. Because what is he used to? He's used to the same system and the same form of government and life (i15).

> *Commonwealth party focus group:*
> We've had a much more direct exposure to the United States than other Latin American countries have had and I feel part of Latin America and also part of the Caribbean but I also recognize a practical reality that we have more than ninety years of close ties with the United States and that has its effect (g1).

> *Statehood party focus group:*
> Since 1898 we have been experiencing an American influence. We can't deny that the culture is no longer solely Puerto Rican; rather, it has been greatly influenced (g6).

> *Commonwealth party focus group:*
> We have been culturally penetrated by the United States . . . for about eighty years (g3).

> *Statehood party focus group:*
> Bobby: Puerto Rico has had ninety-three years of Americanization. I think there's been a substantial process of adaptation to American culture.
> Gloria: We here in Puerto Rico have a lifestyle that is—I won't say copied, but it's somewhat acquired from the United States (g8).

> *University of Puerto Rico focus group:*
> You can see that the American culture has had a lot of influence on the culture here, that parts of the American culture are now ours. It's a mixture. They say that Puerto Ricans are Americanized. I don't

believe that. We've taken things from the Americans for our culture (g11).

Commonwealth party interviewee:
This process has been imperceptible. Without realizing it, every day we are a little less Puerto Ricans and become more the North American prototype. And they have not imposed this by force, but rather through the way they bring us their culture—through communications, through jobs for which the applications are in English, for example (i6).

Two statehood supporters pointed out that it is not only Puerto Rico that is subject to U.S. influence:

Statehood party interviewee:
There's a lot of United States influence in Puerto Rico, just like there is in Caracas and Madrid (i10).

Statehood party interviewee:
Here there's nothing, *nothing*, that any government can control in terms of the Americanizing influence of the United States. Because they haven't been able to control it in Latin America, in Venezuela they haven't been able to control it, they haven't been able to control it in any country in the world (i11).

DISCORD: VALUE OF U.S. INFLUENCE

While respondents agreed that the United States had influenced the island, assessment of the value of that influence varied widely. Most of the disagreement could be classified as partisan, predictably following status preferences. Statehood advocates attributed certain changes that they perceived as positive to the U.S. influence.

Statehood party focus group:
I firmly believe that the American culture has made a very important contribution. . . . The United States came here in 1898. There may have been some initial points of shock but the contribution was very positive, especially in the form of government and freedoms, . . . the type of government, the type of prosperity that the American culture brings (g5).

Statehood party interviewee:
Our aspirations politically and economically are basically United States aspirations. . . . We're not comfortable with just the status quo in terms of our personal economic situation; we want a better job, we want a better future for our children than we've had, we want

to improve economically as a people, we cherish our democratic institutions (i10).

Statehood party focus group:
If you have a car, TV, cable TV now, all the modernism has come from the United States and we can't complain (g8).

Statehood party focus group:
Our culture . . . has been enriched in my view (g6).

Commonwealth and independence supporters valued Puerto Rico's democratic institutions but were unhappy with many other aspects of the U.S. presence.

Commonwealth party interviewee:
We used to be better than we are now. . . now individualism has come as a consequence of our relationship with the United States. Each day we're more like them. . . . The Puerto Rican was never tied to material comforts, but rather human virtues were values that were more important. . . . Individualism, the desire to have more material goods, is beginning to damage the Puerto Rican (i6).

Commonwealth party focus group:
Our customs have been lost and some have been modified. Some essential values are being lost, . . . social norms as well as perhaps the concept of family. . . . The Hispanic has the concept of extended family. . . . The United States is different. . . . It's not that one way is good and the other bad, because theirs has worked there and ours has worked here, but this is a loss of the values that are the foundation of our society (g1).

Independence party focus group:
The North Americans can't leave here until they compensate us for all the social and environmental damage that Americanization has created in Puerto Rico. Until they pay for the lives that the Puerto Rican people have given defending them (g9).

University of Puerto Rico focus group:
Raúl: The roast pig, the *trovadores* . . . there are certain elements of that culture that remain but you realize they're being lost.
Pablo: Too many.
Carla: Exactly . . . now the seven and eight year olds have Ninja Turtles . . . I think all that has been a consequence of the colonial relationship (g11).

PARTISAN INTERPRETATIONS: PERCEIVED THREAT OF ASSIMILATION

Puerto Rican political parties have articulated positions about Puerto Rico's relationship with the United States, including their predictions of the effects of each status option on Puerto Rico. These positions are clearly political assertions intended to bolster each party's agenda at the expense of the rival parties. A statehood party official summed up his party's position with the assertion that "the essence of the Puerto Rican is crystallized in a vision of the future in which as United States citizens we can fully share in the rights, privileges and responsibilities [of citizenship]." In contrast, a commonwealth party leader favored commonwealth status as "the best thing for Puerto Rico" because it allows the island "to be aligned with the United States without losing its national identity" (i4). To an independence party official, however, it is a "miracle that Puerto Rican identity has survived" at all in the current "colonial situation" (i12).

These conflicting perspectives were echoed in the comments of other political leaders. Statehood supporters were adamant that Puerto Rico's culture is resilient and would not be lost if Puerto Rico became a state.

Statehood party interviewee:
There will be no more transformations except those which we ourselves provoke internally. . . . Something dramatic, something crucial that could affect or suppress our culture is impossible through any political change, much less in the change to statehood status (i8).

Statehood party interviewee:
What would we lose? The only thing we don't have is a vote in Congress. Nothing would be lost. . . . Nobody causes traditions to vary, nobody changes them. . . . The customs of Alaska or those of Hawaii have hardly changed. That's why I say that Puerto Rican customs will stay more or less the same (i7).

Statehood party interviewee:
We have a special mixture that we can call the Puerto Rican culture. . . . It's taken a very long time to develop it and . . . it's so ingrained in our people, there's no way that it's going to disappear. . . . Politically there's nothing that can be done for us to lose our culture (i10).

Puerto Ricans in Civic Action interviewee:
Oh, we'll never [lose the differences] because we have been part of the United States for a hundred years and we have not lost them. I mean if we were going to lose anything we would have lost it already (i15).

Statehood party interviewee:
Our customs would be the same, the same ones that Puerto Rico has now (i9).

Statehood party interviewee:
I'm not going to stop responding with my Puerto Rican attitudes .... For example, you give me the opportunity to be courteous and open the door for a woman, I do it in New York and a woman looks at me like I'm some strange being. ... We still have some things that we learned at home. ... It's a way of being, it's not identity, it's a way of being. And they are not going to take away my way of being. ... I am open to the process of cultural absorption, because to me, as Wendell Wilkie said, there's only one world (i11).

Statehood party focus group:
We can't think that the act of changing a political status could limit our culture or diminish it, no, because the culture is part of Puerto Ricans and it is well rooted in us. I would continue being as Puerto Rican as I am now (g5).

Statehood party focus group:
Susana: If our culture and our people have survived five hundred years, why won't it survive five hundred more? And it's not going to change at all.
Guillermo: All cultures evolve. Ours is evolving.
Víctor: The way I see it we can't say that the culture will disappear or won't disappear because that's the future. What we can say is that we will show just like the people of Hawaii did, just like the people of Alaska did, that we will conserve our customs (g6).

Commonwealth and independence supporters did not share this confidence that distinctly Puerto Rican culture and traditions would survive in the event of statehood for the island.

Commonwealth party interviewee:
I have no doubt that if we become a state that would eliminate any remaining impediments to us ceasing to be Puerto Ricans and becoming North Americans (i6).

Commonwealth party interviewee:
If Puerto Rico were a state of Germany, I imagine we'd have to speak German. And I imagine we'd want to participate in German society ... with full rights, privileges, and responsibilities. So it would be absurd that if Puerto Rico were a state we would do what the statehooders claim: maintain a distinct national identity, separate

from the American. Puerto Rico ... would not be a culture in itself, but an element within a larger culture which is the American society. And that is not something that would happen instantly. ... Life would go on as usual, the sun would still rise over Humacao [in eastern Puerto Rico], lights would turn on and off, water would still come out of the tap, people would still speak Spanish. ... But two, three generations from now I have no doubt that Puerto Rico would be completely transformed. And it *should* be transformed if it becomes a state because otherwise it would become a ghetto unable to participate in American life because of the language barrier (i4).

Commonwealth party interviewee:
My principal concern with statehood as I see it is in terms of our nationality, the disappearance of our nationality. The United States is composed of many nationalities. ... In the United States an Italian, a German, ... arrives there and although it's clear that he has his Italian origin, while he is in the United States, he belongs to the Italian minority, the German to the German minority. ... But all together they make the American people. ... We here in Puerto Rico have a nationality. In the United States we're part of a minority, we're a Hispanic minority there. Statehood would do away with Puerto Rico as a people; it would make us one of fifty-one. ...

What would be the worst consequence of statehood? The dissolution of our nationality! ... It wouldn't be the next day. We would continue, the sun would still be warm, ... snow wouldn't fall, and we wouldn't have to speak English the next day. But that's not what it's about. It's that fifty years later, a hundred years later ... in the long run there would have to be adjustments (i5).

Commonwealth party interviewee:
We would be assimilated, we would lose that identity that we Puerto Ricans live so proudly. ... Afterwards Puerto Ricans would lament having lost their identity, their customs, their traditions (i1).

Commonwealth party interviewee:
[Statehood] would be the dissolution of our people. This people would dissolve as one more state. And we would lose the personality that we have in the Caribbean ... and in the whole world of what Puerto Rico is. ... When you integrate yourself fully in a nation, the nation absorbs you (i3).

Commonwealth party focus group:
When you integrate you have to ... become part of the totality of that group. That's why we would lose so many things that identify

us as a people (g2).

Independence party interviewee:
They would absorb us. I think Puerto Rican culture and identity
would suffer greatly if we were a state. . . . I think we would
become or we could become, instead of a culture, a Puerto Rican
identity, an ethnic minority. The concept is different. We do not
want to be an ethnic minority within the North American culture
. . . . We are a nation. So, it's one thing to maintain yourself as
an ethnic minority . . , and that's folklore. . . . But that's not
the aspiration of Puerto Ricans. What we want is to maintain
ourselves as a nation (i12).

University of Puerto Rico focus group member:
I'm afraid, and I say this as the *independentista* that I am, that upon
becoming a state our Puerto Rican character would be completely
lost (g11).

Puerto Rican Socialist Party interviewee:
I think that statehood for Puerto Rico means the death of the Puerto
Rican nationality. Not the next day or in five years, but gradually.
It means our death as a people. . . . When the colonial power
annexes you and makes you part of it, then that's the end of you
(i14).

The fear of the demise of the Puerto Rican nationality was often expressed as
concern that the symbols that are felt to represent that nationality would be
eliminated or displaced. Some symbols, however, were perceived to be under a
greater threat of elimination than others. Respondents had vastly different
reactions to the presence of two media products—Anglo-American music and U.S.
cable television—in Puerto Rico. Imported music was not generally seen as a
threat to the continued vitality of Puerto Rican music. The perceived influence of
cable television, on the other hand, aroused great alarm. Paralleling reactions to
these media were views about traditional Puerto Rican food and Christmas
celebrations. The availability of U.S. food, like music, did not cause concern.
U.S. Christmas traditions, like cable television, elicited considerable concern. A
comparison of these elements reveals a pattern that is linked to the degree that the
interviewees feared the displacement of key symbols of Puerto Ricanness.

COEXISTENCE WITH CULTURAL IMPORTS

Music

Puerto Rico's 111 radio stations broadcast predominantly Spanish-language programming (Subervi-Vélez, Hernández-López, and Frambes-Buxeda 1990: 157). There is one English-language radio station; all of the other radio stations feature Spanish-language announcing and, on popular music stations, varying proportions of Anglo-American and Latin American pop among the musical selections. As one statehood party interviewee rightly pointed out, Puerto Rico is hardly alone in receiving music from the United States.

> They haven't been able to penetrate here.... There's no fully English-language radio station in Puerto Rico; they're all Puerto Rican stations with American music, but you hear more American music in Madrid (i8).

Nonetheless, respondents noted that U.S. popular music was everywhere in evidence, on radio and television, in stores and nightclubs. Many noted changes in listening habits, particularly among young people.

> *Commonwealth party focus group:*
> We've had to accept ... rap music and rock and all that music (g2).

> *Commonwealth party focus group:*
> A lot of music in English has come here, rock and this and that (g4).

> *Statehood party interviewee:*
> We have the natural clash between salsa and [Dominican] *merengue* and rock and rap and all that (i10).

> *University of Puerto Rico focus group:*
> Young people don't write music in Spanish, they write raps. And the groups of rock in Spanish—
> Q: Rock in English or in Spanish?
> A: In English or Spanish, that doesn't come from us. Rock in English is more popular, I think, than rock in Spanish (i11).

> *Commonwealth party interviewee:*
> In music definitely, go to San Juan at night and you'll see, our young people fundamentally are listening to North American music (i6).

Yet, respondents across political parties did not find listening to many varieties of imported music problematic or threatening to their identity. A commonwealth party youth group participant said:

> I have deeper ties to the music from here, Puerto Rico and the Caribbean, but I am also in touch with North American music.... I listen to Sting, Tracy Chapman and that type of music.... I think that to take a position that I like one type better than the

other is sort of illogical. You listen to everything for its individual merit. At least that's what I try to do (g1).

Members of an independence party focus group emphasized that enjoying other music did not make them less Puerto Rican.

> Gabriel: The music you listen to is immaterial. That doesn't identify you. I really like Brazilian music and that doesn't mean I favor Brazil, that I want to be a colony of Brazil.
> Martín: I like heavy metal, psychedelic rock. I listen to traditional Puerto Rican music every morning. Spanish music. I like Dominican *merengue*, and of course the *bomba* and the *plena*. And salsa.
> Jorge: I like all music.
> Ricardo: I play the Puerto Rican *cuatro*. . . . But I also love Andean music. I love [Colombian] *cumbia, vallenato*, I love rock in Spanish, American rock not so much.
> Gabriel: I think it doesn't matter what you listen to as long as you're always aware of who you are (g9).

Similarly, a commonwealth party interviewee asserted:

> I prefer to listen to the Brandenburg concertos of Bach, and maybe some other music, but that doesn't make me German (i4).

The sole respondent who expressed reservations about the wide availability of music from the United States had a very specific fear: that country music from the United States would displace traditional Puerto Rican music if Puerto Rico became a state.

> I'm afraid that in ten years I'll go to a contest of cowboys singing country music instead of seeing [traditional Puerto Rican] *trovadores* singing, or that they'll publicize the cowboy contest more than the *trovadores* and only the old people will go (g11).

Food

Food was also used as an identifying symbol in descriptions of the effects of U.S. influence. In conjunction with mentioning typical Puerto Rican food as an element of Puerto Ricanness, many respondents mentioned the proliferation of U.S. fast-food chains as an example of U.S. influence on the island. Such observations were not overstated; throughout Puerto Rico there are 100 Burger King restaurants, seventy-eight Kentucky Fried Chicken outlets, fifty-four McDonalds, and a full complement of Wendy's, Taco Bells, and other fast-food outlets. For comparison, in the state of Connecticut, which is similar in size and population to Puerto Rico, there are seventy-four Burger Kings, thirty-nine Kentucky Fried Chicken outlets, and 137 McDonald's restaurants.

> *Commonwealth party interviewee:*
> We're invaded by the hamburger and hot dog here. That's part of the Americans; we didn't invent that (i2).

> *Statehood party interviewee:*
> The Puerto Rican is used to eating rice and beans, which is very different from eating mashed potatoes. Now we are getting used to eating mashed potatoes too, and French fries, and fried chicken and all that. And hamburgers. The hamburger has arrived, the hot dog has arrived, but rice and beans is ours (i9).

> *Commonwealth party focus group:*
> Because of the union with the United States we've had to accept the hot dog and the hamburger (g2).

Nonetheless, while many noted that eating habits had been altered by the U.S. presence, this did not seem to cause alarm. The reaction, rather, was similar to the reaction to the influx of music from elsewhere: acceptance of an outside element with the sense that since the Puerto Rican counterpart was also available, the added competition did not pose a problem.

> *Commonwealth party interviewee:*
> Look, I don't have anything against the Americans. I eat hot dogs, and I have a Visa card and a Mastercard (i2).

> *Statehood party focus group:*
> We are not going to stop being Puerto Ricans if statehood comes, we're not going to eat hamburgers, we'll keep eating the same food, we'll keep speaking the same language, we'll continue to love our flag (g6).

> *Statehood party interviewee:*
> Regardless of the influence of whatever culture, I am sure that we could be state number fifty-one of the American nation tomorrow, and the Puerto Rican will never stop eating *gandinga*, rice and pigeon peas, we will never stop roasting pigs on the spit (i7).

Only one interviewee took exception to the proliferation of fast-food chains. The objection was framed in terms of fear of displacement, but it was economic displacement of Puerto Rican business that was feared, rather than the loss of a symbol of Puerto Ricanness:

> *Commonwealth party interviewee:*
> I invite you to walk around out there, and what you'll see are the fast
> food outlets. . . . Now at lunch [the worker] goes to eat a
> hamburger or [chicken] nuggets and then when he leaves instead of
> going to the corner store, which is owned by a Puerto Rican, he goes
> to one of those big chain stores to buy what he needs (i6).

COMPETITION FROM CULTURAL IMPORTS

Most respondents felt that their own identities, as well as their personal
preferences and habits, were not negatively affected by U.S. influence on music
and food. But they were not similarly accepting of the overall exposure to
mainland ways brought by cable television or of United States-style Christmas
celebrations.

Santa Claus

Traditionally, the Puerto Rican celebration of the Christmas season centers on
the Feast of the Epiphany, January 6. Because gifts are brought to children by the
Three Kings on that day, the holiday is commonly referred to as "Three Kings
Day" in Puerto Rico. Analogy with this usage is probably why respondents
invariably referred not to "Christmas" but to "Santa Claus" as they discussed their
observations that the mainland holiday tradition was taking hold in Puerto Rico.

> *Puerto Ricans in Civic Action interviewee:*
> All the kids in Puerto Rico, my generation, grew up with Santa Claus
> (i15).

> *University of Puerto Rico focus group:*
> Pablo: Why is it that Santa Claus has taken hold better than the
>   Three Kings? Simply because Santa Claus comes earlier than
>   the Three Kings. Santa Claus comes on the twenty-fifth [of
>   December], and the Three Kings come on the [sixth of
>   January]. . . .
> Luis: Santa Claus comes *last* because the Three Kings arrive in
>   January, and Santa Claus in December.
> [laughter and applause] (g11).

A commonwealth party interviewee acknowledged Puerto Rico's adoption of U.S.
holidays and then pointed out, perhaps somewhat defensively, that island traditions
are maintained as well:

> Here we celebrate Halloween, yes, and we celebrate Santa Claus. But
> we also celebrate the *Cuatro* Festival, which is Puerto Rican (i2)

The concern expressed about Christmas customs was based on the perception that the traditional Puerto Rican holiday of Three Kings was being displaced.

> *University of Puerto Rico focus group:*
> The thing is, also because of all the Americanization, Santa Claus has been commercialized; the Three Kings have been left aside (g11).

> *Commonwealth party interviewee:*
> Since the American custom is Santa Claus, commerce invades for Santa Claus. It's a struggle, Santa Claus and the Three Kings. . . . Commerce . . . almost forces parents to buy presents for Santa Claus. The Puerto Rican is fighting that. And it overwhelms us, you know? Puerto Rico is the Three Kings. So what we do is we give our child a little inexpensive toy on Santa Claus, and for Three Kings we give him the expensive toy (i1).

The concern about the influence of Santa Claus did not arise simply because a U.S. holiday had been added to the Puerto Rican holiday calendar. No respondent expressed concern about the widespread celebration of the U.S. holiday of Thanksgiving in Puerto Rico. But Thanksgiving does not threaten to replace existing traditions; rather, it is an addition to the catalogue of Puerto Rican holidays at a time of year where there are no local celebrations to be pushed aside. It was the fear that Santa Claus would displace the Three Kings that made this symbol a perceived threat to Puerto Rican identity.

Cable Television

Reactions to holiday celebrations indicated that a tradition that many had identified as distinctly Puerto Rican was felt to be threatened by imported cultural elements. One commonwealth party interviewee expressed similar concerns about the influence of United States-produced mass media products:

> Puerto Rican television, mass media, are in the hands of very conservative people, of people who live the illusion of Americanization. . . . And unfortunately also the communications media have been regulated by the federal government for all these years and there's an American policy against Puerto Rican self-esteem and in favor of Americanization and the glorification of the ideal of American life. . . . The communications media devalue the Puerto Rican self-image and accelerate the process of cultural dependence and assimilation (i4).

Puerto Rican broadcasting, as this interviewee rightly pointed out, falls under the jurisdiction of the U.S. Federal Communications Commission (FCC). Like mainland television, Puerto Rican television works on a free-market model, and the degree of FCC control over content is comparatively limited (Blumenthal and Goodenough 1991: 357–445). This commonwealth party leader was alone among respondents in branding all mass media a threat to Puerto Rican identity. Rather, cable television was singled out as threatening to Puerto Rican culture by some commonwealth and independence supporters who saw it as a carrier of unwanted cultural influence from the United States. Broadcast television was not generally perceived as a threat to Puerto Rican identity.

Puerto Rico's eight broadcast television stations—four commercial, two educational, and two religious—serve the 97 percent of Puerto Rican homes that have televisions. Locally produced programming constitutes approximately one-half of these stations' output. The rest is made up of imports from Spanish-speaking countries and from the United States. Nearly the entirety of broadcast television is transmitted in the Spanish language; programs from the United States are generally dubbed into Spanish, except sporting programs, which carry Spanish-language voice-overs. Cable television is also available throughout the island. Twenty-five percent of Puerto Rican television households subscribe to cable television, most of them in the San Juan area. In contrast to broadcast television, Puerto Rican cable television is dominated by English-language programming on packages of channels from the United States. A study conducted in 1987 showed that 18 percent of cable television programming was in Spanish, almost all of it consisting of the retransmission of Puerto Rican broadcast channels. Whether dubbed into Spanish or in the original English, 89 percent of cable programming was produced in the United States (Flores Caraballo 1993: 4–10; Subervi-Vélez, Hernández-López, and Frambes-Buxeda 1990: 160).

Cable television, unlike music, food, and holiday traditions, is not itself a symbol of Puerto Ricanness. But because most cable programming in Puerto Rico comes direct and unmediated from the mainland, it is closely associated with the United States. An independence party official attributed to the idealized images of U.S. consumer culture on cable television the power to change Puerto Ricans' political status preferences.

> I think cable TV creates more statehood supporters than all the speeches of [statehood party leader] Carlos Romero Barceló (i12).

Others echoed the globalization claims made in other parts of the world concerning media imported from the United States. The frequently expressed fear that imported television programming was influencing young people by easily familiarizing them with U.S. customs and lifestyles seemed to be based on the underlying idea that these customs would supplant Puerto Rican customs in the same way that Santa Claus is seen to be supplanting the Three Kings.

> *Commonwealth party interviewee:*
> Everyone has cable TV and they'd rather watch cable programs than

Puerto Rican channels. What's entering the mind and the heart of the Puerto Rican day after day is the transculturation from a different culture (i6).

Members of an independence party focus group commented that they sometimes found the preponderance of U.S. culture overwhelming:

One of the problems is you always turn on the TV and there's Channel 11 from Atlanta or Channel 30 from New York. . . . You feel besieged (g10).

U.S. programs dubbed into Spanish and shown on Puerto Rican broadcast television elicited little concern, even though the dubbed programs depict the same images of U.S. culture as do the cable programs. Part of the difference in reaction seemed to attach to language. The importance of the Spanish language to Puerto Rican identity makes English-language programming, even if otherwise indistinguishable from much of its Spanish-language counterpart, seem a greater threat.

Commonwealth party interviewee:
Cable TV has put the English language in every living room. And people who have already formed our characters and have a solid base, listen and we watch this as part of cultural growth. But the child who is developing in a society of cable TV, begins to enjoy and understand the humor, American humor, the American way of life, identifies with the American ideal, . . . the clothes, going to the park without a shirt on. And sometimes here . . . one goes to the beach and sees Latinos lying out in the sun. . . . That is an imitation; it's learned. But it's not rational; the American who comes here in winter cooks in the sun because he or she comes escaping from the cold. . . . But we don't need to lie out on the beach, we need to get out of the sun . . . because this is a tropical country (i5).

Comments about music and food, Christmas and cable reveal nuanced views on the vulnerability of symbols to displacement. Puerto Rican leaders did not fear that their culture was being swamped by U.S. culture in an undifferentiated way; rather, they perceived different degrees of pressure on different cultural elements. Even independence and commonwealth advocates were not overly concerned about imported music and food, because they did not feel that they and their culture were giving up anything by coexisting with imports. In contrast, they were concerned about Three Kings Day because they felt that an important holiday tradition was being lost. Opponents of statehood, in particular, feared that cable television was an agent of cultural displacement. Concerns about the influence of cable television at times intertwined with the fear of displacement of the most important symbol of identity in Puerto Rico: the Spanish language.

Language

The centrality of the perceived threat of displacement was particularly clear in discussions of language, a symbol of Puerto Ricanness that respondents had named as central to their sense of identity. The power of Spanish as a defining element of Puerto Ricanness was evidenced by respondents' repeated references to the attempt by the United States to impose English as the language of instruction in schools, an issue that continued to resonate forty-two years after Spanish was reinstated as the school language. The language controversy was described, with greater or lesser historical accuracy, even by respondents who were born long after the issue was resolved. Across the political spectrum, interviewees and focus group participants emphasized that English had not displaced Spanish despite U.S. efforts to that end.

Puerto Rican Socialist Party interviewee:
I don't know if you know that from 1930 until almost 1950 they imposed English as the official language in the schools of the country. That was a disaster. They were forced to reverse [the policy]. They couldn't assimilate [us] (i14).

Independence party focus group:
We all know that when the Americans arrived they wanted to do away with Spanish and the culture and everything. And the Spanish [language], the people wouldn't allow it. Perhaps unconsciously, but there was a struggle against that and finally they changed the whole system and began to teach in Spanish (g10).

Independence party interviewee:
Our culture has been strong, it has been resistant, it has resisted attack. I don't know if you know, but our parents were brought up in a school system where from kindergarten through high school they were required to learn in English. And they overcame that (i12).

Commonwealth party interviewee:
[The United States] placed rectors of public education in Puerto Rico, superintendents in charge of education in public schools, and they gave these people instructions that they had to speak English, and they had to teach in English. And then, imagine the poor Puerto Rican peasants, without knowing the language, having to learn everything in English. . . . But there was resistance in the people and I think that was the first great battle that was fought in Puerto Rico, and I think we won because we still speak Spanish in spite of all that effort and the whole operation that those gentlemen

undertook.... Even though they had iron-handed control over the public education apparatus in Puerto Rico, they didn't succeed. Spanish continued to be spoken, and even though in the elementary and high schools teaching in English was required, the people continued speaking Spanish (i6).

University of Puerto Rico focus group:
They tried to change our language. When the Americans entered here they tried by force to teach English, and they couldn't (g11).

Statehood party focus group:
I don't remember in what year but in the years that my mom and dad were studying, classes were held in English only, and the books were in English. But what happened? The Puerto Rican didn't want to continue in English. And they changed it. Now he speaks Spanish (g8).

When respondents predicted the effects of statehood for Puerto Rico, the displacement of Spanish was a primary issue. With language, as with the other symbols discussed, interviewees were united as to the importance of the symbol and divided, largely along party lines, on whether this manifestation of Puerto Ricanness would be maintained if the statehood option prevailed. Statehood supporters were amenable to adding English to their linguistic repertoires, but even they were not willing to see Spanish pushed aside.

Statehood party interviewee:
Puerto Rico would continue to speak Spanish, but it would also have to learn English to be able to compete ... in the employment market (i9).

Statehood party focus group:
Spanish and English are the two languages most spoken in the world! For a Puerto Rican to speak English and Spanish is a tremendous advantage.... Personally, I'm a statehooder, and there is nobody who is going to stop me from speaking Spanish. What you have to look at is the benefits you get .... If I speak English, what am I doing? Opening new frontiers, improving myself (g7).

Statehood supporters used the example of the failed U.S. attempt to impose English to support their contention that Spanish would be retained under statehood, a claim they made consistently.

Statehood party interviewee:
It seems to me that the Puerto Rican will never lose his language.... We have not lost it nor do I think we'll ever lose it;

it's impossible, it's very difficult. . . . Statehood and Spanish are never going to be opposed. One thing doesn't have anything to do with the other in any way (i8).

Puerto Ricans in Civic Action interviewee:
We have been part of the United States since 1898. And we've been speaking Spanish and Spanish communities in the States are speaking Spanish. Now, it's absurd to say statehood will make us all speak English, just as bad as it would be to say statehood's going to bring snow to Puerto Rico (i15).

While statehood supporters interpreted the historical evidence to mean that Puerto Ricans would retain the Spanish language if it became a state, the lesson that commonwealth and independence supporters drew from the same evidence was not that statehood would be compatible with the Spanish language but that the United States would impose its language, displacing Spanish.

Commonwealth party focus group:
The first thing we'll lose is the language, we're sure we'll lose that. Because there is no state of the fifty states of the United States in which the official language is Spanish (g4).

Commonwealth party interviewee:
In terms of language definitely I don't see how the United States would not impose the English language like they tried to do when they entered Puerto Rico (i6).

Commonwealth party interviewee:
We would lose our identity as a people because . . . what hasn't happened in ninety-three years, which is that we stop speaking Spanish, will happen as soon as we become a state. Because a nation is known by only one language. Obviously, the language that would reign here is English—which isn't a bad thing to learn, but as a second language (i3).

Independence party interviewee:
First of all, the government would impose the use of a common language, which is English (i12).

Puerto Rican Socialist Party interviewee:
You're a state called Puerto Rico and in twenty, thirty years, well, they won't speak Spanish here, because it will be imposed obligatorily that government work be conducted in English, that the legislature be in English, the courts in English (i14).

Statehood advocates have done extensive research into the U.S. legal system as it relates to jurisdiction over language and other issues. They argue that there are legal protections against the most egregious of the perceived threats and have developed the concept of "*jíbaro* statehood"[1] based on states' autonomy to make internal laws.

> *Statehood party interviewee:*
> In the constitutional framework of the United States it is quite clear that the definition of official languages is not a power that has been delegated to Congress. . . . And we visualize that Puerto Rico as a state will . . . have the power to define internally, if so desired, its official languages (i16).

> *Statehood party interviewee:*
> There's not much you can do about the Spanish language. I mean, you could try passing a constitutional amendment, but if you haven't been able to get thirty-three states to declare English your official language in their states, with a simple majority of their legislature, how the hell are you going to get a constitutional amendment which requires ratification by thirty-eight states plus a two-thirds majority in the House and a two-thirds majority in the Senate? (i10).

A commonwealth party interviewee interpreted the same legal issue differently, incorrectly claiming that most states already have "English only" laws.[2]

> [A] danger is that in the long run, we see that the United States is on the way to adopting English as its official government language. Only a few states are lacking. And when there are enough states with "English only" the next step is to propose an amendment to the Constitution that will be ratified. And that would apply to us if we were a state. And it would change us totally. From there a more accelerated process begins that would change our cultural bases (i5).

Differences of opinion arose within several focus groups on the language issue:

> *Independence party focus group:*
> David: We aren't going to have the power to decide if we want Spanish or not. It will be the United States who decides if Spanish or English will be spoken here. . . . We won't be able to decide what we want—the same as now, but worse.
> Alicia: I think it's impossible even in statehood that they could totally change Puerto Rican culture. Whatever happens, if they say, "Speak English!" the person who was speaking Spanish is going to continue speaking Spanish (g10).

University of Puerto Rico focus group:

Luis: In the United States the Constitution doesn't have an official language. That is left to the states. The state of New Mexico has two official languages, English and Spanish. So do other states. If we here decide that the language is going to be Spanish, it stays Spanish. Nobody can impose that. If they imposed it, people here are not going to [suddenly be able to] speak English the next day. . . .

Carla: I don't agree, because it's true that at one stroke the culture is not going to change, but gradually it will happen. It won't be overnight, but one thing will lead to another. It's like a chain reaction and perhaps . . . I won't live to see the drastic change but perhaps my grandchildren, my children will see it (g11).

Statehood party focus groups were open to reflection on the issue of language under statehood, as participants discussed it among themselves.

Statehood party focus group:

Guillermo: If we are speaking Spanish there isn't anyone who can make us change our language.

Susana: Nobody forces me to speak English, nobody can force me to speak another language.

Jaime: But if I had to choose, I would choose statehood because when I look in the paper for a job: "bilingual, bilingual, bilingual" . . . at the moment of truth all the application forms are in English. . . .

Pedro: And it doesn't do us any good to ask for *comida* in Spanish if we aren't going to get it. I'd rather say "food, food, food" and get something to eat.

Jaime: We have a good example: What language did the King of Spain use when he met with . . . Gorbachev? It was English! It worked; they could understand each other (g6).

Statehood party focus group:

Here they often say that we're going to lose the language, that we're going to lose the flag, a lot of political hot air. The language and all those things are part of the culture, and the way I see it, culture evolves. So, state or no state, some day perhaps a thousand years from now, maybe we won't be speaking Spanish in Puerto Rico, even if we were independent, or there would be other customs, because that's how it is. I don't see it as losing, really. Perhaps we will have to make some concessions, which is very different. And that's part of evolution (g8).

International Sports Representation

Like the future of the Spanish language, the future of Puerto Rican international sports representation in the event of statehood for the island was subject to contrasting partisan interpretations. Commonwealth supporters spoke vehemently about the importance of participation in the Olympics and other international competitions and about their certainty that this representation would be lost under statehood.

> *Commonwealth party interviewee:*
> [It's important] having a flag, having an anthem, our national team can represent us as Puerto Rico in international events, having a beauty queen. We've had, I think, two beauty queens. If we were a state and a Puerto Rican beauty were competing in a beauty contest, she would represent the fifty-first state. And if she won, she would be Miss USA. That is, we would lose this type of thing (i1).

> *Commonwealth party interviewee:*
> We would not have our Olympic representation, no international participation. . . . Where does New Mexico compete? What is Louisiana's basketball team? The university teams. But we beat the United States. . . . And our flag is there (i5).

> *Commonwealth party interviewee:*
> Right now, if you take a citizen of any of the states, he or she can't, for example, compete for Texas in the Olympics. Here we compete for Puerto Rico and we play against the United States. And we play against Mexico. And we win or we lose, one of the two. But incorporated into the union. . . . there's no team any more (i3).

> *Commonwealth party focus group:*
> [Under statehood] we lose so many things that identify us as a people. . . . Representation on the Olympic Committee, our Miss Universe participation (g2).

> *Commonwealth party focus group:*
> Verónica: It would be really sad that people here wouldn't go to the Olympics any more. . . .
> Alberto: It's not worth it to be a state and have to merge with a team that we have beaten sometimes. And then the name of Puerto Rico wouldn't be announced any more, it would be the name of the United States (g3).

Statehood advocates offered mixed predictions about sports and statehood. Some respondents' confidence wavered on the issue of whether Puerto Rico would be able to maintain Olympic representation as a state.

Statehood party interviewee:
I think that the only thing that might change at all would be some type of sports relation or something like that. But as a people, if we've maintained [ourselves] for a hundred years united with the United States, I'm sure that we will not change at all (i7).

Statehood party focus group:
Susana: We're not going to lose our Olympic Committee. That is a private franchise that has to pay a fee. Upon becoming a state, we pay our fee and we keep paying our fee and we keep getting medals with our athletes, calling ourselves "Puerto Rico with the United States."
Jaime: But if I had to choose there's no doubt that at least for myself—
Pedro: Statehood.
Guillermo: I think with or without Olympics, statehood is better for us because when a person from the States competes they announce: "This person is from New York, United States." They don't say "United States," they say "New York," they say where he's from. And I think for our athletes they'll say "from Puerto Rico, United States" (g6).

Statehood party focus group:
In sports we would lose, if you want to say lose. But what we have to do is educate the people so they know and see reality. You are going to lose this but in exchange you'll get something else. . . . Which is more important? The pride of playing the [Puerto Rican] anthem in the Olympics, or having food for your children? (g8).

Contrarily, one statehood party official explained that party researchers have investigated the sports issue and have concluded that Puerto Rico would be able to field an Olympic team even as a state.

We are certain that legally speaking we can preserve our sports autonomy within statehood, the reason being that the Olympic Charter allows jurisdictions that are not nations politically to retain Olympic franchises that they've obtained before becoming a state. . . . For example, in the surfing federation, Hawaii competes against the United States, and there's never been any problem with that. The other thing is that it's not as if the United States is trying to eliminate Puerto Rico as a competitor or as if they're jealous of us or anything, so we don't think that within the United States Olympic Committee there's any big push to want to integrate Puerto Rico necessarily, if we don't want to be integrated in the sports world. . . . Our Olympic franchise is an acquired right in the private law. It's not part of the public law. So there's no way that you can take that away from us unless we relinquish it voluntarily, which we would not do (i10).

Commonwealth and independence supporters suggested a conflicting interpretation.

Commonwealth party interviewee:
The Olympic Committee, although the statehooders say one thing, you know that it's not like that. There is just one, the United States has a single Olympic Committee. . . . We would definitely lose our Olympic Committee (i2).

Commonwealth party focus group:
We'll lose [our Olympic Committee] being a state because no state of the United States belongs as a state to the International Olympic Committee because the sports charter—the Sport Act—of the International Olympic Committee does not permit it. Because the Act requires that the United States have a single international team (g4).

Independence party focus group:
Here in Puerto Rico [sports] is very important. . . . If Puerto Rico is incorporated [into the United States] it would immediately stop having an Olympic Committee and we would become part of the North American Olympic Committee. And that would be a great punishment (g9).

THE FEAR OF DISPLACEMENT

With sports as with language and the other elements discussed, whenever interviewees disagreed on how integration into the United States would affect Puerto Rican culture and identity, the same pattern emerged. Puerto Rican political leaders of all parties were clear about the central symbols of their culture and their relationship to them and equally aware of corresponding and potentially competing symbols from the United States. They did not disagree about the value and uniqueness of Puerto Ricanness, as expressed through key symbols that they explicitly recognized as such. Rather, disagreements arose out of differing evaluations of whether those symbols could withstand pressure from competing symbols. In part, the debate over Puerto Rico's status is itself about the potential displacement of symbols of Puerto Ricanness. It is also about economics, defense, and other tangibles, but the central significance of symbols of Puerto Ricanness requires all politicians to address fears of their displacement, leading to the strikingly partisan views presented here. While respondents agreed that the U.S. presence in Puerto Rico did present direct competition to the most salient symbols of Puerto Ricanness, they projected different fates for symbols of Puerto

Rico's uniqueness under statehood.

A large subsection of Puerto Rican politicians—statehood supporters—maintained that Puerto Ricanness was not vulnerable to external pressure and that Puerto Rico's symbols would be maintained under statehood. Those who believed the contrary—commonwealth and independence supporters—voiced doubts about the resilience of those symbols that they deemed most vulnerable to displacement. They expressed more subtle misgivings than the generalized alarm about imported culture that characterizes discussions of globalization; their fears attached not to a vague notion of Puerto Ricanness but to specific elements of Puerto Rican culture that they perceived as being under threat. Their concerns about Americanization were expressed by reference to those symbols of Puerto Ricanness that they believed would be replaced by competing symbols imported from the mainland.

THE VITALITY OF IDENTITY UNDER CHALLENGE

The perception that symbols of identity are under challenge has engendered counterpressure, fortifying the threatened symbols of Puerto Rican identity. Throughout this century, whenever Puerto Ricans have perceived a threat to symbols of their identity, they have responded by demonstrating an increased commitment to those symbols. Arguably, this defensive response to the fear of cultural displacement has had the effect of strengthening a sense of collective identity. Far from destroying Puerto Rico's national identity, the import of U.S. culture has strengthened the sense of Puerto Ricanness by providing a counterexample of what Puerto Ricanness is not.

Identities are always set down in opposition to others. As Walker Connor has noted, "The conception of being unique or different requires a referent, that is, the idea of 'us' requires 'them' " (1972: 344). When a distinct Puerto Rican identity began developing in the nineteenth century, that identity was defined in contrast to the island's Spanish rulers. Although a significant portion of Puerto Rican settlers were Spaniards or descendants of Spaniards, those settlers felt themselves to be different from the Spanish (Pedreira [1936] 1957: 15, 94; González 1987: 77). Throughout the nineteenth century, this sense of difference and the consequent desire for self-government intensified.

Puerto Rican leaders generally welcomed the U.S. takeover of the island because it represented democracy and, they thought, the self-rule they had been seeking from Spain. The reluctance of the United States to bestow self-rule and the attempt by the United States to impose its language and institutions engendered resentment and fierce adherence to Puerto Ricanness. In this way, the U.S. presence in Puerto Rico may have strengthened Puerto Rican identity. Not only by providing a visible "them" that was identifiably different but also by blocking Puerto Rican aspirations and overtly endeavoring to alter Puerto Rican society, the United States supplied a model against which sharply to define "us"—Puerto Ricans.

The theme of difference from the United States has permeated twentieth-century Puerto Rico. Puerto Rican politicians have repeatedly stressed this opposition throughout the century. When arguing against U.S. citizenship in 1914, for example, the resident commissioner pointed out that Puerto Ricans are separated from the United States "by over four hundred years and by more than four hundred leagues, with a different historic process, diverse language, different customs" (*Cong. Rec.* 1914: 6718). Opponents of statehood have welcomed every opportunity to juxtapose "us" against "them" and to interpret Puerto Rican events in light of that juxtaposition. The president of the Puerto Rican independence party described events at the 1979 Pan American Games this way: "In the inauguration ceremonies of the Pan American Games, when our people spontaneously waved thousands of Puerto Rican flags and booed the North American flag, this symbolized their preference in the struggle that is being set up in Puerto Rico between North America and Puerto Rico and it was a protest against the mistreatment of the past eighty-one years of domination" (Berríos Martínez 1983: 32–33). An anti-Vietnam War protester put it starkly in 1969: "[E]ither you're a Yanqui or you're a Puerto Rican" (*New York Times* 1969c).

A sense of separateness has not been recognized only by those wary of the United States. In 1917, the Republican Party of Puerto Rico, which fervently advocated statehood, expressed its gratitude to the United States for granting citizenship to a people "of a race and language different from their own" (Partido Republicano Puertorriqueño 1917: 2). Negative stereotypes of mainlanders cross lines drawn by status preference, as illustrated by comments of focus group participants, who used generalizations about the United States to stress perceived differences between "us" and "them."

> *Statehood party focus group:*
> American women have very messy houses (g8).

> *Commonwealth party focus group:*
> I have had American friends who have lived here and . . . they're somewhat selfish. Perhaps that's how they are raised in other countries (g2).

> *University of Puerto Rico focus group:*
> The American, naturally or because of geography or whatever, is boring (g11).

In the early twentieth century, as the United States overhauled Puerto Rican institutions by fiat, Puerto Ricans' sense of difference was reinforced, and so were their opposition to U.S. domination and their attachment to symbols felt to be under attack. Language is paramount here. Pressure on language offended Puerto Ricans, who were willing to learn English, but not at the expense of Spanish. Throughout the century, language has both engendered opposition and provided an excuse for it. In the early part of the century, according to a specialist on the school language issue, "the movement against teaching English emphasized language as a symbol of national identity and culture, and its strategy was to stress the differences between Puerto Rico and the United States" (Gutiérrez 1987: 68). Anthropologists studying Puerto Rico in the late 1940s concluded that "the Spanish language became a symbol of Puerto Rican national identity only when the United States attempted to enforce the teaching and use of English upon the people" (Steward et al. 1956: 500). This pronounced division of the world along lines of language is still evident in the island.   In revealing terms, a commonwealth party youth group leader emphasized, "We couldn't be Puerto Ricans speaking American—that is, speaking English" (g2).   Commonwealth party governor Rafael Hernández Colón said in defense of his party's 1991 Spanish language law, "We are a culturally differentiated people" (1991a: 1).

At the same time as it has fortified the sense of difference, the U.S. presence in Puerto Rico has undeniably altered Puerto Ricans' behavior. Puerto Ricans may eat more hamburgers and use Visa cards and lie on the beach more than some recognize or care to admit. Many speak fluent English, many live and work in the mainland for short or long periods, many attend mainland universities. These behaviors and others are due to the duration and the magnitude of the U.S. influence in the island.

But, as discussed in Chapter 1, identity is not as much a question of behavior as it is a question of attitudes. It has been defined as "essentially psychological" by Walker Connor (1972: 351), who states that "an individual (or an entire national group) can shed all of the overt cultural manifestations customarily attributed to his ethnic group and yet maintain his fundamental identity as a member of that nation" (341–42). Puerto Ricans are far from shedding their "overt cultural manifestations," but insofar as preferences and behaviors may be changing, this does not indicate that they feel themselves to be less Puerto Rican. As several Puerto Rican respondents asserted, for example, their musical tastes do not determine their identity. Collective identity is a feeling of affiliation with a group—a sentiment. The U.S. presence, by providing a comparison and, at times, a focus for resentment, has fortified Puerto Ricans' identity, their sense of belonging to a group that calls itself Puerto Ricans.

NOTES

1. *Jíbaro* is the Puerto Rican word for "peasant" or "hillbilly," originally referring to small-scale farmers in the central mountains of the island. The word has come to connote "home-grown" Puerto Ricanness.

2. Eighteen states have passed measures declaring English their official language, sixteen of them since the early 1980s (Gurevitz 1994; Perea 1992: 342n.). In the 1990s, bills have also been introduced in Congress seeking to make English the official language of the United States (Perea 1992: 342).

7

The Resilience of Identity

You are going to have a problem systematizing what Puerto
Ricanness is because that cannot be systematized or quantified (i12).

Puerto Rican identity is resilient. After ninety-seven years of partial integration
into the institutions of a large and powerful country with a history and traditions
different from its own, Puerto Ricans retain a strong sense of themselves as Puerto
Rican. The preceding chapters have reviewed the evolution of the relationship
between the United States and Puerto Rico and of Puerto Rican identity, which is
intricately tied to that relationship.

This book has not attempted to formulate an empirical test for defining Puerto
Rican national identity but rather has examined historical and contemporary
evidence to explore how that identity has been perceived and articulated by island
political elites. The insights into processes of collective identity formation and
maintenance provided by their experiences resonate in other areas of the world
where collective identity issues are prominent.

THE MESSAGE OF UNIQUENESS

Puerto Rican political leaders convey a core message about their identity:
Puerto Rican culture, with its unique characteristics, merits preservation. The
notion of uniqueness, unambiguously articulated, lies at the foundation of many of
their observations about Puerto Ricanness. Although political leaders hold
differing views about the U.S. presence in the island, these differences do not
impede their common understanding of Puerto Rico as distinct and separate. Rare
was any indication from any quarter that it would be acceptable to blend in, to

become less distinctive. Former Puerto Rico governor Carlos Romero Barceló, of the statehood party, summed up this feeling when he stated that "to be Puerto Rican is something very special and . . . we who *are* Puerto Rican are not about to give up our identity for anybody" (1978: 7).

This fundamental national identity message was not debated by political opponents in Puerto Rico; what was debated was the ability of Puerto Ricanness to withstand U.S. influence. The point of agreement from which debate emanated was that Puerto Rican uniqueness should be preserved. It is easy to overlook this basic identity message, but it warrants attention because it is the foundation on which collectivities base their sense of separateness.

In Puerto Rico the near-unanimous valuing of the uniqueness of Puerto Rican culture does not translate into unanimity on all of the elements that constitute Puerto Ricanness. Collective identity is not a simple, monolithic phenomenon when it is broken down into particulars. Moreover, the existence of a widely shared perception of collective uniqueness does not mean that the collective necessarily is unique, if such a judgment could be made by objective criteria. Many of the cultural elements identified by respondents as "uniquely" Puerto Rican, in fact, characterize many cultures. But the shared perception of uniqueness and a shared pride in that uniqueness seem to rest at the core of collective identity.

The importance of uniqueness to collectivities can be seen around the world. It has been strongly and repeatedly articulated, for example, in Canada. The province of Quebec has been struggling for years to maintain and promote its Francophone culture, to the point of threatening to secede from Canada if its demands are not met. One of its principal demands is simply recognition in the Canadian constitution as a "distinct society" (*Philadelphia Inquirer* 1992). In Anglophone Canada, meanwhile, there is great concern about the ability of the country to maintain a national identity distinct from the United States (Romanow and Soderlund 1990: 5). In Scotland, there is an established core of support for independence from, or political autonomy within, the United Kingdom. Yet, Scottish uniqueness is asserted even by those who do not favor these options. One political opponent of independence defended her support for the status quo with an avowal of her Scottishness: "I'm a member of the Church of Scotland, the National Trust for Scotland, the Law Society of Scotland—all uniquely Scottish institutions" (Milne 1992: 12). In Japan, belief in the country's cultural uniqueness has been identified as "a salient feature of Japanese mentality" (Manabe 1992: 3). In Somalia, where many in the West perceived only starvation and poverty during the 1992 famine, a Somalian relief worker saw the country's uniqueness being violated by the influx of foreign troops and aid workers insensitive to Somali culture. Saying that Somalis were "just very proud of our own culture," he criticized the newcomers: "They don't know the country and they don't know Somalis. We're different from any other country" (Sly 1992).

Preserving Uniqueness

Implicit in the recognition of uniqueness is recognition of the importance of preserving it. In Puerto Rico, the near-universal pride in Puerto Rican uniqueness was accompanied by a desire to protect and preserve Puerto Rican culture. For commonwealth and independence supporters, especially, the concern for the preservation of Puerto Rican culture was often expressed as a fear of its prospective demise. A commonwealth party leader, for example, predicted that if Puerto Rico integrated into the United States as a state, it would "dissolve and disappear and remain only in the history books as a people that was" (i5). An independence party official expressed the same fear:

> In the same way that individuals believe in their own self-preservation, collective individuals—that is, nationalities—don't believe in killing themselves. And I think it would be sad if that occurred. It has occurred; some nationalities have disappeared. But I hope mine doesn't (i13).

The contrary interpretation put forward by a statehood party leader about the island's fate under statehood nonetheless stressed the notion of preservation:

> Basically statehooders have been on the defensive on this issue, and . . . over the years . . . we've developed an offensive posture to explain not only how Puerto Rico's culture would not be lost under statehood but how it could be improved upon under statehood (i10).

The argument for the preservation of uniqueness was strikingly articulated by a commonwealth party interviewee who spoke about his belief that statehood for Puerto Rico would entail assimilation into U.S. culture:

> What's tragic about that? It's tragic in the same way that it would be to eliminate all the dolphins from the planet, as eliminating the parakeet from [Puerto Rico's rain forest] el Yunque, as eliminating the manatees, as eliminating the buffalo. People try to keep animal species alive, because humanity believes that the variety of species enriches the planet. Well, eliminating a nationality is the same; it's pushing the button to extinguish a nationality, a nation (i4).

The impulse to preserve Puerto Rican uniqueness was expressed with varying degrees of emphasis by Puerto Rican interviewees. This desire, central to national identity concerns in Puerto Rico, has been manifested in many ways elsewhere in the world. While working toward his country's independence, an Estonian leader justified a proposal to restrict the inflow of non-Estonians from the surrounding area "because it's a question of our survival as a nation" (Shipler 1989: 64). Before Latvian independence, three summer schools were established in the United

States to teach children of Latvian immigrants their parents' language and culture "to help Latvia continue to exist as an ethnic entity" (McCrary 1989). The preservation and development of Irish culture were among the "national aims" mandated in Ireland's 1960 Broadcasting Act (E. Hall 1993: 266); many countries' media and cultural policies contain similar provisions.

The premise underlying such statements and policies is that nations merit preservation by their very existence. The socially reinforced sense of belonging to a unique and valued nation may seem too trivial to fight wars over, and, indeed, nationalist wars have many rationales, among them long-standing enmities that are felt to require vengeance. Yet, at the core of many contemporary political confrontations and armed conflicts is the commitment to the preservation of unique nations.

SYMBOLS OF IDENTITY

Members of nations may perceive their nations as unique by reference to those characteristics that they perceive as shared by members of their nation and those that mark outsiders. But these shared characteristics can be difficult to articulate. Instead, members of the nation often define and describe their commonality by reference to symbols that stand for the collectivity, using mental models and symbols to conceptualize things that are not perceptible through the five senses. In Michael Walzer's words, "In a sense, the union of men can only be symbolized; it has no palpable shape or substance" (1967: 194). When asked, "What does it mean to be Puerto Rican?" respondents almost invariably mentioned symbols that they felt represented Puerto Rico, especially when their efforts to articulate their sense of Puerto Ricanness in terms of intangibles foundered.

This does not mean that a collection of shared cultural representations constitutes the entirety of Puerto Rican identity. The whole of national identity is greater than the sum of its symbols. But symbols provide a powerful shorthand for feelings attached to complicated and abstract phenomena. This shorthand is itself intricate; while symbols provide signposts for mapping something more complex, symbolic representations have complexities of their own.

The Mutability of Symbolic Meanings

Although national identity is expressed in a set of symbols that must be sufficiently stable to be shared across a large segment of society, this body of symbols is not static. Symbolic meanings adapt to societal changes, and historical shifts in meaning accumulate and affect the interpretation of the symbols. Accordingly, the significant symbols of Puerto Ricanness have not remained identical over time. The shift in opinion about U.S. citizenship, the recent coining of the symbol of sports representation, and changes in the use of the U.S. and Puerto Rican flags illustrate the potential mutability of symbols of identity over time in one social group or across a populace.

U.S. citizenship has had different meanings in Puerto Rico in the course of this century. Citizenship without statehood was resisted by the majority Unionist Party in 1916 as representing "a citizenship of an inferior order, a citizenship of the second class" (*Cong. Rec.* 1916: 7472) and grudgingly accepted by the party the following year "because it redeems us from our inferiority as colonials" (*La Democracia* 1917). Fixed in the Puerto Rican Constitution thirty-five years later, U.S. citizenship has come to be prized by most Puerto Ricans. Even the independence party has recognized this, including in a proposal for transition to independence a stipulation of permanent dual citizenship for Puerto Ricans alive at the time of independence and open entry to the United States for twenty-five years for those born afterward (Partido Independentista Puertorriqueño, Secretaría de Educación Política).

International sports participation, a comparatively new symbol for the island, has become an important channel through which Puerto Ricans symbolically manifest their Puerto Ricanness. The tensions in Puerto Rico's relationship with the United States are reflected in the juxtaposition of the generalized valuing of U.S. citizenship with the passionate adherence to what is known in Puerto Rico as "sports citizenship," a concept derived from the rules that allow Puerto Rican athletes to represent their island, rather than the country of which they are citizens, in international sporting competitions. Yet before midcentury, "sports citizenship" was an unfamiliar concept in the island and played no role in representing Puerto Rican identity.

Flag display in Puerto Rico illustrates another shift in symbolic meaning. In 1952 commonwealth supporters indicated their pleasure with the new relationship with the United States by displaying the U.S. flag. Forty years on, display of a U.S. flag unaccompanied by a Puerto Rican flag would be interpreted as an indication of support for statehood. The Puerto Rican flag stood for independence from Spain when it was first designed. It came to be seen as representing all Puerto Ricans, regardless of status preference, and was formally adopted in 1952 to represent the commonwealth. Officially, the single-star flag flies alongside the Stars and Stripes, emblematic of an often uneasy relationship.

The Variability of Symbolic Meanings

Symbols not only take on different meanings over time but may also carry different shades of meaning for different individuals or groups at any given time. This variation results from the flexibility of symbolic meanings, from person to person and group to group within a society. Charles D. Elder and Roger W. Cobb explain: "When the symbols of politics are evoked, what is communicated is not strictly a function of the intent of the communicator nor of the manifest content of the message. The meaning of the message is heavily colored by the significance to the receiver of the symbols involved and his or her own interpretation of their meaning. The same symbols may communicate different things to different people" (1983: 10). Since a society is composed of many subgroups that may have different relationships to the society as a whole and to its parts, the emblems of national identity may not have identical meanings to all of the individuals who encounter and interpret them. In the words of Philip Schlesinger (1991: 174), "National cultures are not simple repositories of shared symbols to which the entire population stands in identical relation."

The differences of opinion on Puerto Ricanness among people who all felt themselves to be strongly Puerto Rican illustrate this significant characteristic of collective identity. Some respondents recognized this variation:

> *Independence party focus group:*
> Every person is going to internalize what it is to be Puerto Rican and is going to feel Puerto Rican in a different way (g10).

> *Statehood party interviewee:*
> It's not as simple as saying "What makes up Puerto Rican identity?" ... There are geographical differences within Puerto Rico, socio-economic differences, political differences.... Individuals don't all think the same thing at once, nor do they all act in the same way (i11).

> *Statehood party focus group:*
> It depends on your point of view. There's the conception held by the Puerto Rican who has always lived here, the conception of the Puerto Rican who, for example, lives in the countryside, who lives in the city, who has travelled.... Some people have a positive conception but others have a negative conception too. It depends who you ask (g8).

Notably, those who remarked on this variation were adherents of statehood or independence, positions that have generally held minority standing in Puerto Rico. Their awareness of contrasting viewpoints may reflect a tendency for minorities within a society to be more cognizant of societal variations than are those in the majority.

Variability in symbolic interpretation was illustrated in Puerto Rico by divergent conceptions in the meaning of Puerto Ricanness held by interviewees. Differences were found in respondents' sets of geographical identities, in symbols held to represent Puerto Rico by some respondents but not by others, and in the degree of protection felt necessary for the commonly acknowledged symbols of Puerto Ricanness.

Statehood party members maintained that significant symbols are not endangered, even by Puerto Rico's incorporation into the United States. Their support for becoming part of the United States is based on economic and political considerations; Puerto Ricanness is safe, they argued, and does not factor into their analysis. Confident of the durability of Puerto Rican symbols, statehood supporters have not hesitated to adopt symbols of the United States to represent their political stance.

Commonwealth supporters, in contrast, have chosen in recent years to use mainland symbols only in conjunction with the corresponding Puerto Rican symbols and have often defended their support for commonwealth status in terms of Puerto Ricanness. They reject independence on grounds of economics and political expediency, but they also reject statehood, saying that the most important reason for remaining separate from the United States is to maintain a distinct Puerto Rican identity and culture. They have felt that the symbols of Puerto Ricanness needed protection through such measures as the commonwealth party's law mandating Spanish as the official language of government in Puerto Rico.

Finally, independence supporters value and respect symbols of Puerto Ricanness but emphasized in these interviews that the issue was deeper. They argued that the only way that Puerto Ricanness could be truly expressed was through Puerto Rican independence. While independence party respondents supported protection of symbols, they felt that to be a superficial and inadequate policy.

This brief review suggests a two-tier model of national identity. The first tier, the underlying idea of a Puerto Rican nation, is recognized by political leaders across the major political divide in Puerto Rican society—status preference. Unsystematic observation suggests that this basic notion of Puerto Rico is also widely shared across other social divisions such as gender, race, and class. But the strong sense of Puerto Ricanness manifested by all interviewees cloaked many points of disunity. Overlying the common base is the second tier of Puerto Rican identity: the diverging conceptions of what it means to be Puerto Rican. At this level the shared idea of the nation becomes blurred, subject as it is to the inconsistencies inherent in any human social invention.

Global Symbols

Because of Puerto Rico's unusual political situation, differences of symbolic interpretation are recognized and debated. Despite Puerto Rico's unusual political situation, there remains a common core of symbols taken to represent Puerto Rico. These symbols of identity have gained their meaning and their power through social interaction. Such symbols may seem inconsequential, but they are a kind of social glue. "There are many things that one considers to be unnecessary," mused a member of the 1952 Puerto Rican constitutional convention, "and, nevertheless, it turns out that they are not so unnecessary. For example, I have always believed that a necktie is unnecessary, but custom has made it necessary. Peoples have their symbols and it is custom that, in my judgment, makes it necessary for Puerto Rico to have its flag, have its anthem, and have its coat of arms" (Puerto Rico Constituent Assembly 1952: 2099–100). Custom has converted some representations into symbols that are used and acknowledged around the world. Prominent among these are language, flag, and Olympic team.

Language. The overt purpose of languages is communication, but languages also have the potential to serve as markers of group identity. In the words of John Edwards, "The basic distinction here is between language in its ordinarily understood sense as a tool of communication, and language as an emblem of groupness, as a symbol, a rallying-point" (1985: 17).

The Spanish language, of course, has more than symbolic importance in Puerto Rico. It is the fundamental tool used by most Puerto Ricans for most communication. But in the context of Puerto Rican politics, it also serves as a rallying point for Puerto Rican identity, in direct opposition to the English-speaking United States. Puerto Rican political analyst Juan Manuel García Passalacqua has noted that "since the North American invasion of 1898, the 'language question' has been the subtle way that Puerto Ricans have defended their nationality" (García Passalacqua 1991b). Not only does the Spanish language differentiate Puerto Ricans from English speakers, but position on language also serves as a group marker for people with different political views within the island. Competing conceptions of Puerto Rican identity are expressed within the island through the symbol of language. One analyst maintains that the school language issue never answered to educational concerns but has been, since the beginning, nothing more than a surrogate for the larger political struggle. Even though Puerto Ricans gained control of the educational system in 1949, Edith Algren de Gutiérrez contends that "[s]o long as Puerto Rican citizens remain dissatisfied about the Island's political status, the language issue will be debated" (1987: 1). Exemplifying this assertion, statehood supporters opposed the commonwealth party's Spanish-language law and overturned it upon gaining a legislative majority, because, in the words of statehood party founder Luis A. Ferré, the law "removed [the English language] from its proper place as a symbol of our loyal association with the United States" (Ferré 1991).

This characteristic ability of language to serve as a group marker as well as a means of communication can be seen throughout the world and throughout history. The attempt by conquerors to impose their language on the conquered is a recurrent historical theme. For example, Japan's attempted absorption of its Korean, Taiwanese, and Micronesian colonies in the early twentieth century included requiring the use of the Japanese language (Peattie 1988: 240–41). During the "Japanization" campaign in Korea, students were forbidden from speaking Korean under any circumstances (Kim 1973: 142). Such policies are not a relic of the past. Ethnic Turks living in Bulgaria reported in 1989 that speaking their language in public was punishable by a fine (Haberman 1989). Meanwhile, across the border, Kurds in Turkey were experiencing similar problems; the use of the Kurdish language was subject to restrictions, which were later eased in

Turkey's attempt to deal with its Kurdish minority (Hundley 1992).

Recent world history is replete with examples of militant backlash in reaction to attempts to impose dominant languages on social subgroups. In the Baltic states, where the USSR imposed Russian language and culture when it took over in 1940, this backlash has been particularly visible. Upon becoming independent in 1991, Latvia's new government decreed that Latvian would replace Russian as the official language of the republic, as a way to reverse "Russification" and keep the Latvian language alive (Stets 1991). Similarly, neighboring Estonia turned the tables on Russian residents, who had represented the Soviet rulers, by enacting regulations requiring ethnic Russians to pass an Estonian language test to gain citizenship in the new state (Seplow 1993). In Spain, the efforts of the dictator General Francisco Franco to prohibit the use of languages other than Spanish during his thirty-five-year rule generated fierce resistance, and regional languages have been vigorously promoted since his death in 1975. In a decisive repudiation of Franco's policy, the new Spanish Constitution includes recognition of Spain's regional languages as "a cultural heritage that will be the object of special respect and protection" (Sánchez Goyanes 1980: 147). In India, English as a vestigial colonial language is under attack; two local governments made Hindi the official language of business in 1990, refusing even to answer correspondence written in English (Crossette 1990). In French-speaking Canada, a law prohibiting the use of English or any language other than French on outdoor signs in Quebec was enacted in 1991 (Tierney 1991). These are just a few examples of the power of language as an "in-group symbol" (Gumperz 1982: 7) to mark the boundaries of the group that speaks it and set that group apart from speakers of other languages.

Flag. Unlike languages, flags have a single purpose: to represent something. The function of a flag is to be a symbol; it has no intrinsic meaning until it is invested with meaning by its inventors and through social interaction. The power of flags derives from precisely this singularity of function. While there can be disagreement about which group may claim to be represented by a given flag, as has been the case in Puerto Rico, the sole purpose of flag display is to stand for a group.

Flags are regarded with sometimes militant affection by group members. A Puerto Rican commonwealth party member's passionate proclamation of these feelings was tempered by a degree of self-awareness:

> We love our flag as much as any North American loves the North American flag. We choke up when we see it, we like it, we're proud of it, we like the way it looks, it's very pretty, the brilliant colors of our flag make us feel that it's the prettiest one of all. Of course, we can compare [and see] that there are others that are more or less the same, but ours is ours (g3).

From its creation, the single-star Puerto Rican flag has been a symbolic manifestation of Puerto Rico's separateness from its sovereign power. Its inventors devised it in 1895 as a symbol of their goal of Puerto Rican independence from Spain. During Puerto Rico's years as a U.S. colony, the flag came to represent aspirations of political autonomy or independence. U.S. authorities' opposition to display of the flag during the first half of the twentieth century and, ironically, independence sympathizers' opposition to the official use of the flag to represent a Puerto Rico that was under the U.S. yoke, demonstrate its symbolic importance. Its power was seen in the emotional response to the flag's gaining official status in 1952 and in the controversy over which flag or flags to display at the 1979 Pan American Games. Statehood supporters have demonstrated the most obvious variation in the symbolic representation of Puerto Rican identity with their refusal to endorse the 1991 referendum unless it included the right to the flags, as well as the anthems and languages, of both Puerto Rico and United States, and with their jubilant waving of U.S. flags to celebrate the defeat of the 1991 referendum.

The socially constructed power of flags to represent peoples and their aspirations—and in so doing to threaten the power structure—can be seen wherever clashes occur. As the United States did early in the occupation of Puerto Rico, dominant states have tried and failed to prohibit the display of rebel groups' flags as symbols of insurgency. The Kurdish flag has been illegal in Turkey (*New York Times* 1992a), as were flags of at least some of the Soviet republics before the breakup of the Soviet Union. Estonian leaders claim that the ban on the Estonian flag fell in a demonstration in 1988, when so many people carried the flag that the police were unable to arrest them all (Shipler 1989). Before the 1993 peace agreement between Israel and the Palestine Liberation Organization, display of the Palestinian flag in the occupied territories was illegal (Brown 1993). In all of these cases, the flags in question represented groups whose autonomist goals threatened authorities; the flags were prohibited solely because they symbolized that threat. The absence of a flag can similarly provoke authorities. A Spanish prosecutor sought a fine and prison sentence for a local mayor in the Basque region who displayed town, province, and Basque flags at City Hall during local festivities, but did not display the flag of Spain (Calvo 1995).

Sports. The literal arena of sporting competition is a third principal symbol of contemporary Puerto Rico. A Puerto Rican independence party official voiced the fundamental national identity message in the context of sports when he stated that Puerto Rican participation in international sports contests was "the *only* expression of our uniqueness that can be legitimately exhibited internationally" (Rodríguez Orellana 1991: 13).

Sports representation as a symbol of group identity is strikingly significant in Puerto Rico and elsewhere. When Australia was awarded the Summer Olympic Games for the year 2000, the country's prime minister exulted, "There couldn't be a greater indication to the world that Australia is a nation with its own identity" (Engel and Gittings 1993). International sports competitions provide a sanctioned outlet for the expression of national feeling. Recent world realignments have been accompanied by changes in sports representation to channel such expression. Estonia formed an Olympic Committee in 1989, on the way to becoming independent (Shipler 1989: 62). The flag-bearer for Latvia in the 1992 Winter Olympics enthused that his delegation was "so happy to be here, to show the world that we are a country like other countries, not a part of Russia" (Longman 1992). The former Yugoslav republics of Slovenia and Croatia sought and gained recognition by the International Olympic Committee in 1992, as soon as they became separate states (*New York Times* 1992b). Conversely, when twelve former Soviet republics competed together as the Commonwealth of Independent States (CIS) at the 1992 Summer Olympics, the president of the Russian Olympic Committee bemoaned the effect of the breakup of the Soviet Union on CIS athletes and coaches: "It's a loss of national identity. It's impossible to play in such a mood" (Hiatt 1992).

These three symbols—the historic ones of language and flag and the modern one of sports representation—have become internationally recognized as differentiators of nations and states. Part of their power derives from precisely that international acknowledgment. Other symbols speak to smaller audiences. Few outsiders would distinguish a Puerto Rican *plena* from other Caribbean or Spanish-language music, yet to a Puerto Rican the association is unmistakable. The poetry of Robert Burns may be a school chore or an aesthetic pleasure to many, but to a Scot it likely carries deeper significance. The Catalan *sardana* dance, the U.S. Thanksgiving holiday, the Japanese tea ceremony are powerful cultural symbols that do not communicate a national identity message to the outside world in the standardized way that languages or flags or Olympic competitions do but that evoke intense feelings of identification from within.

THE FEAR OF SYMBOLIC DISPLACEMENT

Symbols of identity are subject to change over time and in society, but such change is often unwelcome. Within a nation, the threat that some symbols of identity will be displaced by others may be equated with a loss of uniqueness.

The U.S. presence in Puerto Rico has presented direct competition to the most salient symbols of Puerto Ricanness, and the internal debate about Puerto Rican identity has been framed in terms of the ability of symbols of Puerto Ricanness to withstand this competition. The fear of displacement in Puerto Rico was particularly revealed through contrasting attitudes toward different components of imported culture and media. Some imports—notably music and fast food—were perceived as merely supplementing Puerto Rican culture and media; these were not deemed a threat to local culture and did not arouse consternation. Other imported cultural products—especially Christmas celebrations and cable television—were seen as threatening entirely to displace existing symbols of identity. In these cases, many respondents expressed anxiety about the survival of Puerto Rican culture.

The fissure along status preference lines makes this variation particularly obvious in Puerto Rico, but the notion of displacement of key symbols of cultural identity by imported symbols provides a useful framework for thinking about reactions to imported media and culture anywhere. To those inside a culture, the potential elimination of particular traditions and symbols of that culture is more readily perceived and thus more conceptually straightforward than generalized allusions to identities and lifestyles. The rather clear-cut anxiety over displacement may underlie protest about globalization, but it has been obscured by contentions about culture and values that do not lend themselves to empirical evaluation.

The fear of displacement may be unfounded; such a perception does not necessarily mean that displacement is actually occurring. But to point out that the fear of cultural displacement is not the same thing as displacement itself is not to dismiss this fear as unreasonable. Local symbols may, indeed, be vulnerable to displacement. The supplanting of local symbols by imported ones is one way that imported media and cultural products could function to diminish collective identity or identities in a receiving society. But the concern voiced about threatened symbols may itself be symbolic, a means of articulating a more diffuse feeling that the nation's distinctive identity is being lost. While displacement of a symbol might not actually be imminent, the articulation of the fear of displacement may communicate deeper anxieties.

Conversely, modification or displacement could take place over time without arousing fears of displacement. This has occurred with food traditions all over the world, as noted by Raymond Sokolov: "Dishes that were novelties as recently as the nineteenth century—most tomato dishes in most northern countries, for example—are now part of what passes for an authentic tradition stretching back to Noah" (1991: 13). Because symbols and the identities they stand for are not static, because identity is more dynamic than the symbols that represent it, it can accommodate shifts in symbolic representation over time. As the Puerto Rico example indicates, what seems to be important is not whether particular symbols are actually replaced by others but whether members of the group *perceive* that symbols of their identity are threatened.

US VERSUS THEM: COLLECTIVE SELF-AWARENESS

Displacement is perceived as a threat when imported culture brings potentially competing symbols. Considerations of globalization have tended to assume that imports weaken identity, but a case can be made for precisely the opposite effect: defensive response to the fear of cultural displacement may have the effect of strengthening identity. Puerto Ricans demonstrated clear awareness of which symbols derived from their own culture and which came from elsewhere, and they responded to perceived pressure on their culture by defending the cultural elements that they considered their own. Anthropologists studying Puerto Rico in the late

1940s noted that the development of national consciousness in the island "became manifest in opposition to United States cultural patterns as American sovereignty intensified cultural ambivalence and a sense of conflict" (Steward et al. 1956: 501).

The history of Puerto Rico demonstrates that exposure to other cultures, whether through conquest, international agreements, proximity, or mass media, can create a basis for recognizing what is unique about one's own culture. This comparison generates increased awareness of "them" and may elicit stronger self-defense on the part of "us." Deliberate efforts from without to change cultural symbols tend to induce resistance. For example, Japan's assimilationist policies during its occupation of Korea from 1910 to 1945 generated "a tremendous upsurge of identity awareness under a Japanese yoke" (Mesler 1973: 223). In China, "[p]rogrammed attempts since 1949 to speed up the process of sinifying the remaining minorities has led to increased ethnic consciousness and . . . resentment on the part of the minorities" (Connor 1972: 351–52). As one anthropologist has observed, "Ethnic identity is often the result of conflict rather than its cause" (U.S. Institute of Peace 1994).

Political agreements may be felt to threaten identities by reducing institutional autonomy, but they, too, may supply comparisons that can strengthen identity. A citizen of Luxembourg recently commented about Luxembourg's position as a small country literally and metaphorically surrounded by large ones in the European Union: "There is no danger of us losing our national identity because we are different. We are not German and not French, but something in between" (Carvel 1994).

The perceived pressure on identity from voluntarily imported and freely consumed mass media is of a different nature. This pressure has been held by some to be even more insidious than deliberate pressure. But like other forms of pressure on identity, imported media may provide models against which to compare, highlighting the difference between them and us. Walker Connor has noted that "advances in communication and transportation tend also to increase cultural awareness. . . . Not only does the individual become more aware of alien ethnic groups; he also becomes more aware of those who share his identity" (1972: 329). A study in Korea found that watching U.S. armed forces television generated opposition to imported culture and was associated with "an intensely protective attitude toward Korean culture" in some viewers (Kang and Morgan 1990: 299). Discussing the effect of imported popular culture in New Zealand, an observer concluded, "New Zealanders know what it is to be a 'Kiwi' by knowing what we are *not*: we are not Australian, we are not British, and we are not American" (Lealand 1994: 37). A study of television viewers in Wales found that in interpreting a television program, their understanding of "Welshness" was "frequently defined in terms of what they considered were 'un-Welsh' and typically English traits" (Griffiths 1993: 21). A Puerto Rican friend commented that seeing such unfamiliar things as snow and winter coats on television programs as a child "did not make me forget what I *was*; it made me know what I was *not*."

CULTURE, POLITICS, AND IDENTITY

Of the many possible approaches to the topic of identity, the framework of examination developed here highlights these characteristics: collective identity is expressed as a message of uniqueness; this uniqueness is expressed through symbols that are neither static over time nor monolithic across social groups; fear of the displacement of symbols may generate resistance; and exposure to others, by force or otherwise, can bring about greater collective self-awareness.

The first two points are often overlooked or taken for granted in analyses of identity. The centrality of the message of uniqueness as a significant component of group identity is crucial. And awareness of the mutability of symbols and symbolic meanings and of the variability of symbols of identity is important when considering the vulnerability of national and other collective identities to external pressures. Claims about any type of influence on national identity seem hollow without consideration of the dynamic nature of national identity within a society and over time.

The second two points challenge generalized assumptions about the vulnerability of local identities to external influence. They suggest an explicit means to examine reactions to imported culture and media: vague concerns about globalization can be better understood by identifying specific fears of cultural displacement. Further, they posit that pressure on identity can generate a vital counterpressure; the importation of symbols that compete with established symbols of identity can strengthen identity.

These observations emerge from examining the experience of national identity from the point of view of insiders. What members of a nation think about their own national identity matters. Their views are particularly useful for consideration of claims related to the effects of globalization and media flows on national identity. A central weakness of that literature has been the absence of considerations of the experience of national identity and therefore how it might be affected by imported cultural, commercial, and media products.

Beginning in 1898, the United States sought to remake Puerto Rican society into something akin to its own, to remodel islanders' attitudes and institutions to more closely resemble those of the sovereign power. Puerto Rico has indeed been shaped by the U.S. presence. The overt coercive pressure to "Americanize" in the early years of U.S. sovereignty was not without effect, particularly on Puerto Rico's legal, educational, and military structures. The U.S. legacy is reflected as well in the island's political institutions; Puerto Rico's stable democratic system contrasts sharply with the political arrangements of its Caribbean neighbors.

Since the establishment of internal self-government, other factors attributable to the United States—notably, commercial ones—have also greatly shaped Puerto Rican culture. But although U.S. influence on Puerto Rican social patterns and institutions is undeniable, the symbols of Puerto Rican identity have not given way to U.S. replacements. Puerto Rican political elites, variously motivated, have consistently sought to defend Puerto Rico's uniqueness. In almost a century of U.S. sovereignty over Puerto Rico, island leaders have attempted to communicate to the United States two interrelated messages: Puerto Ricans are a distinct people who require self-government, and Puerto Rico's uniqueness is worth preserving.

Pressure to "Americanize" and constant exposure to the United States have not made Puerto Ricans into a people who feel they are simply a part of the larger whole of the United States. Rather, this pressure and the visibility of the United States in Puerto Rico have heightened awareness of the differences between the island's Hispanic-Caribbean culture and the culture of the U.S. mainland. The steadfast adherence to symbols that represent differentiation from the United States indicates that Puerto Ricans have felt that their identity has been encroached upon. The vigor of their defense of Puerto Ricanness has responded to the aggressiveness of the United States' efforts to subdue it. A shared feeling of Puerto Ricanness has remained strong as Puerto Ricans perceive more subtle pressures on identity.

This sense of Puerto Rican distinctiveness is the result of complex social processes that are not readily contained. It has prevailed, in part, through the intrinsic dynamism as well as the deliberate cultivation of symbols of identity. There is no reason to believe that Puerto Ricans are unusual in maintaining their sense of uniqueness in the face of outside pressures. Collective identity is resilient and durable, and these qualities make it a pervasive force throughout the contemporary world.

Appendix

Field Research Notes

The contemporary portion of this study was based on interviews and focus groups conducted in November and December 1990 and April and May 1991. These two periods were close enough in time that I believe the two sets of data can be considered together as a single-point snapshot data set. Perhaps more important than their temporal proximity is that this period marked a relative lull within a highly charged period in Puerto Rican politics, falling between the proposal of the plebiscite in 1989 and the referendum campaign in 1991. The most significant event related to this project that took place during the course of the interviews was the passage in early April 1991 of the Spanish language law. As the culmination of a long process, the passage of the law was not unexpected, and although respondents specifically mentioned the law in the second set of interviews and not in the first set, language issues were sufficiently salient that they were mentioned by virtually all respondents, before and after the passage of the law. Overall, the timing of the interviewing was propitious, as the two years of plebiscite negotiations had served to refocus the ever-present status question, obliging political parties to rearticulate their positions and voters to reassess theirs.

STUDY SUBJECT GROUPS

The category of political elites comprises many levels of politicians, officials, appointees, financial supporters, lobbyists, party staff, and volunteer activists. For this study I narrowed the focus to two groups: politicians, as shapers of identity, and young political activists, as future leaders and a specific audience for the politicians' messages. I was concerned only about the notions of identity held by Puerto Ricans resident in Puerto Rico; the identity question for Puerto Ricans resident in the U.S. mainland is a different matter.

Young people are important in Puerto Rican politics. In the political stalemate of recent years, in which the two dominant parties have split the bulk of the votes almost evenly, party recruitment of voters-to-be has been an important electoral strategy. As voter registration rates on the island are high, registration drives aimed at adults are not fruitful. The high voter turnout limits the value of "get-out-the-vote" efforts (García Passalacqua 1984: 139). Therefore, the prime source of new party members is young people reaching voting age. The president of the independence party youth group, saying, "We are three hundred thousand new voters," noted that the group's message was directed at "the youth of this country" (g9). A member of the commonwealth party's youth wing detailed his group's strategy:

> If the person is still too young to register to vote, [we] convey the message that our party is the best alternative for the country and that he or she can join, affiliate with our party, and be active in our organization in the seventy-eight municipalities, and work in political campaigns, in political education in our organization. Youth have an important role in our party because youth mean the victory or defeat of any party (g2).

Each of the major parties has an organized youth section as part of its recruitment and organizing efforts. The groups carry out their own activities and participate in party activities. The islandwide president of each party's youth group is part of the party's decision-making hierarchy. Members of these youth sections were the participants in ten of the eleven focus groups I conducted; members of a University of Puerto Rico organization made up the eleventh group.

FIELD RESEARCH METHOD

Interviews

I chose to do what Lewis Anthony Dexter, following David Reisman, terms "elite interviewing" of politicians. Reisman used the term for "people in important or exposed positions" who "may require VIP interviewing treatment on the topic which relates to their importance" (1964: 528n). Dexter expands the term to apply to any interviewee "who in terms of the current purposes of the interviewer is given special, nonstandardized treatment." The aim of "elite interviewing" is to discover the presuppositions of the interviewee. Definition and structuring of the topic at hand are left to the interviewee, who is encouraged to "introduce to a considerable extent . . . his notions of what he regards as relevant" (Dexter 1970: 5).

Focus groups

This discussion of the rationale and process of focus groups is based on works of Robert K. Merton (1987), Richard A. Krueger (1988), and David L. Morgan (1988), as well as personal experience. Focus groups are another way to penetrate the ideas and conceptions of interviewees rather than fitting answers and observations into a predetermined framework. A focus group is a moderated group discussion focused on the topic of interest—an "organized process of listening," in Krueger's words. In the early 1940s, Merton and his colleagues developed procedures for generating qualitative information through guided group discussions. This method found its way to market researchers, who used the technique to evaluate consumer responses to products and advertising campaigns (Merton 1987: 558–61). Apparently, market researchers dubbed this data-gathering method the "focus group" and developed specific guidelines for its application in their field. Their techniques were later readopted by social scientists (Morgan 1988: 21; Krueger 1988: 20). Some social scientists, sensitive to accusations from market researchers that they did not properly apply the method, renamed their data-gathering technique "peer group conversations" (Morgan 1988: 77). My group interviews diverged from standard market research techniques in that they were with smaller groups and, in some cases, with groups of acquaintances rather than strangers, both conditions that Krueger finds acceptable (1988: 105–6). In any case, I call them focus groups for ease of reference.

As a research technique, focus groups occupy a space between interviewing and participant-observation; focus group discussions are less structured and have less researcher participation than do interviews, but the groups are scheduled, and participants assemble for the express purpose of the research, removed from the natural setting called for in participant-observation data gathering (Morgan 1988: 53). The focus group method is based on the idea of minimal moderator intervention in a group discussion. Ideally, the participants interact with each other rather than with the moderator, allowing, as with elite interviewing, the participants' ways of conceptualizing the topic to emerge (Morgan 1988: 17). Focus groups differ from elite interviewing because of the dynamic produced in a focus group. "The hallmark of focus groups," says David Morgan, "is *the explicit use of the group interaction to produce data and insights that would be less accessible without the interaction found in a group"* (Morgan 1988: 12). Morgan and Krueger both maintain that focus groups are useful for open exploration of topics, suggesting the value of focus groups for exploratory research on a topic as multilayered as identity.

Questionnaire

The open-ended interview and focus group methods allow respondents to set the agenda. I also wanted to be able to compare respondents' views on key elements of identity. Because the interviews and focus groups were conducted as unprompted discussions, I felt there was a marked possibility of a salience factor intervening. If I asked a respondent, "What, to you, is Puerto Ricanness?" at the moment that he or she happened to be looking out the window at the Puerto Rican flag or to have just returned from a lunch of rice and beans, flag or food might be at the front of the respondent's mind, overriding other elements that at other moments might be of equal importance.

For this reason, I designed a brief questionnaire for interviewees and focus group participants to fill out after the interview was completed. The questionnaire asked respondents to rank the importance of a series of items that could be associated with Puerto Rico. The purpose of this questionnaire was to have a basis for comparison of the significance of the same elements to respondents. This would not eliminate the influence of immediate past experience (including the interview itself), but asking respondents to rank the importance of each item on a list provided a way to partially neutralize the salience factor by generating a comparable measure on identical items. (See pp. 183–85 for questionnaire).

SAMPLE SELECTION

Interviews

To learn how Puerto Rican identity is conceptualized by its shapers, I sought to interview party members at various levels in each party's hierarchy. I did not have any specific individuals in mind. As Dexter notes, "[I]n elite and specialized interviewing it is not usually possible to determine by any mechanical method who should be interviewed. . . . [D]ifferent interviewees make quite different and unequal contributions to the study" (1970: 39).

To select interviewees, I employed a rough quota system, stratifying by Puerto Rican political parties, type of post held, and island regions. The political party stratification was crucial. I wanted representation of the three major parties on the island as well as other political entities. I tried to interview roughly equal numbers of statehood and commonwealth supporters, reflecting their balanced electoral strength. I interviewed fewer independence officials, again to reflect their smaller electoral strength, but independence advocates made up a higher percentage of the interviewees than their electoral strength of approximately 5 percent (See Table 3). I stratified for post held in order to get viewpoints of members at different points in each party's structure, such as holders of local and islandwide elective office and party appointees of several stripes. The geographical stratification, while quite rough, was intended to capture any differences that might reflect the varied cultures of Puerto Rico's urban and rural, coastal and inland areas.

To find the specific interviewees, upon arrival in Puerto Rico I contacted several people who had been suggested to me by friends and advisers. These people, in turn, suggested others, and in this way I accumulated names to drop and

Table 3.   **Respondents' Political Party Affiliations**

In-depth interviewees			Focus group participants		
Party	N	%	*Party*	# of groups	%
Commonwealth	6	42%	Commonwealth	4	36 %
Statehood	5	36%	Statehood	4	36 %
Independence	2	14%	Independence	2	18 %
Socialist	1	7%	Univ. of P.R.	1	0.9%
total	14			11	

was able to reach potential interviewees. Most interviews involved many phone calls to establish contact and schedule a time and, in some cases, a preliminary meeting with the interviewee or an assistant to screen me and my project. At all times I had numerous queries out to potential interviewees. As they responded, I scheduled interview times. The interview subjects were ultimately those I was able to schedule, maintaining the predetermined stratifications, during my time in the island.

There are several ways that this procedure could result in a biased sample. The most obvious bias, and an inescapable one, is that I was able to interview only people who were willing to take the time to talk with a stranger. One evident demographic bias is gender: the in-depth interviewees were all male, as my attempts to schedule interviews with visible female politicians were unsuccessful. (Two subjects of the shorter interviews were women.) This is not a vast misrepresentation of the Puerto Rican political system, which, like the U.S. system on which it is modeled, is overwhelmingly male-dominated. Another possible bias is the age distribution of the in-depth interviewees. The sample is slightly tilted toward younger politicians, with seven in the forty-one-to-fifty age group and with the other eight distributed equally on either side (see Table 4). While junior party officials may have different opinions from those of their more powerful senior colleagues, their opinions as expressed in these interviews were congruent with those of the senior politicians.

To justify my belief that overall this is not a biased sample or at least not systematically biased, I will briefly discuss the process of arranging interviews. My search for an elected independence party official to interview illustrates the process. The independence party holds two seats in the fifty-three-member Puerto Rican House of Representatives and one in the twenty-seven-member Senate. I wanted to interview one of these three elected officials; I had no preference among them. After several calls to all three, I was referred to a legislative aide, who asked to meet with me. After discussing the project, he agreed to schedule me for an interview with his boss the following week. After the interview, he asked if he could be of any further help. When I replied that I had been trying for several weeks to get an interview with a prominent commonwealth party senator, he

Table 4.   Respondents' Ages

	In-depth interviewees	Focus group participants
Age	N	N
< 21	0	13
21-30	1	22
31-40	2	0
41-50	7	0
51-60	3	0
> 60	1	0
total	14	35

telephoned the senator directly, bypassing the secretarial maze that I had been navigating. "Senator," he said, "do me a favor. Give me fifteen minutes to talk to a friend." He escorted me to the senator's office, personally introduced us, and left me to what became an extensive interview that I likely would not have been able to arrange myself.

Personal connections were helpful in gaining access to mayors. Local mayors are important in the Puerto Rican political structure, and their activities are quite distinct from those of legislators and other San Juan-based politicians who deal with politics at the islandwide level. Unlike legislators, the mayors do not spend their time interacting with one another at the capitol in San Juan. This was all the more reason to do local interviewing, but it increased the difficulties of access. Personal ties, however insubstantial, proved to be the most—indeed, the only—effective channel for reaching mayors. For example, the mayor of one town agreed to meet with me through the help of an acquaintance who teaches at a school attended by the mayor's nephew. This shaky series of links provided a lead-in sufficient to arrange an interview. I approached another mayor through a friend whose parents had grown up in his town. Using this rather tenuous reference, my friend undertook the preliminary footwork to set up the interview.

In one case I had no personal connection. I wanted to interview the mayor of a town outside San Juan. I called the mayor's office daily for two weeks, explained the project to several secretaries, and requested an interview. After at least ten calls, the mayor's personal secretary promised that the mayor would see me the following week. I arrived at the appointed hour and was told that the mayor was on his way. When he had not arrived after ninety minutes, the secretaries suggested interviewing an assistant mayor instead, an offer that I accepted.

At this point I had interviewed one statehood party mayor, one statehood party assistant mayor, and one commonwealth party mayor, all from different parts of the island. I wanted to balance this by interviewing another commonwealth party mayor, so I asked several well-connected friends for referrals. The first interview that came through was with a mayor of a town in the mountainous interior of the

Table 5.   **In-Depth Interviewees:**
Party, Geographic Location, and Type of Post Held

Type of post	elected		appointed	
Location	San Juan	else-where	San Juan	else-where
Commonwealth	2	2	1	1
Statehood	2	1	1	1
Independence	1	0	1	0
Socialist	1	0	0	0
total	6	3	3	2

island, who agreed to talk with me at the request of a legislative aide (of another party) whom I had met in the process of legislative interviews. This incident was typical. Other interviews were arranged in the same manner, through the cooperation of interviewees who took an interest in the project. One focus group participant had a connection with Felisa Rincón de Gautier, the nonagenarian former mayor of San Juan. He insisted that I speak with her and arranged a half-hour interview.

Altogether I interviewed nineteen politicians. Five of these interviews, including the one with Rincón de Gautier, were too brief to be entirely comparable with the others. Therefore, when categorizing the interviews as a body, I refer only to the fourteen in-depth interviews. The interviewees included two members of the Puerto Rican Senate, three members of the House of Representatives, three mayors and one assistant mayor, one legislative aide, and three party officials (See Table 5). Outside of the three major parties, I interviewed representatives of two other political organizations—the Puerto Rican Socialist Party, which favors independence, and Puerto Ricans in Civic Action, a nonpartisan group that advocates statehood.

Focus groups

Determining the appropriate number of focus groups for a research project is not a precision undertaking. Morgan notes that "one important determiner of the number of groups is the number of different population subgroups required" (1988: 42). As I had with politicians, in arranging focus groups I stratified for the subgroups of interest: political parties and residents of different parts of the island. I aimed for approximately equal numbers of statehood and commonwealth groups and fewer independence groups and for participants from throughout the island. Political party youth groups were easy to find through each party's headquarters, and members were generally amenable to participating in the project. Members of a nonpartisan University of Puerto Rico organization called Students United for Peace also readily agreed to participate.

Altogether I conducted eleven focus groups: four each with commonwealth and statehood youth group members, two in San Juan and two elsewhere; two independence groups with participants of mixed geographical provenance; and the University of Puerto Rico group of mixed party affiliation and hometown. Each focus group had three to seven participants, for a total of forty-three participants. The usefulness of focus groups is said to be exhausted when participants' responses become predictable (Morgan 1988: 42) or when little new information surfaces (Krueger 1988: 97). Applying these criteria, I conducted more than enough focus groups.

THE INTERVIEW AND FOCUS GROUP PROCESS

All of the focus groups were conducted in Spanish. The interviews were conducted in Spanish, with two exceptions, both of them statehood party interviewees who asked to do the interview in English, one "to practice my English," the other for the benefit of an overseas reporter who was present.

I presented each interviewee with a letter of introduction explaining the project in general terms and asking permission to tape-record the interview and to cite him or her in my writings. Although none of the interviewees declined to be quoted by name, I have presented interviewee responses anonymously. I tape-recorded all of the interviews and focus groups, with the exception of one interview with an author and former legislator, who explained that "as a man of the written word," he preferred not to be recorded in unconsidered conversation. In that instance, I took written notes with the interviewee's permission.

After the preliminaries, I began the interview with a few questions specific to each individual: how long they had held their current post, previous party activities, their political background. I then explained that I was interested in both their personal point of view and party policy and that I would ask about each in turn. For the interviews and focus groups I used as a flexible guide the instrument discussed in the next section. A few broad questions with clarifying questions posed at appropriate moments in the discussion were usually sufficient to elicit the information of interest. Interviews lasted fifty to seventy minutes. After each interview, I asked the interviewee to fill out the questionnaire on identity issues and basic demographic information.

The focus groups were conducted in a similar manner. When the participants had assembled, I introduced myself to the group as a whole, explained the nature of the project in general terms, and answered, again in general terms, any questions they had. I emphasized that I was interested in their ideas and different points of view and that there were no right or wrong answers (Morgan 1988: 52; Krueger 1988: 25). In most cases one participant of each group signed the letter of agreement to tape-record the session on behalf of the group. I have assigned pseudonyms to focus group participants when citing their comments.

The focus group instrument was the same as the interview instrument. I began again with a question about what they associate with Puerto Rico and let them talk among themselves. Occasionally, I asked if there were disagreements or encouraged a shy or interrupted participant to speak. In most cases the groups went very smoothly. There was no problem in getting participants to talk; the greatest challenge was to keep them from all talking at once.

The group discussions lasted sixty to seventy-five minutes. After the group was finished and the tape recorder turned off, participants often had questions about me and my work and how I had become interested in Puerto Rico. These post-focus group conversations, this time with the focus group participants asking the questions, lasted as long as thirty to forty minutes.

INSTRUMENT

Interviews and focus groups

The interviews and focus groups were built around three large conceptual questions. Several lesser questions were inserted when necessary to focus the discussion or move it forward. The first question was deliberately open: "To you, what is *puertorriqueñidad*, what does it mean to be Puerto Rican?" The idea was to get respondents' unprompted responses about what the island represented to them. The ease with which interviewees addressed this question indicated that it was not overly vague. Elaboration on the question was usually sufficient to provide ample discussion of Puerto Rican symbols and traditions.

After probing as much as possible on Puerto Ricanness, I asked the second principal question: "What are your concerns about each status option?" This question, a focused, partisan way to explore the same issues, was intended to clarify respondents' conceptions of the essence of Puerto Rico by eliciting comments about what they felt would be changed under each status option. I also asked about the party's message concerning Puerto Ricanness and about the party's channels for getting that message to the public.

The third principal question was a series of five self-identification questions in the form, "Do you feel Caribbean," "Do you feel Latin American," and so on for Hispanic, *estadounidense* (from the United States), and Puerto Rican. This series of questions was intended to explore the relative weight of each of those possible self-identifications. These questions, too, generally elicited extensive elaborations. Finally, to give respondents the chance to bring up issues that had not been covered, I asked if there was anything that they wanted to add.

Survey questionnaire

After the first round of interviews and focus groups, I designed the survey questionnaire. I took from those interviews a list of all the elements that had been mentioned by respondents as part of Puerto Ricanness, whether they were mentioned by many respondents or by few. I selected twenty-five varied items from this list and added five elements that nobody had mentioned but that were plausibly Puerto Rican. This total of thirty items made up the first part of the questionnaire. Item 31—"others?"—provided space for respondents to write in any other item they may have felt was important. Respondents were asked to indicate the importance of each item to their personal conception of what it meant to be Puerto Rican on a scale of 1 to 7. The second part of the questionnaire asked respondents to rank in order of importance to their own self-identity the five terms that had been discussed in the interview: Caribbean, Hispanic, Latin American, North American or *estadounidense*, and Puerto Rican. Finally, I asked for demographic information: age, sex, occupation, hometown, party affiliation, and so on. (See pp. 183–85 for questionnaire.)

Once the instrument had been developed and tested, I delivered it to all respondents from the first round of data collection and requested that they fill it out. All interviewees complied willingly, as did all of the focus group members that I was able to find; seven focus group members eluded me, but as they were distributed through all the focus groups conducted, I do not think there is any systematic bias to their not being represented in the final data. During the second round of data collection, I asked each respondent to fill out the questionnaire immediately after the interview or focus group. Although it is possible that responses may differ depending on whether the questionnaire was filled out immediately after the interview or several months later, no apparent differences in data resulted.

POSSIBLE INTERVIEWER EFFECTS

My position as an outsider may have affected the responses to the questions I asked during the interviews and focus groups. On the positive side, all interviewees and focus group participants evidenced a need to make me understand their perspectives. They were insistent on explaining in detail their views and the reasons for their positions. This was useful in getting respondents to go beyond rehearsed and superficial statements about issues that are constant topics of Puerto Rican political discourse. It is conceivable that speaking to an outsider allowed politicians and political activists to express their views more candidly than they might have thought advisable in addressing political opponents or Puerto Rican voters.

On the negative side, it is possible that my own identity as *estadounidense* had an inhibiting effect on the interviewees. Several apologized before making mildly negative comments about the United States, indicating that I was not to take these comments personally. One interviewee said:

> Don't take it badly that I say that I'm Puerto Rican first and then North American. . . . I'm telling you how I feel (i3).

A focus group member stated:

> I've had experiences with North American classmates and they keep their distance. I apologize, [I know] you are North American, but that is the truth (g4).

Nonetheless, respondents, particularly focus group participants, did not seem constrained in their criticism of the United States by my nationality, as evidenced by these excerpts.

> *Commonwealth party focus group:*
> I'm more interested in going to a Latin American country, getting to know it, than going to the United States. I tell you this frankly . . . I've never been attracted to going to the United States (g4).

> *University of Puerto Rico focus group:*
> I have never lived in the United States. I have family who have lived in the United States and, well, frankly, I wouldn't want to live there (g11).

ANALYSIS

To analyze the data, I transcribed the tapes of all of the interviews and focus groups verbatim and set out to look for patterns. Organizing the information was a matter of reading the transcripts repeatedly and categorizing respondents' comments by individual, party affiliation, and so on. I made a chart of all responses (see Figures 1 and 2, pp. 71–72), and excerpted responses on selected subjects. Beyond the questions posed in the interviews, I had no predetermined framework for classifying the information gathered; the organizational scheme emerged from patterns that became apparent upon reviewing the interview material.

The information culled from these interviews and focus groups could have been organized in many different ways. For this study, I chose to arrange the material around three key aspects of Puerto Rican identity: "What is Puerto Rico?" and what constitutes Puerto Ricanness; "What am I?" based on the self-identification questions; and respondents' views on the influence of nearly a century of U.S. presence in the island.

Figure 3.   Interview And Focus Group Instrument

I. *Introductory questions specific to the individual interviewee, the focus group, and the individual focus group participants:*

  (*interview*)
  1. What is your role in the party?
  2. How long have you held your current post?
  3. What other posts have you held?

  (*focus group*)
  To each individual in the group:
  1. What is your age?
  2. Have you ever lived in the United States?
       If so, for how long and at what age?

  To the group as a whole:
  1. What is the role of the youth organization in the party?

II. *General questions. Same set of questions for interviews and focus groups.*

  1. To you, what is *puertorriqueñidad*, what does it mean to be Puerto Rican? (PROBE extensively)

  2. What are your concerns about each status option, both from your personal point of view and in terms of your party's policies?

  3. Do you feel Caribbean?
     Do you feel Hispanic?
     Do you feel Latin American?
     Do you feel North American or *estadounidense*?
     Do you feel Puerto Rican?

  4. Is there anything else that you would like to add or comment on?

Figure 4.   **Questionnaire**

I. The following words and phrases have been mentioned by some people as things that they associate with Puerto Rico. Please indicate the importance of each of these words and phrases to your personal conception of what it means to be Puerto Rican, using a scale of 1 to 7, from lesser to greater importance.

| 1=unimportant | 4=of medium importance | 7=extremely important |

example:
| *pasteles* | 1 | 2 | 3 | 4 | 5 | 6 | 7 |

If *pasteles* are of medium importance to you in your personal concept of what it means to be Puerto Rican, indicate this by circling the number 4.

| *pasteles* | 1 | 2 | 3 | ④ | 5 | 6 | 7 |

	unimportant					extremely important	
1. customs	1	2	3	4	5	6	7
2. way of dressing	1	2	3	4	5	6	7
3. food	1	2	3	4	5	6	7
4. the *bomba* and the *plena*	1	2	3	4	5	6	7
5. the flag	1	2	3	4	5	6	7
6. the Olympic team	1	2	3	4	5	6	7
7. the *coquí*	1	2	3	4	5	6	7
8. Latin personality	1	2	3	4	5	6	7
9. *parrandas*	1	2	3	4	5	6	7
10. rice and beans	1	2	3	4	5	6	7
11. non-punctuality	1	2	3	4	5	6	7
12. hospitable people	1	2	3	4	5	6	7
13. *trovadores* competitions	1	2	3	4	5	6	7
14. rum	1	2	3	4	5	6	7
15. the Spanish language	1	2	3	4	5	6	7
16. individualism	1	2	3	4	5	6	7
17. the anthem	1	2	3	4	5	6	7
18. Santa Claus	1	2	3	4	5	6	7

Figure 4 (continued)

19. beaches	1	2	3	4	5	6	7
20. expressive people	1	2	3	4	5	6	7
21. *décimas*	1	2	3	4	5	6	7
22. the Three Kings	1	2	3	4	5	6	7

23. mixture of Taíno, Spanish and African cultures

	1	2	3	4	5	6	7
24. family	1	2	3	4	5	6	7
25. the *jíbaro*	1	2	3	4	5	6	7
26. consumerism	1	2	3	4	5	6	7
27. the island	1	2	3	4	5	6	7
28. the Catholic religion	1	2	3	4	5	6	7
29. salsa music	1	2	3	4	5	6	7
30. history	1	2	3	4	5	6	7

31. others? _____

_____

II. Rank the following words in order of relative importance in terms of how you define yourself, beginning with the most important (1), and ending with the least important (5).

1=the most important   5=the least important

_____ Caribbean

_____ Hispanic

_____ Latin American

_____ North American (*estadounidense*)

_____ Puerto Rican

III. Please provide the following information.

1. Sex (circle)   M   F

2. Age
_____ under 21
_____ 21-30
_____ 31-40
_____ 41-50
_____ 51-60
_____ over 60

3. Occupation _____

4. In what town did you grow up? _____

5. Where do you live now? _____

6. Have you ever lived in the United States? _____

6a. if you have lived in the United States, how many years did you live there?
_____ years.

7. Party affiliation (please circle)

PNP
PIP
PPD
other _____
none

Thank you very much for your participation.

Bibliography

Abbad y Lasierra, Fray Iñigo. [1788] 1970. *Historia Geográfica, Civil y Natural de la Isla de San Juan Bautista de Puerto Rico*, 3d ed. Introduction by Isabel Gutiérrez del Arroyo. Río Piedras, PR: Editorial Universitaria.

Acosta, Ivonne. 1987. *La mordaza: Puerto Rico 1948–1957*. Río Piedras, PR: Edil.

Allen, Charles H. 1900. *Address of His Excellency Charles H. Allen to the Two Branches of the Legislature of Porto Rico*. 4 December. San Juan, PR: El País.

Amdur, Neil. 1979. "Cheers and Jeers Mark Games' Start." *New York Times*, 2 July: C1.

Andelman, David A. 1980. "Groups Claiming F.A.L.N. Ties Raid Offices of Bush and Carter." *New York Times,* 16 March: 1.

Anderson, Benedict. 1983. *Imagined Communities: Reflections on the Origin and Spread of Nationalism*. London: Verso.

Anderson, Robert W. 1965. *Party Politics in Puerto Rico*. Stanford: Stanford University Press.

———. 1988. "Political Parties and the Politics of Status." *Caribbean Studies* 21(1–2): 1–43.

Barrett, Laurence I. 1993. "State of Anticipation." *Time*, 8 November: 47–48.

Bauza, Nydia. 1991. "Culminan el escrutinio." *Nuevo Día*, 17 December: 20.

———. 1993. "Con fecha una nueva consulta." *Nuevo Día*, 23 November: 5.

Baymont, Henry. 1952. "Senado aprueba Constitución. La envían a Presidente Truman para firma." *El Mundo*, 2 July: 1, 16.

Beirne, Charles. 1975. *The Problem of "Americanization" in the Catholic Schools of Puerto Rico*. Río Piedras, PR: Editorial Universitaria.

Berríos Martínez, Rubén. 1983. *La independencia de Puerto Rico: Razón y lucha*. Mexico: Editorial Línea.

———. 1993. "A mis compatriotas." *Nuevo Día*, 13 November: 65.

Bhana, Surendra. 1975. *The United States and the Development of the Puerto Rican Status Question 1936–1968*. Lawrence: University of Kansas Press.

Bird, Roger, ed. 1988. *Documents of Canadian Broadcasting*. Ottowa: Carleton University Press.

Bjornson, Richard. 1986. "National Identity Concepts in Africa: Interplay between European Categorization Schemes and African Realities." In Peter Boerner, ed., *Concepts of National Identity: An Interdisciplinary Dialogue.* Baden-Baden: Nomos Verlagsgesellschaft: 123–39.

Black, Ruby. 1936. "Tydings presenta un Proyecto de Ley para la celebración de un plebiscito sobre la independencia de Pto. Rico." *La Democracia*, 25 April: 1.

Blumenthal, Howard J., and Goodenough, Oliver R. 1991. *This Business of Television.* New York: Billboard Books.

Boerner, Peter, ed. 1986. *Concepts of National Identity: An Interdisciplinary Dialogue.* Baden-Baden: Nomos Verlagsgesellschaft.

Brameld, Theodore, with the assistance of Ona K. Brameld and Domingo Rosado. 1959. *The Remaking of a Culture: Life and Education in Puerto Rico.* New York: Wiley.

Brown, Derek. 1993. "Bethelehem's Christmas Marred by Row about Flag." *Guardian*, 22 December: 9.

Cabranes, José A. 1979. *Citizenship and the American Empire: Notes on the Legislative History of the United States Citizenship of Puerto Ricans.* New Haven, CT: Yale University Press.

Calvo, Nacho. 1995. "Denuncian a un edil del PNV por no izar la bandera española en las fiestas locales." *Diario 16 Andalucía*, 5 January: 18.

Cámara de Representantes. 1991. "El idioma del gobierno es el español." *Nuevo Día*, 27 March: 52.

Camargo, Nelly de, and Noya Pinto, Virglio B. 1975. *Communication Policies in Brazil.* Paris: UNESCO.

Carlo, Dario. 1952. "Independentistas le rindieron culto a bandera puertorriqueña." *El Mundo*, 26 July: 2, 26.

Carr, Raymond. 1984. *Puerto Rico: A Colonial Experiment.* New York: New York University Press.

Carrasco, Olga. 1993. "A la carga con las consultas." *Nuevo Día*, 22 November: 4.

Carvel, John. 1994. "A Fine Old State to Be In." *Guardian*, 27 December: 18.

Castro Pereda, Rafael. 1991a. "Firme la voluntad." *Nuevo Día*, 15 March: 63.

———. 1991b. "Una difícil papeleta." *Nuevo Día*, 20 December: 77.

Cebollero, Pedro A. 1945. *A School Language Policy for Puerto Rico.* English ed. San Juan: Imprenta Baldrich.

Clark, Victor S., et al. 1930. *Porto Rico and Its Problems.* Washington, DC: Brookings Institution.

Clay, Jason W. 1989. "Epilogue: the ethnic future of nations." *Third World Quarterly* 11(4): 223–33.

Comisión Estatal de Elecciones. 1991. "De esto se trata el referéndum." *Nuevo Día*, 11 October: 54–55.

———. 1992. "Escrutinio de Elecciones Generales 1992." Mimeo.

———. 1993. "Estas son las definiciones de las fórmulas de status político de acuerdo a los partidos que las promulgan." *Nuevo Día*, 10 November: S–2.

Congressional Record. 1914. 15 April: 6718–20.

Congressional Record. 1916. 5 May: 7468–94.

Congressional Record. 1922a. 2 March: 3301–10.

Congressional Record. 1922b. 7 March: 3479.

Congressional Record. 1922c. 24 April: 5913–15.

Congressional Record. 1928. 12 April: 6325–49.

Congressional Record. 1936a. 23 April: 5925–27.

Congressional Record. 1936b. 1 June: 8459–61; 8562–66.

Congressional Record. 1946. A2894–95.

Congressional Record. 1947: 658–87.

Congressional Record. 1962. 11 July: 13175.

Connor, Walker. 1972. "Nation-Building or Nation-Destroying?" *World Politics* 24(3): 319–55.

Covas Quevedo, Waldo D. 1991. "Celebran un 'hispánico triunfo' sobre la estadidad." *Nuevo Día,* 5 April: 10.

———. 1993. "Mudo para el Norte medio Puerto Rico." *Nuevo Día,* 29 January: 5.

Crossette, Barbara. 1990. "Campaign to Oust English Is Revived in India." *New York Times,* 27 May: 4.

Dalbor, John B. 1969. *Spanish Pronunciation: Theory and Practice.* New York: Holt, Rinehart and Winston.

Dávila Colón, Luis R., ed. 1984. *Breakthrough from Colonialism: An Interdisciplinary Study of Statehood.* 2 vols. Río Piedras, PR: Editorial de la Universidad de Puerto Rico.

Davis, George W. 1899. "Report of Brigadier General George W. Davis, USV, on Civil Affairs of Puerto Rico." In U.S. War Department. 1900. *Annual Reports of the War Department for the Fiscal Year Ended June 30, 1899.* 56th Cong., 1st Sess., H. Doc. 2. Washington DC: Government Printing Office.

La Democracia. 1917. "Atavismo colonial." 2 March: 4.

La Democracia. 1921. "Los discursos pronunciados por el Gobernador Interino, señor Benedicto, y por el Gobernador señor Reily, en la ceremonia celebrada en la mañana de hoy en el Teatro Municipal." 30 July: 1, 3.

La Democracia. 1922. "La magna asamblea del Partido Unionista." 13 February: 1, 3–6.

La Democracia. 1929. "Proyecto de programa político de la Unión de Puerto Rico." 26 August: 5.

La Democracia. 1936. "Barceló comenta los proyectos de Tydings." 25 April: 1, 4.

Deutsch, Karl W. 1966. *Nationalism and Social Communication: An Inquiry into the Foundations of Nationality.* 2d ed. Cambridge: MIT Press.

Dexter, Lewis Anthony. 1970. *Elite and Specialized Interviewing.* Evanston, IL: Northwestern University Press.

El Día. 1932. "Un motín de serias proporciones en San Juan." 18 April: 4.

Dorfman, Ariel, and Mattelart, Armand. 1972. *Para leer el pato donald: comunicación de masa y colonialismo.* Mexico: Siglo Veintiuno.

Edwards, John. 1985. *Language, Society and Identity.* Oxford: Basil Blackwell in association with André Deutsch.

Elder, Charles D., and Cobb, Roger W. 1983. *The Political Uses of Symbols.* New York: Longman.

Engel, Matthew, and Gittings, John. 1993. "Sydney Wins the Right to Stage Olympiad 2000." *Guardian,* 24 September: 1.

English First. 1993. "¡Aviso Electoral!" *Nuevo Día,* 11 November: 49.

Epstein, Erwin H., comp. 1970. *Politics and Education in Puerto Rico: A Documentary Survey of the Language Issue.* Metuchen, NJ: Scarecrow Press.

Erikson, Erik H. 1959. *Identity and the Life Cycle.* New York: International

Universities Press.

Estado Libre Asociado. 1991. "Declaración del Español como Idioma Oficial para Usarse en el Gobierno de Puerto Rico." Carta Circular Núm. 01-91. 10 April.

Estrada Resto, Nilka. 1991a. "Tildan de 'burla' la amenaza de impugnar el proyecto del idioma." *Nuevo Día*, 4 April: 24.

———. 1991b. "De gala el idioma español." *Nuevo Día*, 6 April: 4.

———. 1993a. "Abrumadora preferencia por el español en una consulta" *Nuevo Día*, 9 January: 16.

———. 1993b. "Alianza intelectual contra el proyecto de Rosselló." *Nuevo Día*, 14 January: 14.

———. 1993c. "Tirijala tripartito por la permancencia olímpica." *Nuevo Día*, 15 October: 14.

European Commission. 1994. "Strategy Options to Strengthen the European Programme Industry in the Context of the Audiovisual Policy of the European Union." Green Paper. April.

Feldman, Saul D. 1979. "Nested Identities." *Studies in Symbolic Interaction*, vol. 2: 399–418.

Fernández, Ronald. 1987. *Los Macheteros: The Wells Fargo Robbery and the Violent Struggle for Puerto Rican Independence*. New York: Prentice-Hall.

Fernández Vanga, E. 1946. "El veto a la ley del idioma." *El Imparcial*, 6 November: 5.

Ferrao, Luis Angel. 1993. "Nacionalismo, hispanismo y élite intelectual en el Puerto Rico de la década de 1930." In Silvia Alvarez-Curbelo and María Elena Rodríguez Castro, eds., *Del nacionalismo al populismo: Cultura y política en Puerto Rico*. Río Piedras, PR: Ediciones Huracán: 37–60.

Ferré, Luis A. 1969. "Mensaje sobre el estado del País." *Actas de la Cámara de Representantes del Estado Libre Asociado de Puerto Rico*. 29 January: 75–87.

———. 1991. "La gran mentira." *Nuevo Día*, 11 April: 71.

Flores Caraballo, Eliut Daniel. 1993. "El impacto de las nuevas tecnologías de comunicación en los procesos políticos y culturales de Puerto Rico." Paper presented to the Symposium Trasmisión de Información y Conocimiento tras 500 años de Desarrollo Tecnológico, Universidad del Sagrado Corazón, San Juan, Puerto Rico, 19 October.

Foraker Act of 1900. (Organic Act of April 12, 1900, secs. 1–41). *U.S. Statutes at Large* 31: 77–86.

Francis, E. K. 1976. *Interethnic Relations: An Essay in Sociological Theory*. New York: Elsevier.

Galib Bras, Salomé. 1991a. "Sigue en el candelero el asunto del plebiscito." *Nuevo Día*, 14 March: 24.

———. 1991b. "Innecesario el referéndum." *Nuevo Día*, 16 March: 17.

Galvez Maturana, S. 1952. "Por fin Puerto Rico ha dejado de ser un pueblo sin bandera." *El Mundo*, 25 July: 32.

García, Ivonne. 1993. "Parties Mainly Use TV to Tout Status." *San Juan Star*, 31 October: 10–11.

García, Pepo. 1993. "La semana entrante las vistas sobre el inglés." *Nuevo Día*, 8 January: 12.

García Martínez, Alfonso L., ed. 1982. *Puerto Rico: Leyes fundamentales*. Río Piedras, PR: Edil.

García Passalacqua, Juan Manuel. 1984. *Puerto Rico: Equality and Freedom at Issue*.

New York: Praeger.

———. 1991a. "La verdad sobre la estadidad." *Nuevo Día*, 21 February: 77.

———. 1991b. "La decisión clave." *Nuevo Día*, 15 March: 61.

———. 1991c. "¿Qué es un americano?" *Nuevo Día*, 23 May: 77.

Garde, Roger de la, Gilsdorf, William, and Wechselmann, Ilja, eds. 1993. *Small Nations, Big Neighbour: Denmark and Quebec/Canada Compare Notes on American Popular Culture* (Acamedia Research Monograph series: 10). London: John Libbey.

Gellner, Ernest. 1983. *Nations and Nationalism*. Ithaca, NY: Cornell University Press.

Gleason, Philip. 1983. "Identifying Identity: A Semantic History." *Journal of American History* 69(4): 910–31.

González, José Luis. 1987. *El país de cuatro pisos y otros ensayos*. Río Piedras, PR: Ediciones Huracán.

González Bracero Jr., Emilio. 1991. "Puerto Rico Must Push for Self-Determination." *San Juan Star*, 24 April: 17.

Griffiths, Alison. 1993. *"Pobol Y Cwm:* The Construction of National and Cultural Identity in a Welsh-Language Soap Opera." In Phillip Drummond, Richard Paterson, and Janet Willis, eds., *National Identity and Europe: The Television Revolution*. London: British Film Institute: 9–24.

Guardian. 1994. "Kurds Offer Olive Branch to Turkey." 17 August: 7.

Gumperz, John J., ed. 1982. *Language and Social Identity*. Cambridge: Cambridge University Press.

Guralnik, David B., ed. 1970. *Webster's New World Dictionary of the American Language*. New York: World.

Gurevitz, Mark. 1994. "States Designating English as the Official State Language." Congressional Research Service Report for Congress, Library of Congress, 31 August.

Gutiérrez, Edith Algren de. 1987. *The Movement against Teaching English in the Schools of Puerto Rico*. Lanham, MD: University Presses of America.

Haberman, Clyde. 1989. "Flow of Turks Leaving Bulgaria Swells to Hundreds of Thousands." *New York Times*, 15 August: 1.

Hall, Eamonn G. 1993. *The Electronic Age: Telecommunication in Ireland*. Dublin: Oak Tree Press.

Hall, Zoë. 1993. "Jurassic Perplexity." *Guardian International*. 29 December: sec. 2, p. 12.

Harper, Richard Conant. 1980. *The Course of the Melting Pot Idea to 1910*. New York: Arno Press.

Hayes, Carleton J. H. 1960. *Nationalism: A Religion*. New York: Macmillan.

Hernández Agosto, Miguel. 1993. "La estadidad: desastre económico comprobado." *Nuevo Día*, 14 October: 85.

Hernández Colón, Rafael. 1991a. "Mensaje del Gobernador del Estado Libre Asociado de Puerto Rico Hon. Rafael Hernández Colón con motivo de la firma del proyecto de ley que declara el español como idioma oficial de Puerto Rico." 5 April. Mimeo.

———. 1991b. "An Open Letter to Fellow Citizens of the United States from the Governor of Puerto Rico." *New York Times*, 9 April: A25.

Hiatt, Fred. 1992. "Squabbles Soften Firm Confidence of Russian Chief." *Philadelphia Inquirer*, 19 July: G6.

Hobsbawm, E. J. 1990. *Nations and Nationalism since 1780: Programme, Myth, Reality.* Cambridge: Cambridge University Press.

Hobsbawm, Eric, and Ranger, Terence, eds. 1983. *The Invention of Tradition.* Cambridge: Cambridge University Press.

Horne, Donald. 1986. *The Public Culture: The Triumph of Industrialism.* London: Pluto Press.

Hroch, Miroslav. 1985. *Social Preconditions of National Revivial in Europe.* Trans. Ben Fowkes. Cambridge: Cambridge University Press.

Hull, Harwood. 1928. "Porto Ricans Give Lindbergh Message, Asking for Freedom." *New York Times*, 4 February: 1, 4.

Hundley, Tom. 1992. "Turkey Cracking Down on Kurds." *Philadelphia Inquirer*, 24 March: C9.

Hunt, William H. 1902a. *Second Annual Report of the Governor of Porto Rico covering the Period from May 1, 1901 to July 1, 1902.* 57th Cong., 2nd Sess., S. Doc 32.

———. 1902b. *Message of the Hon. William H. Hunt, Governor of Porto Rico, to the Legislative Assembly, 2nd Session, January 2, 1902.* San Juan, n.p.

———. 1903. *Third Annual Report of the Governor of Porto Rico covering the Period from July 1, 1902 to June 30, 1903.* 58th Cong., 1st Sess., S. Doc 26.

Hunter, Robert J. 1966. "A Historical Survey of the Puerto Rican Status Question, 1898–1965." In United States–Puerto Rico Commission on the Status of Puerto Rico, *Status of Puerto Rico: Selected Background Studies.* Washington, DC: Government Printing Office: 50–145.

International Commission for the Study of Communication Problems. 1980. *Many Voices, One World.* Paris: UNESCO.

Isaacs, Harold R. 1975. *Idols of the Tribe: Group Identity and Political Change.* New York: Harper and Row.

Kang, Jong Geun, and Morgan, Michael. 1990. "Culture Clash: Impact of U.S. Television in Korea." In L. John Martin and Ray Eldon Hiebert, eds., *Current Issues in International Communication.* New York: Longman: 293–301.

Kedourie, Elie. 1960. *Nationalism.* London: Hutchinson.

Kim, Eugene C. 1973. "Education in Korea under the Japanese Colonial Rule." In Andrew C. Nahm, ed., *Korea under Japanese Colonial Rule.* Kalamazoo: Center for Korean Studies, Institute of International and Area Studies, Western Michigan University: 137–45.

Kristof, Nicholas D. 1992. "Restlessness Reaches Mongols in China." *New York Times*, 19 July: E4.

Krueger, Richard A. 1988. *Focus Groups: A Practical Guide for Applied Research.* Newbury Park, CA: Sage.

Laws of Puerto Rico. 1948.

Laws of Puerto Rico Annotated. 1982. Oxford, NH: Equity.

Lealand, Geoff. 1988. *A Foreign Egg in Our Nest? American Popular Culture in New Zealand.* Wellington: Victoria University Press.

———. 1994. "American Popular Culture and Emerging Nationalism in New Zealand." *National Forum* 74(4): 34–37.

Lerner, Daniel. 1958. *The Passing of Traditional Society: Modernizing the Middle East.* Glencoe, IL: Free Press.

Lerner, Daniel, and Schramm, Wilbur, eds. 1967. *Communication and Change in the*

Developing Countries. Honolulu: East-West Center Press.

Lewis, Gordon K. 1963. *Puerto Rico: Freedom and Power in the Caribbean.* New York: Monthly Review Press.

Longman, Jere. 1992. "New Light on Olympic Torch: Games Open amid Ceremony, Change." *Philadelphia Inquirer*, 9 February: A1, A4.

Luce, Edward. 1993. "Broadcasters Speak Out against Free Trade in TV Shows." *Guardian*, 8 October: 17.

Luciano, María Judith. 1990. "Caldeada la aprobación del español." *Nuevo Día*, 25 October: 4.

————. 1991a. "Culpan al 'Spanish Only.' " *Nuevo Día*, 13 June: 5.

————. 1991b. "Reto al referéndum en los tribunales." *Nuevo Día*, 19 September: 7.

————. 1991c. "Mensajes ocultos en la consulta." *Nuevo Día*, 16 October: 12.

————. 1993a. "Argumentos filosos en la confrontación." *Nuevo Día*, 16 January: 7.

————. 1993b. "Anticipa dos millones de sufragios." *Nuevo Día*, 10 November: 5.

————. 1993c. " 'Asegura' Kennedy la ciudadanía." *Nuevo Día*, 10 November: 7.

MacAloon, John J. 1984. "La Pitada Olímpica: Puerto Rico, International Sport, and the Constitution of Politics." In Stuart Plattner, ed., *Text, Play, and Story: The Construction and Reconstruction of Self and Society*, 1983 Proceedings of the American Ethnological Society. Washington, DC: American Ethnological Society.

Mackenzie, W. J. M. 1978. *Political Identity.* Manchester, England: Manchester University Press.

Maldonado-Denis, Manuel. 1972. *Puerto Rico: A Sociohistoric Interpretation.* Trans. Elena Vialo. New York: Random House.

Manabe, Kazfumi. 1992. "Japanese Cultural Identity: Old Tradition, New Technology." Paper presented at the Forty-Second Annual Conference of the International Communication Association, 21–25 May. Mimeo.

Marquis, Christopher. 1991. "As Olympic Team Competes, Islanders Weep with Pride." *Miami Herald*, 5 May: 20A.

Martínez, Andrea. 1993. "Rosselló le sale al paso a Palau sobre el idioma." *Nuevo Día*, 16 October: 19.

McCrary, Lacy. 1989. "School Preserves Latvian Roots." *Philadelphia Inquirer*, 5 August: B1.

McPhail, Thomas L. 1987. *Electronic Colonialism.* Newbury Park, CA: Sage.

Merton, Robert K. 1987. "The Focussed Interview and Focus Groups: Continuities and Discontinuities." *Public Opinion Quarterly* 51: 550–66.

Mesler, David P. 1973. "Korean Literature of Resistance: A Case for Chŏng Pi-sŏk." In Andrew C. Nahm, ed., *Korea under Japanese Colonial Rule.* Kalamazoo: Center for Korean Studies, Institute of International and Area Studies, Western Michigan University: 220–30.

Milne, Kirsty. 1992. "Flodden or Culloden, It's Time to Move On." *New Statesman and Society*, 13 March: 12–13.

Morales, Vicente. 1979. "Amenazan con llevarse los Juegos." *Nuevo Día,* 5 January: 3.

Morales Carrión, Arturo. 1983. *Puerto Rico: A Political and Cultural History.* New York: Norton.

————. 1990. *Puerto Rico and the United States: The Quest for a New Encounter.* San Juan: Editorial Académica.

Morales Padrón, Francisco. 1962. "Primer intento de independencia puertorriqueña." *Caribbean Studies* 1(4): 11–20.

Morgan, David L. 1988. *Focus Groups as Qualitative Research.* Newbury Park, CA: Sage.

Moynihan, Daniel Patrick. 1993. *Pandaemonium: Ethnicity in International Politics.* Oxford: Oxford University Press.

Mulero, Leonor. 1993. "Simon 'vende' la estadidad." *Nuevo Día,* 5 November: 8.

El Mundo. 1948a. "Gobernador Piñero dió ayer su aprobación para llevar equipo." 25 March: 1.

El Mundo. 1948b. "Señalan falla en enseñanza del inglés." 4 July: 1, 18.

El Mundo. 1948c. "Liberales aceptan la estadidad como aspiración suprema, pero otros detalles demoran la fusión, Muñoz sugiere status especial para Puerto Rico." 5 July: 1, 14.

El Mundo. 1948d. "Puerto Rico en Londres." 14 July: 6.

El Mundo. 1948e. "Inauguración de las Olimpiades fué acto de pompa y esplendor." 30 July: 1.

El Mundo. 1948f. "Los tres candidatos a la gobernación electiva." 24 October: 32.

El Mundo. 1952a. "Benítez cree que los opositores a Sección 20 atacaban la ONU." 11 July: 1, 16.

El Mundo. 1952b. Advertisements for Farmacias Moscoso and Cadierno Hnos. Distributors. 25 July: 20.

El Mundo. 1952c. "Se inaugura Estado Asociado. Gob. recalca que la bandera es de todos." 26 July: 1, 22.

El Mundo. 1952d. "Todd iza bandera." 26 July: 4, 26.

Muñoz Marín, Luis. 1954. "Puerto Rico and the U.S., Their Future Together." *Foreign Affairs* 32(4): 541–51.

———. 1980. *Mensajes al pueblo puertorriqueño pronunciados ante las cámaras legislativas 1949–64.* San Juan: Inter-American University Press.

———. 1984. *La historia del Partido Popular Democrático.* San Juan: Editorial El Batey.

Nafziger, James A. R. 1988. *International Sports Law.* Dobbs Ferry, NY: Transnational.

Negrón de Montilla, Aida. 1975. *Americanization in Puerto Rico and the Public School System 1900–1930.* Río Piedras, PR: Editorial Universitaria.

———. 1990. *La americanización de Puerto Rico y el sistema de instrucción pública 1900–1930.* 2d ed. Río Piedras, PR: Editorial de la Universidad de Puerto Rico.

New York Times. 1898. "Miles Announces Landing." 27 July:1.

New York Times. 1899a. "The Puerto Rican Crisis." 21 February: 7.

New York Times. 1899b. "Puerto Rico's New Schools." 18 December: 6.

New York Times. 1946. "6,000 San Juan Students Strike." 9 November: 6.

New York Times. 1969a. "Tension Remains at Puerto Rico U." 5 October: 35.

New York Times. 1969b. "13 Puerto Ricans Injured in Clash." 9 November: 41.

New York Times. 1969c. " 'Yanqui Go Home' Echoes in Puerto Rican Streets." 24 November: 4.

New York Times. 1992a. "26 Are Killed as Kurds Clash with Turkish Forces." 22 March: 4.

New York Times. 1992b. "I.O.C. to Meet on Yugoslavs." 8 June: C3.

Nuevo Día. 1991a. "Puerto Rico vence a Estados Unidos." 16 August: 1.

Nuevo Día. 1991b. "El pueblo votó por el statu quo." 11 December: 8.

Nuevo Día. 1993. "A defender el café boricua." 25 October: 10.

Oliveras, Cándido. 1962. "Acerca de la enseñanza en los idiomas español e inglés: entrevista con Cándido Oliveras." Reprinted from *El Día* June 25, 1962. In Erwin H. Epstein, comp., 1970, *Politics and Education in Puerto Rico: A Documentary Survey of the Language Issue.* Metuchen, NJ: Scarecrow: 101–18.

Osuna, Juan José. 1949. *A History of Education in Puerto Rico.* Río Piedras, PR: Editorial de la Universidad de Puerto Rico.

Padilla, Victor M. 1959. "Ike dice E. U. decidiría sobre estadidad a base del resultado de plebiscito aquí." *El Mundo,* 22 August: 7.

Pagán, Bolívar. 1959. *Historia de los partidos políticos puertorriqueños, 1898–1956.* 2 vols. San Juan: Librería Campos.

Partido Estadista Republicano. 1959. "Carta del Presidente." *El Imparcial,* 24 August: 8.

Partido Independentista Puertorriqueño. 1991. "Dale el Sí." *Nuevo Día,* 20 October: 50.

———. 1993. "El voto que cuenta." *Nuevo Día,* 13 November: 9.

———. Secretaría de Educación Política. n.d. "Transición: Posterior a la proclamación de la independencia."

Partido Nuevo Progresista. Comisíon Estadista. 1982. "El impacto de la estadidad en el olimpismo puertorriqueño." Mimeo.

Partido Popular Democrático. 1993a. "Plebiscito en Puerto Rico." *Nuevo Día,* 10 November: 13.

———. 1993b. "Pensionado." *Nuevo Día,* 10 November: 99.

Partido Republicano Puertorriqueño. [1899] 1917. "Primera Plataforma del Partido Republicano Puertorriqueño." *El Tiempo,* 3 March: 2, 4, 6.

———. 1917. "¡Loor al Partido Republicano!" *El Tiempo,* 3 March: 1, 2.

Peattie, Mark R. 1988. "The Japanese Colonial Empire, 1895–1945." In Peter Duus, ed., *The Cambridge History of Japan. Volume 6: The Twentieth Century.* Cambridge: Cambridge University Press: 217–70.

Pedreira, Antonio. [1936] 1957. *Insularismo.* Reprint. San Juan: Biblioteca de Autores Puertorriqueños.

Perea, Juan F. 1992. "Demography and Distrust: An Essay on American Languages, Cultural Pluralism, and Official English." *Minnesota Law Review* 77: 269–373.

Perlez, Jane. 1991. "An Insurgency Seeks to Become a Nation." *New York Times,* 30 June: E5.

Philadelphia Inquirer. 1992. "Panel Suggests Changes to Placate Quebec." 1 March: A8.

La Prensa (New York). 1946. "Dicen a Truman vede proyecto de idioma en P. Rico." 22 August: 2.

Puerto Rico. Constituent Assembly. 1952. *Diario de Sesiones.*

———. Constitutional Convention. 1952. *Notes and Comments on the Constitution of Puerto Rico.* Washington, DC: n.p.

———. Supreme Court. 1965. "People vs. Superior Court." *Puerto Rico Reports,* 92: 580–90.

Pye, Lucian W. 1962. *Politics, Personality and Nation Building: Burma's Search for Identity.* New Haven, CT: Yale University Press.

Reguero, José Rafael. 1993. " 'Protegida' la cultura." *Nuevo Día,* 19 October: 24.

Reisman, David. 1964. *Abundance for What? and Other Essays.* Garden City, NY: Doubleday.

Renan, E. [1882] 1939. "What Is a Nation?" In Alfred Zimmern, *Modern Political Doctrines.* London: Oxford University Press: 186–205.

Rivera, Ramón Luis. 1993. "La Estadidad: igualdad y progreso." *Nuevo Día,* 23 October: 74.

Robertson, Ian. 1987. *Sociology.* 3d ed. New York: Worth.

Rodríguez Bou, Ismael. 1966. "Significant Factors in the Development of Education in Puerto Rico." In United States–Puerto Rico Commission on the Status of Puerto Rico, *Status of Puerto Rico: Selected Background Studies.* Washington, DC: Government Printing Office.

Rodríguez Fraticelli, Carlos. 1993. "Pedro Albizu Campos: estrategias de lucha y luchas estratégicas." In Juan Manuel Carrión, Teresa C. Gracia Ruiz, and Carlos Rodríguez Fraticelli, eds., *La nación puertorriqueña: ensayos en torno a Pedro Albizu Campos.* San Juan: Editorial de la Universidad de Puerto Rico: 121–38.

Rodríguez Orellana, Manuel. 1991. "The Dog That Did Not Bark: Reflections on the Congressional Process concerning the Status of Puerto Rico: 1989–1991." Paper presented at the *Destino '91* conference. Yale University, New Haven, CT, 6 April. Mimeo.

Rohter, Larry. 1993. "3 Ex-Presidents Join the Debate on Puerto Rico." *New York Times,* 13 November: 8.

Romanow, Walter I., and Soderlund, Walter C. 1990. "Media Imperialism North American Style: Canada's Efforts to Protect Its Cultural Sovereignty." Paper prepared for presentation at the Tenth Anniversary Conference, Speech Communication Association of Puerto Rico, San Juan, Puerto Rico. Mimeo.

Romero Barceló, Carlos. 1978. *Statehood Is for the Poor.* San Juan. n.p.

Roosevelt, Theodore. [1894] 1926. "American Ideals." In *The Works of Theodore Roosevelt,* vol. 13. New York: Scribner's.

Roosevelt, Theodore Jr. 1937. *Colonial Policies of the United States.* Garden City, NY: Doubleday, Doran.

Root, Elihu. 1899. "Annual Report." In U.S. War Department. 1904. *Five Years of the War Department following the War with Spain 1899–1903, as Shown in the Annual Reports of the Secretary of War.* Washington, DC: Government Printing Office.

Rosario, Ruben del. 1980. *Vocabulario Puertorriqueño.* 3d ed. Río Piedras, PR: Edil.

Rosario Natal, Carmelo, ed. 1989. *Escudo, himno y bandera: Origen e historia de los símbolos de Puerto Rico.* Río Piedras, PR: Edil.

Rossbach, Udo. 1986. "Documenting Publications Related to the Concept of National Identity." In Peter Boerner, ed., *Concepts of National Identity: An Interdisciplinary Dialogue.* Baden-Baden: Nomos Verlagsgesellschaft.

Rosselló, Pedro. 1991. "El idioma." *Nuevo Día,* 9 February: 57.

Rowe, L. S. 1904. *The United States and Porto Rico with Special Reference to the Problems Arising Out of Our Contact with the Spanish-American Civilization.* New York: Longmans, Green.

Rustow, Dankwart A. 1967. *A World of Nations.* Washington, DC: Brookings Institution.

Sánchez Goyanes, Enrique. 1980. *Constitución española comentada.* Madrid: Paraninfo.

Schiller, Herbert I. 1976. *Communication and Cultural Domination.* White Plains, NY: M. E. Sharpe.

Schlesinger, Philip. 1991. *Media, State and Nation: Political Violence and Collective Identities.* London: Sage.

Seplow, Stephen. 1993. "Estonia's Edgy Russians." *Philadelphia Inquirer,* 30 May: C5.

Seppänen, Paavo. 1984. "The Olympics: A Sociological Perspective." *International Review for the Sociology of Sport* 19(2): 113–27.

Serrano Geyls, Raúl, and Gorrín Peralta, Carlos I. 1980. "Puerto Rico y la estadidad: Problemas constitucionales (parte II)." *Revista del Colegio de Abogados de Puerto Rico* 41: 1–28.

Seton-Watson, Hugh. 1977. *Nations and States: An Enquiry into the Origins of Nations and the Politics of Nationalism.* Boulder, CO: Westview Press.

Shipler, David. K. 1989. "A Reporter at Large: Symbols of Sovereignty." *New Yorker,* 18 September: 52–99.

Silva, Rolando A. 1993. "Lo peor de dos mundos." *Nuevo Día,* 6 November: 70.

Sly, Liz. 1992. "Tradition of Distrust Calls for Tact." *Philadelphia Inquirer,* 10 December: A15.

Smith, Anthony D. 1981. *The Ethnic Revival.* Cambridge: Cambridge University Press.

———. 1983. *Theories of Nationalism.* 2d ed. New York: Holmes and Meier.

———. 1988. "The Myth of the 'Modern Nation' and the Myths of Nations." *Ethnic and Racial Studies* 11(1): 1–26.

———. 1991. *National Identity.* London: Penguin.

Smolowe, Jill. 1980. "F.A.L.N. Linked to 100 Bombings." *New York Times,* 16 March: 44.

Sokolov, Raymond. 1991. *Why We Eat What We Eat: How the Encounter between the New World and the Old Changed the Way Everyone on the Planet Eats.* New York: Touchstone.

Starowicz, Mark. 1993. "Citizens of Video-America: What Happened to Canadian Television in the Satellite Age." In Roger de la Garde, William Gilsdorf, and Ilja Wechselmann, eds., *Small Nations, Big Neighbour: Denmark and Quebec/ Canada Compare Notes on American Popular Culture.* London: John Libbey: 83–102.

Stets, Dan. 1991. "Citizenship in Doubt for Latvia's Russians." *Philadelphia Inquirer,* 16 September: 1.

Steward, Julian H., et al. 1956. *The People of Puerto Rico.* Urbana: University of Illinois Press.

Subervi-Vélez, Federico, Hernández-López, Nitza M., and Frambes-Buxeda, Aline. 1990. "Mass Media in Puerto Rico." In Stuart H. Surlin and Walter C. Soderlund, eds., *Mass Media and the Caribbean.* New York: Gordon and Breach: 149–76.

Symmons-Symonolewicz, Konstantin. 1985. "The Concept of Nationhood: Toward a Theoretical Clarification." *Canadian Review of Studies in Nationalism* 12(2): 215–22.

Talbot, Winthrop. 1917. *Americanization.* New York: H. W. Wilson.

Tierney, Christine. 1991. "Quebecers Don't Ask Rest of the World to Pardon Their French." *Philadelphia Inquirer,* 26 December: A12.

The Times (Puerto Rico). 1917. Editorial. 5 March: 7.

Todd, Roberto H. 1967. *Génesis de la bandera puertorriqueña*. 2d ed. Madrid: Ediciones Iberoamericanas.

Tomlinson, John. 1991. *Cultural Imperialism*. London: Pinter.

Trías Monge, José. 1981. *Historia Constitucional de Puerto Rico*. Río Piedras, PR: Editorial Universitaria.

Turner, John C. 1982. "Towards a Cognitive Redefinition of the Social Group." In Henri Tajfel, ed., *Social Identity and Intergroup Relations*. Cambridge: Cambridge University Press: 15–40.

U.S. Congress. 1906. *Sixth Annual Report of the Governor of Porto Rico*. 59th Cong., 2nd Sess., Doc 135.

————. 1932. *Correct the Spelling of the Name of the Island of Porto Rico*. 72d Cong., 1st Sess., H. Doc. 585.

U.S. Geographic Board. 1933. *Sixth Report of the United States Geographic Board*. Washington, DC: Government Printing Office.

U.S. House Committee on Public Lands. 1950. *To Provide for the Organization of a Constitutional Government by the People of Puerto Rico: Hearings on H.R. 7674 and S. 3336*. 81st Cong.

U.S. Institute of Peace. 1994. "Ethnicity and Conflict—A Cross-Disciplinary Debate." *Journal*, February: 5, 9.

United States–Puerto Rico Commission on the Status of Puerto Rico. 1966. *Status of Puerto Rico: Selected Background Studies*. Washington, DC: Government Printing Office.

U.S. Secretary of the Interior. 1906. *Report of the Commissioner of the Interior for Porto Rico to the Secretary of the Interior, U.S.A.* Washington, DC: Government Printing Office.

U.S. Senate. 1900. *Education in Porto Rico*. Letter from the Secretary of War. 56th Congress, 1st sess. S. Doc. 363.

U.S. War Department. 1932. *Annual Report of the Chief of the Bureau of Insular Affairs*. Washington, DC: Government Printing Office.

Walzer, Michael. 1967. "On the Role of Symbolism in Political Thought." *Political Science Quarterly* 82(2): 191–204.

Wells, Henry. 1969. *The Modernization of Puerto Rico: A Political Study of Changing Values and Institutions*. Cambridge: Harvard University Press.

WIPR. 1991. "Vea hoy la transmisión especial . . ." *Nuevo Día*, 5 April: 21.

Wolin, Sheldon. 1989. *The Presence of the Past: Essays on the State and the Constitution*. Baltimore: Johns Hopkins University Press.

Zamosc, Leon. 1994. "Agrarian Protest and the Indian Movement in the Ecuadorian Highlands." *Latin American Research Review* 29(3): 37–68.

Index

About the Author

NANCY MORRIS is a lecturer in the Department of Film and Media Studies at the University of Stirling in Scotland.

ISBN 0-275-95228-2

HARDCOVER BAR CODE